IMPROVING EFFECTIVE COVERAGE IN HEALTH: DO FINANCIAL INCENTIVES WORK?

IMPROVING EFFECTIVE COVERAGE IN HEALTH: DO FINANCIAL INCENTIVES WORK?

Damien de Walque, Eeshani Kandpal, Adam Wagstaff

Jed Friedman, Sven Neelsen, Moritz Piatti-Fünfkirchen,
Anja Sautmann, Gil Shapira, and Ellen Van de Poel

Policy Research Report

Contents

Figures

Foreword

Countries have made years of significant progress to improve access to health services. However, important gaps in equity of access to high-quality health care remain due to fragile primary health care systems. And now, the COVID-19 (coronavirus) pandemic has put decades of progress at risk. The question we all face now is how to reclaim prepandemic gains while accelerating equity and progress for greater impacts and health for all.

Financial incentives or performance pay to frontline health facilities and workers were rolled out in many countries in the mid-2000s as an innovative approach to confronting the challenge of poor health outcomes in low-income economies. It was a significant departure from previous financing models, which had little link to outcomes and results. Performance-based financing (PBF) projects included such financial incentives as well as other critical reforms related to transparency and accountability. Moreover, these new projects were accompanied by an extensive portfolio of impact evaluations funded by the World Bank's Health Results Innovation Trust Fund.

These programs—and, indeed, this report—would not have been possible without the unprecedented multidisciplinary collaboration between client governments and World Bank research and operational staff, spanning 15 years and nearly 40 countries, driven by the desire to not only inform country programs with rigorous evidence but also contribute to the global dialogue on improving health systems. *Improving Effective Coverage in Health: Do Financial Incentives Work?* builds on this substantial investment in knowledge and evidence in this critical area to examine the results from PBF. Although focused on low-income countries and primary services, the scope of the studies is impressive. The largest programs studied here, such as those in Argentina, Cameroon, Nigeria, Tajikistan, Rwanda, and Zimbabwe, each covered millions of households. The report collates this work and brings additional analysis to provide an assessment of the evidence on performance pay specifically as well as of the broader results from PBF projects.

Several powerful, high-level findings emerge from this report. The report documents that PBF projects produced gains in health outcomes compared with the status quo, although these gains did not necessarily result from the specific financial incentives and associated monitoring components of projects. Whereas transparency, accountability, and direct frontline facility financing produced results, the evidence does not show additional benefits that outweigh the costs of performance pay to frontline workers. Specifically, many aspects of quality care improvements are well outside the control of health workers. Thus, impactful health financing reform might mean pivoting from performance pay while retaining other important aspects of PBF projects that do yield similar results. The report also looks at the demand side, emphasizing that cash transfers and vouchers can be part of the solution for more effective coverage in low-demand settings.

The operational and policy messages in this report are compelling, as detailed in the concluding chapter. Health facilities can deliver better results when they have budget autonomy, flexibility, and unified payment systems, and health facilities' budgets can be output oriented and impactful even without explicit performance pay. In contexts in which the time might be right for performance pay, emerging technologies can be used to reduce implementation costs of rollout and monitoring.

Although the analysis in this report draws on evidence that predates the COVID-19 crisis, the findings are more critical than ever as the world navigates recovery and has an unprecedented opportunity to rethink the way countries build health systems, finance them, and deliver services toward the goal of health for all.

Carmen M. Reinhart
Senior Vice President of
Development Economics
and Chief Economist
The World Bank

Mamta Murthi
Vice President
Human Development
The World Bank

March 2022

Acknowledgments

This report was developed under the leadership of Adam Wagstaff, who was the manager of the Development Research Group's Human Development Team at the time of his passing, at the age of 61, on May 10, 2020. Adam needs no introduction as one of the world's leading lights on health financing and health system reform.

In the planning sessions for this report, he articulated a strong vision for a forthright, evidence-based take on the tough subject of designing health financing reform that is sustainable and scalable. He was particularly interested in documenting the impacts of such reform on the quality of care delivered and equity. Adam drove this report's focus on effective coverage. While pushing us intellectually, Adam also advocated for the clear communication of this research and the translation of analytical findings into concrete action items that policy makers could refer to when developing health financing programs. His intellectual curiosity and rigor led the team to ask important, policy-relevant questions and to answer them as well as the evidence permits without shying away from admitting what we do not know.

We are grateful for having had the opportunity to know Adam, work with him, and learn from him. While we deeply miss him, his warmth, sense of humor, and collegiality have inspired and motivated us throughout the process of working on this report. In his absence, we have endeavored to write a report on which we hope Adam would be happy to see his name.

This report was produced by a team led by Damien de Walque, Eeshani Kandpal, and Adam Wagstaff, with Jed Friedman, Sven Neelsen, Moritz Piatti-Fünfkirchen, Anja Sautmann, Gil Shapira, and Ellen Van de Poel.

The team sincerely thanks Francisca Ayodeji Akala, Harold Alderman, Paulin Basinga, Sebastian Bauhoff, Kathleen Beegle, Mickey Chopra,

Mariam Claeson, Jishnu Das, Asli Demirgüç-Kunt, Shantayanan Devarajan, Tania Dmytraczenko, David Evans, Francisco Ferreira, Deon Filmer, Guenther Fink, Emanuela Galasso, Roberta Gatti, John Giles, Amanda Glassman, Michele Gragnolati, Stuti Khemani, Aart Kraay, Joe Kutzin, Ken Leonard, Magnus Lindelow, Benjamin Loevinsohn, Bruno Meessen, Manoj Mohanan, Mamta Murthi, Ayodeji Oluwole Odutolu, Berk Özler, Elina Pradhan, Carmen Reinhart, Daniel Rogger, Norbert Schady, Mahvish Shaukat, Gaston Sorgho, Juan Pablo Uribe, Petra Vergeer, Christel Vermeersch, Monique Vledder, David Wilson, Sophie Witter, Michael Woolcock, and Feng Zhao for their comments at various stages of this work. Fozia Aman, Salome Drouard, Pablo Amor Fernandez, Diwakar Kishore, Sneha Lamba, Carolina Lopez, Mayra Saenz, and Jeanette Walldorf provided outstanding research assistance. We thank Antonn Park for editing this report. We also gratefully acknowledge support from the following World Bank–managed trust funds: Health Results Innovation Trust Fund; Global Financing for Women, Children and Adolescents; and the Knowledge for Change Program.

About the Authors

Lead authors

Damien de Walque is a lead economist in the Development Research Group (Human Development Team) at the World Bank. His research interests include health and education and the interactions between them. de Walque's current work is focused on evaluating the impact of financial incentives on health and education outcomes. He is working on evaluating the impact of HIV/AIDS interventions and policies in several African countries. On the supply side of health services, he is managing a large portfolio of impact evaluations of results-based financing in the health sector. de Walque has also edited a book on risky behaviors for health (smoking, drugs, alcohol, obesity, and risky sex) in developing countries. He holds a PhD in economics from the University of Chicago.

Eeshani Kandpal is a senior economist in the Development Research Group (Poverty and Inequality Team) at the World Bank. Her research examines two types of financial incentives: (1) cash transfers to poor households and (2) pay-for-performance contracts with health workers and facilities to improve the provision of primary health care. She is particularly interested in design elements like the targeting mechanisms of cash transfers and optimal pricing regimes for health service delivery as well as spillovers from incomplete contracts or targeting methods. Kandpal holds a PhD in applied economics from the University of Illinois at Urbana-Champaign.

Adam Wagstaff was research manager in the Development Research Group (Human Development Team) from 2009 until his passing in May 2020. His DPhil in economics was from the University of York; before joining the World Bank, he was a professor of economics at the University of

Sussex. He was an associate editor of the *Journal of Health Economics* for 20 years and published extensively on a variety of aspects of the field, including health financing and health systems reform; health, equity, and poverty; the valuation of health; the demand for and production of health; efficiency measurement; and illicit drugs and drug enforcement. Much of his recent work had been on health insurance, health financing, vulnerability and health shocks, and provider payment reform. Wagstaff had extensive experience with China and Vietnam but also worked on countries in Africa, Central Asia, Europe, Latin America, and South Asia as well as countries in East Asia. Outside health economics, he published on efficiency measurement in the public sector, the measurement of trade union power, the redistributive effect and sources of progressivity of the personal income tax, and the redistributive effect of economic growth.

Contributing authors

Jed Friedman is a lead economist in the Development Research Group (Poverty and Inequality Team) at the World Bank. His research interests include the measurement of well-being and poverty as well as the evaluation of health and social policies. His current work involves investigating the effectiveness of health financing reforms, the nutritional and development gains from early childhood investment programs, and the incorporation of new approaches to survey-based well-being measurement. Friedman holds a PhD in economics from the University of Michigan.

Sven Neelsen is an economist in the World Bank's Health, Nutrition, and Population Global Practice, where he focuses on the measurement and tracking of Sustainable Development Goal 3.8—Universal Health Coverage—and is involved in evaluating and implementing health financing reforms in low- and middle-income countries. He has extensively studied the impacts of health coverage extensions and health shocks on out-of-pocket medical payments, health service coverage, and household consumption among the poor in Peru and Thailand. Neelsen has a PhD in economics from Ludwig Maximilian University of Munich.

Moritz Piatti-Fünfkirchen is a senior economist at the World Bank working at the nexus of public financial management and health. He is interested in how to balance fiscal control with service delivery needs and has written extensively on the use of financial management information systems. His work is currently focused on reforms in the Africa region, where he leads various analytical programs, including those on how to deploy disruptive technology solutions. Before joining the World Bank, Piatti-Fünfkirchen worked as an advisor in the Ministry of Health in Zanzibar/Tanzania, where he supported the government in budget management and the introduction of health finance reforms. He holds an MSc in economics for development from Oxford University and an MA in economics from the University of Aberdeen.

Anja Sautmann is a research economist in the World Bank's Development Research Group (Human Development Team). Her research asks how households and individuals make decisions, from health care for children to daily consumption to marriage, and how incentives and individual behavior shape optimal policy design. Much of her work concerns demand for public primary care in Mali. Before joining the World Bank, Sautmann was an assistant professor at Brown University (2010–17) and the director of research, education, and training at the Abdul Latif Jameel Poverty Action Lab at the Massachusetts Institute of Technology (2017–20). She received her PhD in economics from New York University and is an affiliate of the CESifo research network.

Gil Shapira is an economist in the World Bank's Development Research Group (Human Development Team). His research involves analyzing demographic and health issues in developing countries. His current work includes investigating the effectiveness of health financing reforms, the indirect impacts of the COVID-19 pandemic, and the drivers of gaps and inequalities in quality of health services in Sub-Saharan Africa. Shapira received his BA in economics from Columbia University and his PhD in economics from the University of Pennsylvania.

Ellen Van de Poel leads the Health Financing work program within the Global Financing Facility (GFF). Her team supports countries in developing and implementing strategies to increase domestic resources for health and improve the efficiency of health spending. Before joining the GFF, Van de Poel was an associate professor of health economics at Erasmus University Rotterdam (Netherlands). Her research focused on evaluating health financing reforms and the measurement of equity in health and has been published in leading journals. She received her PhD from the Erasmus School of Economics.

Overview

Key messages

1. Financial incentives or performance pay to frontline health facilities and workers emerged as an innovative means to improve the quantity and quality of health services delivered. This approach to health financing arose from the frustrating status quo of poor health outcomes in low- and middle-income countries despite increased service utilization.
2. This report provides new evidence and reviews the existing literature to assess the results from the introduction of such financial incentives.
   a. The report pays special attention to impacts on effective coverage, a measure that adjusts simple coverage of care with the quality of care provided.
   b. It asks which constraints to poor quality of care can be addressed by financial incentives for health workers.
   c. It further asks what has been the impact of such incentives in general on utilization and quality of care.
   d. Finally, it asks how offering these incentives compares with some key policy alternatives: cash transfers, vouchers, and direct financing of frontline facilities.
3. A range of rigorous studies show that performance-based financing (PBF) projects, which include performance pay among other critical features, including transparency and accountability reforms, resulted in gains in coverage but far fewer, if any, improvements in the quality of health services delivered.
4. Compared with business-as-usual, PBF projects offer gains of a similar magnitude as those from direct facility financing (DFF) approaches, which transfer equivalent funds and have transparency and accountability reforms as do PBF projects but do not have specific incentives for health workers and the associated monitoring.

5. Policy makers may find PBF appealing because of the accountability provided by its link to results. DFF reforms should thus incorporate measures like portals or dashboards that track the flow of funds and provide timely information on the quality and efficiency of health care delivery. In addition, performance pay or household targeted cash transfers may supplement the financing of improvements in selected indicators.

Outline of the report

Improving Effective Coverage in Health: Do Financial Incentives Work? is arranged as follows:

- **Overview**—The Overview provides a summary of the key findings and messages of the report.
- **Chapter 1: Introduction**—Chapter 1 describes the lay of the land in the service delivery of maternal and child health care, focusing on how care is financed with and without additional demand- or supply-side incentives. It also introduces the conundrum of increasing coverage but persistently poor health outcomes, which motivates the need to look at effective coverage and financial incentives for effective coverage.
- **Chapter 2: Effective Coverage: A Framework Linking Coverage and Quality**—Chapter 2 attempts to answer the question "What is effective coverage, what are its implications for efficiency?"
- **Chapter 3: Quality of Care: A Framework for Measurement**—Chapter 3 focuses on the question "How does quality of care relate to effective coverage, how to measure it, and what constrains it?"
- **Chapter 4: Decomposing the Constraints to Quality of Care Using Data on Antenatal Care Consultations from Five Sub-Saharan African Countries**—Chapter 4 presents new evidence on the constraints to quality of antenatal care.
- **Chapter 5: Performance-Based Financing Improves Coverage of Reproductive, Maternal, and Child Health Interventions**—Chapter 5 presents evidence on the impact of performance-based financing on service delivery, quality of care, human resources, and equity thus far.

- **Chapter 6: Policy Alternatives to Performance-Based Financing**— Chapter 6 offers key counterfactuals, including demand-side incentives and direct facility financing, using a systematic review and pooled analysis. It presents a deep dive into direct facility financing.
- **Chapter 7: Performance-Based Financing as a Health System Reform and Cautionary Evidence on Performance Pay and Irrelevant Care**—Chapter 7 describes the role of performance-based financing in the development of health systems: avoiding nonindicated care and wasted resources, integrating quality measurement into health systems, and measuring the broader impacts of health financing reform.
- **Chapter 8: Conclusion and Operational Implications**—Chapter 8 operationalizes key aspects of performance-based financing given the evidence presented.

Introduction

Financial incentives or performance pay links payments to health facilities and workers to the quantity and quality of services they deliver. These performance incentives came on the scene in health financing as a consequence of a frustrating status quo: health outcomes have remained poor in low- and middle-income countries (LMICs) despite sustained investments in health service delivery and concomitant increases in the utilization of services over the past two decades (Eichler and Levine 2009). Performance-based financing (PBF) projects—which include performance pay among other critical features, including public financial management reform, health facility autonomy, decentralization, supportive supervision for the frontlines, and community engagement—held appeal for development agencies and donors because of their explicit links to transparency and accountability. Since the late 2000s, more than US$2.5 billion has been invested in PBF projects in primary health service delivery in low-income countries. This report examines the evidence on the impact of performance pay specifically, and PBF projects more broadly, on coverage, effective coverage, health outcomes, as well as clinical and infrastructure quality.

Much of this report uses effective coverage as a measure of performance. Effective coverage is a metric that combines simple health coverage with minimum content and quality. Considering the content and quality of care is crucial to understanding why service utilization increases may not translate into improved health outcomes. While the content and quality of care may seemingly be in the locus of control of frontline health facilities and workers—after all, it is up to the health worker to provide relevant care in any patient-provider interaction—there are other constraints to quality that are not under the facility or worker's control.

To understand why the content and quality of care might be inadequate and the scope for performance pay to improve it, the report delves into the constraints to content of care through a theoretical framework and an empirical application to antenatal care (ANC) in five Sub-Saharan African countries. This framework decomposes the constraints to quality of care and describes the various levels at which they lie (Ibnat et al. 2019). These constraints can include inadequate physical capacity at the health facility level; health worker knowledge, which is typically produced further up the health system, in medical schools; and health worker effort, which is the only component that is directly in a health worker's locus of control and thus potentially responsive to performance pay to the worker. For instance, in a centralized health system where frontline health facilities do not receive an adequate operating budget—which too often is the institutional reality in many low-income countries—if a piece of equipment breaks or there is a drug stockout, a health worker may not be able to provide necessary care because they lack the infrastructure to do so. Performance pay can incentivize frontline health facilities and workers, but it only addresses constraints to quality at these levels. However, the data show that gaps in physical infrastructure and the availability of drugs and supplies are substantial. In other words, many constraints to quality are not within the health facility or worker's locus of control, suggesting that performance pay may only have limited potential in improving coverage, effective coverage, or the quality of care.

Next, the report takes a broad-based look at the impact of performance pay and broader PBF projects in high-income country and LMIC health systems and provides new evidence from multiple rigorously designed impact evaluations. The evidence shows that PBF projects have led to gains in primary health service delivery even in low-income, centralized health systems. However, questions of comparative efficacy and effectiveness arise when the impacts of PBF projects are juxtaposed against other interventions related to financial incentives on the demand and supply sides. On the demand side, the report considers conditional cash transfers (CCTs) and vouchers, while on the supply side, it considers direct facility financing (DFF), which shares many features of PBF projects in terms of providing an operating budget to the frontlines as well as autonomy over how to disburse that budget, but does not include performance pay.

The results show that financial incentives on the demand and supply sides can increase coverage. However, such incentives typically work on the margins, while large gains in effective coverage remain an elusive goal. The discussion and interpretation of these findings highlight the importance of the institutional setting. Performance pay may make sense in decentralized, high-quality health systems that already support facility financing and autonomy as well as accountability and transparency. In contrast, its potential may be more limited in centralized, under-resourced health systems that have key gaps at various points. The report further shows that incentives on the demand and supply sides may work on margins that complement each other by addressing different constraints. It highlights the role of baseline coverage, content, and quality; the provider's effort response to price; and task complementarity as key determinants of the impact of performance pay on purchased indicators. The report also provides cautionary primary evidence that performance pay can incentivize the provision of inappropriate, unnecessary, or irrelevant care. It argues for the integration of health care quality and efficiency measurement into health system reform, with attention paid to both the underprovision of needed care as well as the provision of unnecessary or irrelevant care, which can become an important dimension of quality as health care systems mature. Taken together, these findings shed light on how program teams and policy makers may fruitfully combine demand- and supply-side financing and highlight various questions they should ask when selecting the indicators for which performance pay may be used. The report concludes with a consideration of the operational implications of these findings, especially with regard to the design of a sustainable and scalable health financing reform that aims for substantial improvement in effective coverage.

Why effective coverage?

The ultimate goal of development efforts in health is the production of better health in LMIC populations. Such investment is still much needed because all over the developing world, coverage for health services remains low, especially among the poor, notwithstanding progress made during the push toward the Millennium Development Goals (Wagstaff, Bredenkamp, and Buisman 2014). For example, equitable access to affordable health care is not a reality for many women, men, children, and adolescents in the developing world, resulting in more than six million deaths from preventable causes each year (WHO 2020). This is true both for basic services, such as maternal and child health, as well as for services aimed at preventing and treating the emerging threat of noncommunicable diseases. Indeed, Kruk et al. (2018) show that the majority of LMIC neonatal and maternal deaths are "amenable," which is to say that they could be prevented by improving the quality of care.

This assessment is even starker if, beyond access to medical services, effective coverage is considered, that is, coverage with effective services at a minimum level of quality and content. A framework for effective coverage presents how this concept can be decomposed into the product of coverage (those in need getting care) and quality (correct or successful treatment among those getting care). Estimates of effective coverage and its two components for six conditions (pregnancy, child malaria, child diarrhea, hypertension, tuberculosis, and HIV) using household survey data first establish that effective coverage—and by extension, quality of care—is currently still shockingly poor for many health conditions in many environments. Figure O.1 illustrates with the example of ANC how looking at coverage versus effective coverage provides a very different perspective. It shows the effective coverage contours and their components, coverage and quality, for ANC for a large set of LMICs using data from the Multiple Indicator Cluster Surveys. Each dot represents a survey with the name of the country abbreviated and the survey year. Coverage, on the horizontal axis, is measured as the percentage of women giving birth who had at least one ANC visit. Quality is defined as the proportion among them who had at least four ANC visits, with at least one of those visits with a skilled provider, and for whom, during their ANC visits, blood pressure as well as blood and urine samples were taken. Many countries are situated in the upper right corner of the figure, indicating both high coverage and quality and thus high effective coverage. However, there is another group of countries lower down, on the right side of the graph, for which coverage is high but quality is lower (20–60 percent).

The estimates in the report further explore whether it is coverage or quality that is the bottleneck to better effective coverage varies by condition and country. Using the example of HIV treatment, the results also indicate substantial variation by household wealth and that although over the past decades, there has been substantial progress in coverage of the poor—often

Figure 0.1 Effective coverage contours for antenatal care

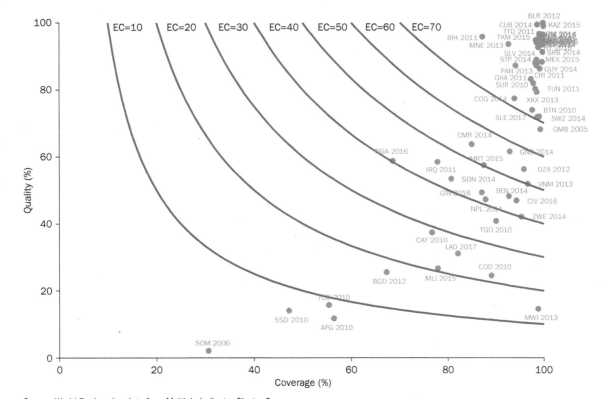

Source: World Bank, using data from Multiple Indicator Cluster Surveys.

Note: Coverage: percent of women giving birth who had 1+ antenatal care visits. Quality: of those covered, the percent who had 4+ visits, 1+ visits with a skilled provider, blood pressure taken, and blood and urine samples taken (correct treatment). EC = effective coverage. ISO 3166-1 alpha-3 codes are used for the country abbreviations (https://unstats.un.org/wiki/display/comtrade/Country+codes+in+ISO+3166).

more than wealthier households, even if the levels remain too low—important gaps in quality translate into stark inequity in effective coverage.

Regional and topical focus of the report

Driven by the burden of disease in low-income countries and the fact that most care in LMICs is provided at the primary level, the introduction of financial incentives has mostly focused on frontline health workers—those at the primary level—and specifically maternal and child health services.

Thus, this report focuses on maternal and child health services, with most of the primary evidence coming from Sub-Saharan Africa. This is because evidence suggests that poor quality, over and above access, is the key constraint to improving maternal and neonatal mortality—including for antenatal care, as discussed in figure O.1. In addition to most maternal and neonatal deaths being "amenable" to improvements in quality (Kruk et al. 2018), maternal and neonatal diseases are among the top two contributors to the burden of disease in low-income countries (IHME 2020). Indeed, the five Sub-Saharan African countries that are used for detailed analysis in this report—Cameroon, the Central African Republic, the Democratic Republic of Congo, Nigeria, and the Republic of Congo—contribute almost 20 percent of the global burden of maternal mortality (Kassebaum et al. 2014). The report also reviews and spotlights relevant evidence from high- and middle-income countries (for example, Argentina, Armenia, the Kyrgyz Republic, Tajikistan, the United Kingdom, and the United States) and includes evidence related to the impact of financial incentives for curative care as well as the prevention of noncommunicable diseases.

Of the 26 completed or ongoing impact evaluations of World Bank–funded PBF pilots in health, 19 focus on maternal and child health service delivery in Sub-Saharan Africa (RBFHealth website).[1] This report draws on 22 of these 26 studies, albeit to varying degrees. The analysis focuses on a subset of eight countries, whose selection was driven by data needs. The analysis of the constraints to quality of care requires direct clinical observations of patient-provider interactions for ANC provision. Most of the impact evaluations did not include these data, but the analysis in this report relies on the five that did. Similarly, comparison of PBF with the key policy counterfactual of DFF draws on impact evaluations from the five countries (Cameroon, Nigeria, Rwanda, Zambia, and Zimbabwe) in the impact evaluation portfolio that included this alternative. Thus, not only do the analysis and evidence presented here represent a lion's share of the contributors to poor health outcomes, but also, they provide evidence that is relevant for a number of low-income country contexts.

Performance pay

A large set of interventions has been proposed and implemented to address the twin issues of low quality of care and inadequate access to high-quality care in low-income countries. But little progress has been made, particularly in terms of health outcomes. Due to frustration with the status quo of substantial gains to service utilization but a persistently high and stagnating number of preventable deaths, performance pay gained prominence (Eichler and Levine 2009). Promising early evidence of the effectiveness of financial incentives to health workers in the form of performance pay came from high-income countries, including the United States, the United Kingdom, and many other countries (Doran et al. 2006). In addition, the early evidence on the PBF package—performance pay combined with public financial management reform, health facility autonomy, decentralization, supportive supervision for the frontlines, and community engagement— from two low-income countries, Burundi and Rwanda, was also promising. Donors and governments were attracted by the transparency, accountability, and link to results espoused by PBF programs (Fritsche, Soeters, and Meessen 2014), and significant investments flowed into PBF projects in primary health, with US$2.4 billion in International Development Association financing (Gergen et al. 2017). Notably, these donor finances also included a significant level of funding for rigorous impact evaluations. This report takes a step back and looks at all the evidence, relying heavily on the impact evaluations of PBF pilots in low-income countries, especially the provision of maternal and child health services at the primary level in Sub-Saharan Africa, to assess the impact of PBF.

The report also highlights the salience of the institutional setting. Much of the evidence on the effectiveness of performance pay to improve health services and outcomes is from high- and middle-income countries. To be precise, much of the high-income country experience is from implementing performance pay for selected indicators, with no supplementary interventions. The health systems in question are already high quality, decentralized, transparent, and have accountability measures. Further, all the health facilities, including those on the frontline, have operating budgets and autonomy. Many of the applications of performance pay in low-income settings are in a different type of health system. Figure O.2 depicts the case of the modal health system in a low-income setting. Typically, these systems are centralized, with no operating budget provided to frontline health facilities, and no autonomy over facility management, staffing, or procurement of equipment, drugs, or supplies. The report draws on evidence from impact evaluations that examined the effectiveness of PBF projects, which include performance pay and a host of other reforms to autonomy, transparency, and accountability. As such, it is difficult to make a one-to-one comparison of performance pay interventions in high-income countries with the results from studies of PBF projects.

Figure 0.2   Lay of the land in centralized health systems in low-income countries

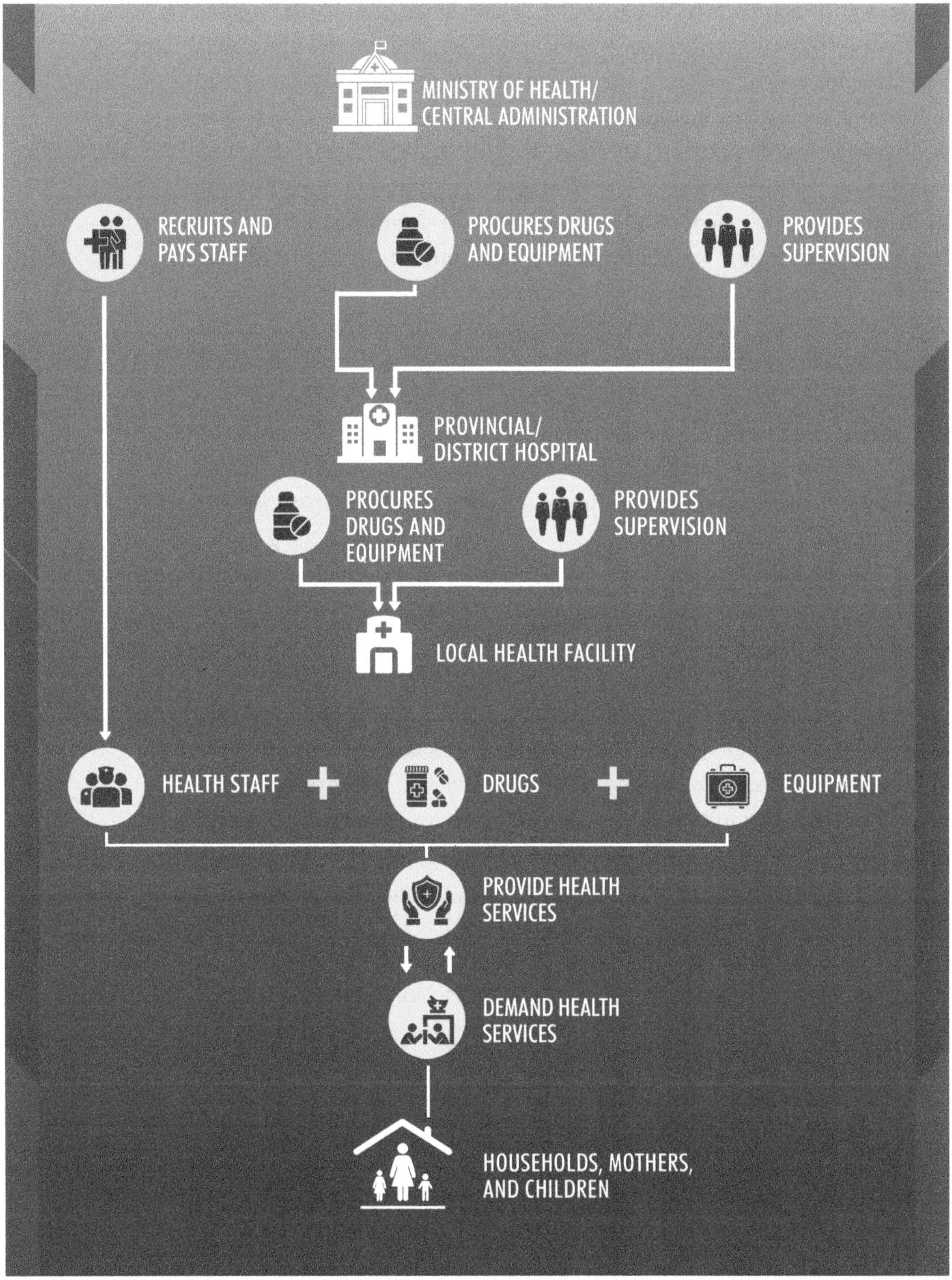

Source: World Bank.

Understanding constraints to effective coverage

Substantial evidence suggests that the quality of care in many LMICs is low, especially for the poor (Kruk et al. 2018). Performance-based incentives assume that facilities or providers can respond to the quality-related incentives by improving quality. Understanding why effective coverage lags coverage requires understanding why the rate of relevant treatment is not 100 percent. As this report shows, low rates of effective coverage can arise for a variety of reasons, and not all of them are in the health facility or health worker's locus of control. Service utilization rates can still at times be poor in low-income countries, especially for preventive care (Mills 2014). In addition, health conditions are often misdiagnosed, and even when they are well diagnosed, the correct treatment or interventions might not be prescribed or implemented (Das, Hammer, and Leonard 2008). In other words, even when care is accessed, the quality of the care received can be poor, hence leading to a gap between coverage and effective coverage.

The question central to understanding whether financial incentives such as performance pay would significantly improve quality—and thus increase effective coverage—is one of where the various constraints to quality lie and the degree to which each constraint matters. For instance, health facilities and workers may not be able to change demand-side constraints leading to low service utilization. On the supply side, low effective coverage might be due to (1) poorly trained staff who do not know how to treat a patient, an issue that is addressed upstream in the system at medical schools and through professional training; (2) lack of physical capacity, such as essential equipment, drugs, or supplies, remedying which is likely not in the individual health worker's locus of control—indeed, in centralized systems, this may not even be under the frontline health facility's control; (3) lack of effort from the providers even if they have all the necessary knowledge and physical capacity (Ibnat et al. 2019); or (4) the different treatment of patients depending on their socioeconomic status (Fink, Kandpal, and Shapira 2021). As this decomposition of the constraints to quality demonstrates, only effort and perhaps some of the gaps arising from physical capacity are within the scope of the health worker or health facility's locus of control. However, much underperformance remains unexplained by these two factors, and thus it is unlikely to be addressed by performance pay or even the broader PBF programs.

The report illustrates and quantifies the relative sizes of the different constraints to quality, and thus the limits to the potential impact of a financial incentive intervention to frontline health workers and facilities, using an empirical application of the three-gap model to a five-country data set of ANC consultations in Sub-Saharan Africa. The report finds evidence of constraints along many margins, starting with infrastructure. As shown in figure O.3, despite decades of investments in infrastructure, poor structural quality is widespread. Facilities in some countries are better provisioned than others, but in all the countries examined, facilities that are supposed to provide maternity care often lack even the basic infrastructure and equipment for such care, with particularly poor availability of test kits for the diagnosis of sexually transmitted diseases and consumables such as tetanus toxoid injections. Many of the associated actions—for instance, giving a pregnant woman a tetanus toxoid injection or screening her for HIV—have clear links to maternal and neonatal health outcomes (Carroli, Rooney, and Villar 2001). These gaps in availability thus represent significant shortfalls in health facilities' ability to provide high-quality ANC.

Beyond gaps in infrastructure, the report documents poor performance compared with international protocol. In particular, it finds that underperformance is widespread. As presented in figure O.4, in all five countries, health workers are only performing about 50 to 60 percent of the World Health Organization essential protocol for ANC. To assess levels of idle capacity, the observed levels of performance are linked to structural capacity and health worker knowledge. The findings show that up to a third of all underperformance can be attributed to idle capacity; that is, a third of the time, health workers have all the knowledge and equipment to provide a certain component of ANC but still fail to do so. The report also documents significant variation across and within countries (and between and within facilities) in such idle capacity, suggesting that even in the country with the poorest overall level of care (the Democratic Republic of Congo), some women receive ANC that is comparable in quality to the care provided in the country with the highest level of care (Cameroon).

As shown in figure O.5, poor quality of care in the form of deviations from protocol not only implies undertreatment, but also can include inappropriate or irrelevant treatment. Generally, the rates of overtreatment are low but can be as high as 25 percent. This finding is striking because the measurement of preventive care is not even geared at picking up overtreatment, and much of the overtreatment in LMICs may be in the form of irrelevant medication usage (Kwan et al. 2019; Lopez, Sautmann, and Schaner 2022), which is not measured in the data. Indeed, there are only two robust measures of inappropriate or irrelevant treatment in ANC—the provision of tetanus vaccines

Figure 0.3 Availability of drugs and consumables, equipment, and other supplies for providing antenatal care

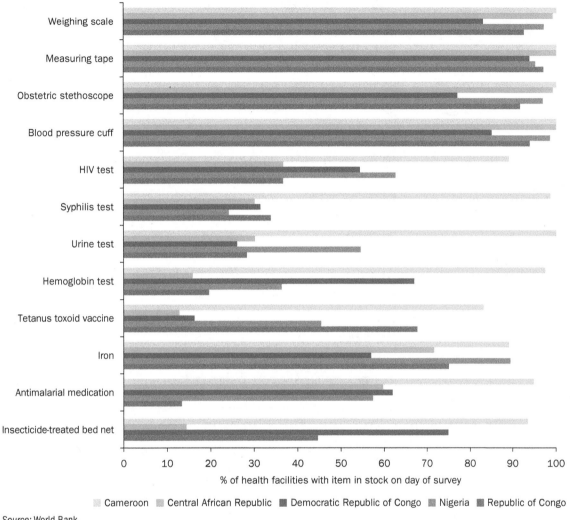

% of health facilities with item in stock on day of survey

Cameroon   Central African Republic   Democratic Republic of Congo   Nigeria   Republic of Congo

Source: World Bank.

in pregnancy without checking whether the woman has already received a tetanus vaccine, and the too-early provision of prophylactic malaria treatment that is not only unnecessary but may even be harmful to fetal development (Peters et al. 2007; Hernándes-Díaz et al. 2000). Yet, unnecessary or irrelevant care provision is found for both measures in all the contexts studied. Although most of the evidence on irrelevant treatment focuses on curative care and not preventive care, this finding motivates the concern surrounding inappropriate treatment and more careful assessment of it. Finally, the finding

Figure 0.4   Know-can-do gaps in the provision of antenatal care

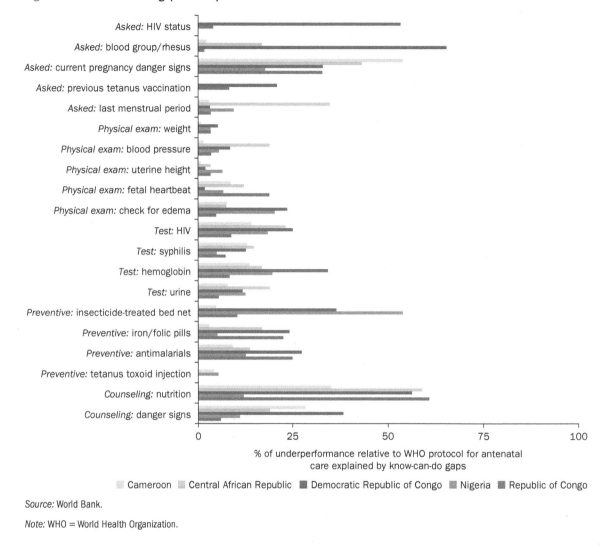

Source: World Bank.

Note: WHO = World Health Organization.

highlights that low effort by providers results in both undertreatment and irrelevant or inappropriate treatment—often concurrently.

The results further suggest that poor effort by providers is not easily explained by attributes like facility level, provider age, grade or experience, or even patient characteristics like age and education, which may be hypothesized to affect provider performance. Such effort gaps may explain up to a third of all underperformance relative to the protocol for ANC, suggesting that "simply" removing structural and knowledge constraints will not suffice in improving the quality of care. The report also reviews evidence showing

Figure 0.5 Provision of unnecessary care in antenatal care provision in five Sub-Saharan African countries

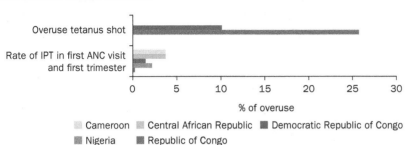

Source: World Bank.

Note: Overuse of tetanus toxoid vaccination is defined as the provision of this vaccine without checking documentation to see whether the woman has already received one for the current pregnancy. IPT refers to the initiation of prophylactic malaria treatment, using prescription sulfadoxine/pyrimethamine. The guidelines recommend prophylactic malaria treatment starting in the second trimester of pregnancy. Overuse of IPT is defined as the provision of such treatment in the woman's first antenatal care visit in her first trimester. ANC = antenatal care.

the presence of a steep wealth-quality gradient, which indicates that wealthier patients receive better quality of care—even at the same facility. However, the evidence also suggests that conditional on the quality of care, wealthier patients pay more than poorer patients. Taken together, these findings highlight the need for interventions that improve the physical capacity of facilities, address key gaps in medical training, *and* bolster health worker effort (whether by offering financial incentives or other means).

Key findings on financial incentives in primary health care provision in low-income countries

Much of the world, especially high- and middle-income countries, is in the midst of a push away from compensating public sector health providers through low-powered incentives like salaries and fixed facility budgets, toward high-powered incentives involving a mix of salaries/budgets and bonuses as well as facility-level funds linked to performance. A concrete example from Nigeria illustrates how these interventions work: including direct financing and health worker incentives, a facility might receive US$12 for each institutional delivery, US$1.20 for an ANC visit, and US$0.80 for a fully immunized child. In addition to such performance pay, a PBF project would include directly transferring operating budgets to facilities and granting autonomy over how to use these funds, paired with requirements to report on the use of funds for transparency and accountability and, in some instances, community oversight for health promotion and increased service utilization. Of course, these projects function on top of an existing system of primarily input-based financing. The strength of the incentive thus depends on the baseline level of financing, which may be an important driver of program impact, but which data limitations have prevented from quantification.

The report starts with a rapid overview of the design and characteristics of performance pay approaches in health—largely drawing on high- and middle-income country experience, highlighting the potential of performance pay in improving worker effort. Then, it delves into the evidence on PBF projects. The findings show that in most contexts, PBF projects have resulted in some improvements in terms of coverage. Often, this is institutional delivery, but the findings suggest that the performance pay aspect of PBF projects is likely not the driving force for such improvement.

As shown in figure O.6, some of the largest impacts of the PBF projects studied in this report are observed on structural quality, meaning the quality of infrastructure and equipment at facilities, aspects that performance pay arguably would not affect. Consistent with the discussion on

Figure O.6 Impacts of performance-based financing on facility physical capacity in Cameroon and Nigeria

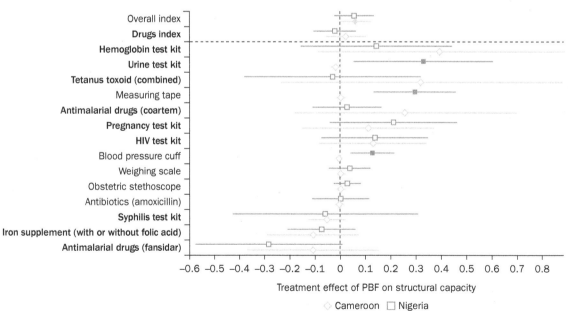

Sources: World Bank, based on Khanna et al. 2021 and de Walque et al. 2021.

Note: Markers above the dashed line refer to summary indexes; those below the line represent the individual components of those indexes. Solid markers indicate statistically significant estimates ($p < .05$); markers that are open indicate imprecise estimates. "Whiskers" around markers represent 95% confidence intervals. Components of the drugs index are in **bold** along the y axis. PBF = performance-based financing.

the various constraints to quality, the report shows that PBF projects have small impacts on most aspects of idle capacity, suggesting that such projects may do little to improve clinical quality of care beyond the improvements in structural quality (figure O.7). If anything, as figure O.7 shows, the significantly estimated impacts of PBF on idle capacity are positive. In other words, PBF increases some dimensions of idle capacity—which means that providers respond to PBF by leaving out additional aspects of care that they could perform. However, some of the earlier PBF programs studied in this report only incentivized structural quality rather than clinical or process quality, while later pilot programs incentivized all the dimensions of quality. The report highlights such a "later generation" program (in box 6.1, in chapter 6) implemented in the Kyrgyz Republic, which used anatomical models to train and provide supportive supervision on the correct provision of high-impact maternal

Figure O.7   **Impacts of performance-based financing on idle capacity—or the know-can-do gap—in Cameroon and Nigeria**

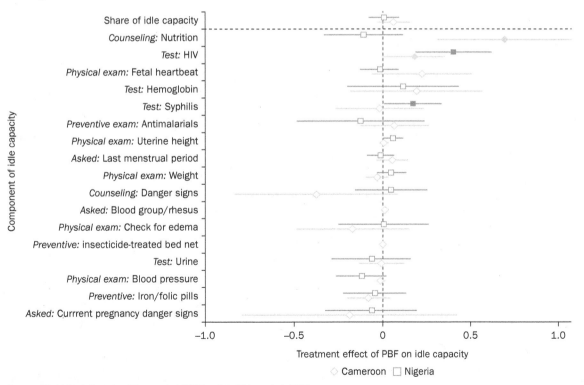

Sources: World Bank, based on Khanna et al. 2021 and de Walque et al. 2021.

Note: Markers above the dashed line indicate a summary effect. Solid markers indicate statistically significant estimates ($p < .05$); markers that are open indicate imprecise estimates. "Whiskers" around markers represent 95% confidence intervals. PBF = performance-based financing.

and neonatal care. The evaluation of this pilot indeed found that such training can significantly improve clinical quality.

Nonetheless, the fact that the relatively larger impacts of many PBF projects are on structural quality rather than idle capacity may indicate that the performance pay aspect of PBF projects is not a key driver of any observed gains from PBF projects. Even in the example of the Kyrgyz Republic, the impacts of training on quality appear in an arm where no performance pay was provided, only the training. This finding in turn calls into question the cost-effectiveness of this particular financial incentive approach to improve health. The report also finds mixed but limited evidence of impacts on equity, with PBF projects reducing the disparity in the quality of care received by wealthy and poor women in one instance but increasing it in another.

Moreover, whether performance pay works as a financial incentive might be questioned. Evidence from Argentina and Nigeria suggests that performance pay may mostly work to signal the importance of the services being purchased. This in turn implies that there may be scope to improve the cost-effectiveness of PBF projects if there are other ways to improve effort by signaling such importance rather than through offering high financial incentives that also require third-party verification. Such third-party verification costs can add significantly to overall program costs—up to a third of all administrative costs in one estimate (Zeng et al. 2021)—but they can be substantially reduced through the use of risk-based algorithms (Grover, Bauhoff, and Friedman 2019).

The report provides a cautionary tale from high-cost systems that performance pay may lead to increases in inappropriate care or overtreatment in response to misaligned pecuniary incentives. It reports primary evidence, which is limited in nature due to data challenges, that such a response to performance pay may occur in low-income country health systems as well. In addition to potential harm to patients, or at the very least the desirability of avoiding unnecessary treatment, the provision of unnecessary treatment is also related to sustainability.

Performance pay and key demand- and supply-side counterfactuals

The existing literature and this report thus yield some evidence of gains in coverage and structural quality from the introduction of PBF projects, but they call into question the impact of the performance pay aspect of these projects. This finding is further explored by comparing PBF projects with

DFF. The key difference between PBF and DFF projects is specifically the performance pay component; they share other features, including public financial management reform, health facility autonomy, decentralization, supportive supervision for the frontlines, and community engagement. DFF transfers equivalent funds to that of the performance pay component of PBF projects but without a conditionality mechanism.

Using harmonized data from five countries—Cameroon, Nigeria, Zambia, Zimbabwe, and the early Rwanda pilot—that piloted a DFF approach (de Walque et al. 2021; Khanna et al. 2021; Friedman, Das, and Mutasa 2017; Friedman et al. 2016; Basinga et al. 2011), the report finds that often both PBF and DFF projects represent notable improvements over business-as-usual in moving forward with the desired transformation of health systems. However, as shown in figure O.8, except for institutional

Figure O.8 Comparison of the pooled impact of performance-based and unconditional facility financing in five Sub-Saharan African countries (Cameroon, Nigeria, Rwanda, Zambia, and Zimbabwe)

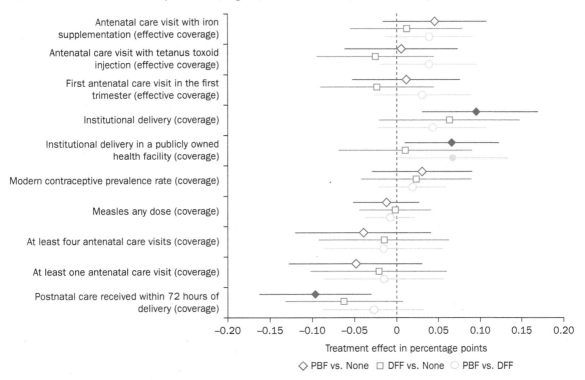

Sources: World Bank, based on de Walque et al. 2022.

Note: Solid markers indicate statistically significant estimates (*p* < .05); markers that are open indicate imprecise estimates. "Whiskers" around markers represent 95% confidence intervals. DFF = direct facility financing; PBF = performance-based financing.

deliveries, PBF projects do not lead to incremental gains over DFF projects, even when the DFF arm disbursed significantly less than the overall PBF package. This is further evidence that suggests that performance pay may yield muted or limited results as opposed to the other aspects of PBF projects, and it calls into question the rationale for financial incentives in the form of performance pay in PBF projects. The report examines several reasons that might explain why institutional deliveries may be more responsive to PBF interventions than to DFF, including assessing differences in program design and the relative importance of the price paid versus the salience of the task itself.

An alternative to financial incentives for health workers is offering such incentives on the demand side, such as CCT programs, which are present in 64 countries, and vouchers, which give beneficiaries free or subsidized access to health services for which providers are reimbursed on a fee-for-service basis. Neelsen et al. (2021) undertake a systematic review and meta-analysis comparing studies of health outcomes from PBF projects, voucher programs, and CCTs. With the necessary caveats inherent in the meta-analysis methodology, the results, presented in figure O.9, suggest that financial incentives, on average, improve maternal and child health service

Figure O.9 Impacts of PBF, vouchers, and conditional cash transfers on the utilization of maternal and child health services: Results from a meta-analysis

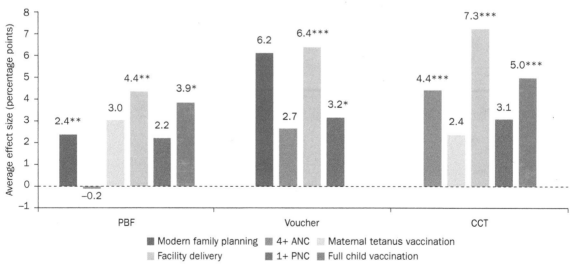

Source: Neelsen et al. 2021.

Note: ANC = antenatal care; CCT = conditional cash transfer; PBF = performance-based financing; PNC = postnatal care.

***$p < .01$, **$p < .05$, *$p < 0.1$.

indicators, but the mean effect sizes are modest, ranging between 2 and 7 percentage points. PBF projects (which provide such incentives as well as many other features) have a significant positive mean effect on the use of modern family planning, facility births, maternal tetanus, and child vaccination but not on ANC or postnatal care visits.

Comparison of the supply- and demand-side incentives shows that the mean effects are similar in size and significance across PBF projects, vouchers, and CCTs. Only for ANC visits is there a statistically significant difference between effect sizes across these intervention types, with CCTs being significantly more effective than PBF projects and vouchers. The overall similarity of effect sizes underscores the need for cost-benefit analysis since each of these three approaches to financial incentives comes with different costs of implementation. The cost- and cost-effectiveness analysis of PBF programs is nascent (see Zeng et al. (2018) and Shepard et al. (2020) for examples) and there are very few comparative cost studies. Nevertheless, the choice of specific schemes—whether deployed individually or in combination—should be driven first and foremost by the nature of the barrier to service utilization and provision (a topic covered in box O.1.). A CCT would not have an impact if there is no health facility, and a PBF program would not have any impact if patients cannot afford care at a health facility.

Looking forward: Research and operational implications

The evidence discussed in this report highlights that supply-side incentives, specifically performance pay for frontline health workers and facilities, can yield limited results, but the goal of financing the frontlines is not a marginal one. The question is how to achieve the goal of universal health coverage in a sustainable, effective, and efficient manner. The explicit results orientation might make performance pay more politically palatable. It is likely that this link to results and transparency has crowded-in much-needed donor financing, including for the research on which this report builds. But the report also highlights the importance of the institutional setting in which the reform is being implemented. There is little evidence to support performance pay in centralized, under-resourced, unfinanced health systems, whereas other aspects of reforms related to autonomy, transparency, and accountability in PBF and DFF projects have resulted in notable improvements in health outcomes over business-as-usual.

Box 0.1 In Focus: Action items for task teams working on health financing reform

This report presents evidence showing that meaningful improvements in health system performance can be achieved when financial and managerial autonomy is extended to health providers directly. Such direct financing not only requires that health facilities receive a transfer of resources, but also that they are made accountable for delivery of services and prudent financial management. At the same time, the report casts doubt on the need for performance pay as a starting point in health financing reform in under-resourced settings. The report may thus give rise to reasonable questions about how policy makers can design a health financing reform that finances health service providers directly—in a way that is transparent and accountable, and only using performance pay options when they are carefully contextualized.

This box pulls together various relevant findings from across the report to provide action items for teams working on health financing reform projects aimed at improving effective primary health care coverage in low-income countries in a sustainable and scalable way. It broadly categorizes these actions into four stages: diagnostics to identify barriers to high-quality care, identification of relevant policy options, questions about sustainability and scalability of supply-side interventions, and measurement.

Diagnostics to identify the relevant barriers to access to high-quality care

Teams designing health financing projects may benefit from tracking the following indicators ahead of time, with the goal of deciding whether performance pay is appropriate for any of the indicators targeted by the project:

1. How different are the coverage and effective coverage rates for the key indicators?
   a. Using Demographic and Health Survey (DHS) or other nationally representative household data, calculate coverage and effective coverage for the indicators of interest.
   b. The indicators that have the largest gaps between coverage and effective coverage may represent "low-hanging" fruit for health projects focused on quality improvements to target.
2. What are the baseline levels of coverage?
   a. As chapter 6 shows, performance pay may not make a lot of sense in catchment areas and for indicators where coverage levels are already very high.
   b. Especially low levels of coverage may reveal demand-side issues, indicating a role for vouchers and cash transfers.
   c. Teams may thus consider using demand-side incentives to shore up demand for the least used essential services and then test low levels of performance pay for selected indicators.
   d. The "sweet spot" for performance pay may be for indicators where baseline utilization has room for improvement but is not so low as to be indicative of demand-side barriers.
3. Are there gaps in the structural capacity to provide essential health services?
   a. What are the essential items (equipment, supplies, drugs, and other consumables) that are required to provide the services of interest?
   b. Are they available, stored as per guidelines, in frontline facilities?

(Continued)

Box 0.1 *continued*

4. Similarly, are there gaps in provider knowledge for the provision of essential health services?
   a. If yes, at what level are these gaps typically addressed?
   b. Medical school curricula may be slower to update, but in-service training modules may supplement formal medical training in some instances.
5. For the indicators for which performance pay may be considered, how high is idle capacity, which is the portion of care that could have been provided given health worker knowledge and health facility infrastructure, but is not performed by the provider?
   a. Performance pay may only make sense for indicators that have a high degree of idle capacity.
   b. If idle capacity does not explain underperformance for an indicator, other approaches, including facility financing and demand-side incentives may make more sense.
6. What is the country's capacity to finance facilities directly through prevailing public financial management systems?
   a. Implement the diagnostic proposed by Piatti-Fünfkirchen, Hadley, and Mathivet (2021).

Identification of relevant options

Take a comprehensive health systems approach:
   o Map out the various financing flows across sources and ensure that these are complementary.

o The practical question should not be "performance-based financing (PBF) or direct facility financing (DFF)," but rather how, across all sources, facilities are being paid and what a purposeful incentive structure would look like.
o Demand-side options, where feasible, may be combined with supply-side interventions as they address a different set of issues than PBF or DFF.

Scalability and sustainability of supply-side approaches

Where supply-side schemes seem most opportune, or in the context where such schemes have been in place for a while, the following are some questions to ask about scalability and sustainability:

1. If facilities do not have a budget under their control, what needs to be done to send financing directly to them? This may require policy and legal reform. Options may include the following:
   o Setting up dedicated block grants for facilities (as is being done in Burkina Faso).
   o Recognizing facilities as vendors and paying them similarly to how private service providers would be reimbursed (as is being done in Uganda).
   o Integrating facilities into the budget as dedicated spending units (as is being done in Tanzania).
   o Recognizing facilities as extrabudgetary units that receive an intergovernmental transfer (this is more appropriate for larger hospitals and is done in many countries, for example, Rwanda).

(Continued)

Box 0.1 *continued*

2. If procurement is centralized, consider options for shadow budgets for facilities that are drawn down where facilities purchase inputs from a central repository at a discounted price.
   o Enable options to procure emergency drugs from the private sector if otherwise not available.
3. If frontline facilities do not receive routine supportive supervisory visits, consider adding visits from the district health team. The verification visits in PBF trials provide a good template for such supervision, even if it is decoupled from performance pay.
4. If there is no community oversight, consider engaging the community in facility management, such as through citizen scorecards and meetings with village development committees.
5. If there are substantial delays in salary payments, consider public expenditure tracking system reforms to improve the timeliness of salary payments.
6. Explore fintech innovations, such as mobile money, to facilitate payments to remote providers while leaving a digital footprint of the transaction.
7. Strengthen basic financial management capacity at the facility level to ensure financial accountability and build confidence in prudent use of resources by financial institutions.
8. Performance pay is not the only way of making payments to providers output oriented: catchment population size and composition, disease burden, and remoteness can be leveraged to serve key needs without performance pay.

   o Pay for performance should be considered with care and only added at the margins once a functional facility payment system is in place.
   o Use the diagnostics section above to identify candidate indicators for performance pay or fee-for-service.
9. How to sequence interventions correctly:
   o Teams may wish to start with 18–24 months of demand-side interventions paired with DFF.
   o Mobile money, portals, and dashboards can provide accountability, but they can also be used to start changing the orientation of frontline facilities and staff into a more results-linked one.
   o Repeat the diagnostics exercise and then consider whether it makes sense to add performance pay for any of the indicators.

Measurement

This report and these action items highlight the importance of good data at the household and health facility levels.

1. National health facility censuses that include at least a representative sample of private providers are large investments but provide a wealth of detail.
2. DHS and other nationally representative household surveys can be leveraged to track coverage and effective coverage.
3. DHS-Service Provision Assessment and Service Delivery Indicator surveys provide a wealth of useful data on the structural capacity of representative frontline health facilities.

(Continued)

Box 0.1 *continued*

4. Irrelevant care should be tracked, not just the underprovision of necessary care. As the report highlights, the threat of misaligned incentives through performance pay is that of the provision of irrelevant care. This has implications for patient welfare and the cost-effectiveness of the health system.
5. Measuring clinical quality can be tricky. Direct observations are expensive, but they provide in-depth pictures of care provision. Where available, balance scorecards and other routinely tracked data reported through PBF portals can provide valuable insights.
6. Administrative data from birth and other civil and vital registries can provide routinely updated data on health outcomes.

Resources brought to the frontlines through PBF projects have significantly improved the structural quality of primary health facilities.

So, the question arises as to the value of performance pay relative to its limited benefits. Performance pay requires verification, which is complex and can be costly to implement. In one example, the costs were estimated to be about 20 percent of all administrative costs (Zeng et al. 2021). Although risk-based verification algorithms may reduce such costs of performance pay, other measures, like dashboards and business plans (as in DFF projects), may offer similar accountability and transparency but at lower cost and with greater simplicity. In addition, the costs of performance pay can be unpredictable for the government and the health facility, which makes performance pay hard to scale unless it is well aligned with the government's public financial management system. This also raises questions about its sustainability. Of course, DFF may also require alignment with public financial management systems—for instance, having health facilities recognized as spending units in the charter of accounts is not always a straightforward process—but DFF does not face the challenge of budget unpredictability faced when scaling PBF programs.

The policy options for improving health services through financial incentives are undoubtedly on a continuum. For instance, one low-cost option may be to identify areas where baseline demand is particularly weak for certain types of services, ensure a minimum standard of quality of care in a public facility—using direct financing—followed by household-level cash transfers to see how much they increase a given indicator, and only then consider performance pay to frontline health workers and facilities. The future of performance pay—as one health financing approach in an arsenal of several options—should not be a "yes" or "no" question but rather a "how" and "in what sequence" question. Box O.1 discusses in detail how task teams might approach these questions.

Chapter 8 considers the future of approaches to strengthening health systems, including PBF and DFF. PBF schemes offer strong accountability toward external donors, which has likely contributed to their popularity. These schemes incorporate important innovations beyond performance pay, for instance, accountability and transparency linked to decentralization and funding of the frontlines. In contexts where payment mechanisms such as DFF appear more appropriate, as discussed in box O.1, policy makers may want to incorporate accountability measures that satisfy the reporting demands of donors. This is especially the case in heavily donor-dependent countries where it could be argued that—at least in the short term—PBF schemes should serve as a tool for improving donor alignment around a package of services, much more than a tool for changing the public provider payment function. Thus, sustainable health financing reform may not incorporate performance pay while retaining other important aspects of PBF interventions.

The report concludes in chapter 8 with a discussion of the operational insights from the evidence presented. It draws four main messages from the findings presented in the report for the design of sustainable and scalable health financing reform. First, sustainability is about more than just money, and risk and uncertainty can lead to interventions being unsustainable even if the financing is available. Second, health facilities can often benefit from budget autonomy, flexibility, as well as unified payment systems, and their budgets can be output oriented without being linked to performance pay. Third, performance pay must make sense in the broader health system context—in other words, a substantial portion of the constraints to quality must be within the health worker's locus of control; the public financial management system should have a way to make and, if necessary, scale the performance payments; a purchasing unit, whether dedicated or not, should exist; and the budget structure should be able to handle the unpredictability of performance pay. Fourth, emerging technologies can be used to reduce the implementation costs of performance pay approaches. For instance, mobile payments to facilities may help deliver necessary accountability reform alongside the decentralization and direct financing of frontline health facilities. The report calls for the collection and analysis of data to track the constraints to effective coverage and the design of health financing interventions that are informed by such data.

The design of financial incentives in health care and the best way to measure quality of care at scale to support such incentive schemes are a difficult policy problem in which open questions remain. Even with many questions still unanswered, this report presents research that highlights the limits of complex PBF interventions, particularly compared with "lighter touch" policy options such as DFF. The research discussed in this report makes the case that health financing reform can—indeed, should—include accountability and transparency even if it does not include performance pay. The report discusses several rigorous methods for measuring the quality and efficiency of care and offers thoughts on scaling up such measurement. The research collated here also demonstrates the value of fixing the fundamentals: decentralizing, financing the frontlines, and incentivizing the utilization of preventive health services can be meaningful reforms by themselves. That said, in all the countries studied here, much room for improvement remains on many measures of health system performance. As countries seek to leverage health financing reform to develop high-quality health systems, the report argues that there is a need for an expanded suite of policy options, including but not limited to PBF, which can help countries address all the barriers they face to improving effective coverage.

Note

1. Initially 36 impact evaluations of PBF pilot programs in health were funded, but to our knowledge, only 25 have been or are expected to be completed (https://www.rbfhealth.org/impact).

References

Basinga, P., P. J. Gertler, A. Binagwaho, A. L. Soucat, J. Sturdy, and C. M. Vermeersch. 2011. "Effect on Maternal and Child Health Services in Rwanda of Payment to Primary Health-Care Providers for Performance: An Impact Evaluation." *The Lancet* 377 (9775): 1421–28.

Carroli, G., C. Rooney, and J. Villar. 2001. "How Effective Is Antenatal Care in Preventing Maternal Mortality and Serious Morbidity? An Overview of the Evidence." *Paediatric and Perinatal Epidemiology* 15: 1–42.

Das, J., J. Hammer, and K. Leonard. 2008. "The Quality of Medical Advice in Low-Income Countries." *Journal of Economic Perspectives* 22 (2): 93–114.

de Walque, D., J. Friedman, E. Kandpal, M. Saenz, and C. Vermeersch. 2022. "Performance-Based Financing versus Direct Facility Financing for Primary

Health Service Delivery: Pooled Evidence from Five Sub-Saharan African Countries." World Bank, Washington, DC.

de Walque, D., P. J. Robyn, H. Saidou, G. Sorgho, and M. Steenland. 2021. "Looking into the Performance-Based Financing Black Box: Evidence from an Impact Evaluation in the Health Sector in Cameroon." *Health Policy and Planning* 36 (6): 835–47.

Doran, T., C. Fullwood, H. Gravelle, D. Reeves, E. Kontopantelis, U. Hiroeh, and M. Roland. 2006. "Pay-for-Performance Programs in Family Practices in the United Kingdom." *New England Journal of Medicine* 355 (4): 375–84.

Eichler, R., and R. Levine. 2009. *Performance Incentives for Global Health: Potential and Pitfalls.* Washington, DC: Center for Global Development.

Fink, G., E. Kandpal, and G. Shapira. 2022. "Inequality in the Quality of Health Services: Wealth, Content of Care, and Price of Antenatal Consultations in the Democratic Republic of Congo." *Economic Development and Cultural Change.* https://doi.org/10.1086/713941.

Friedman, J., A. Das, and R. Mutasa. 2017. "Rewarding Provider Performance to Improve Quality and Coverage of Maternal and Child Health Outcomes: Zimbabwe Results-Based Financing Pilot Program: Evidence to Inform Policy and Management Decisions." World Bank, Washington, DC.

Friedman, J., J. Qamruddin, C. Chansa, and A. K. Das. 2016. "Impact Evaluation of Zambia's Health Results-Based Financing Pilot Project." World Bank, Washington, DC.

Fritsche, G. B., R. Soeters, and B. Meessen. 2014. *Performance-Based Financing Toolkit.* Washington, DC: World Bank.

Gergen, J., E. Josephson, M. Coe, S. Ski, S. Madhavan, and S. Bauhoff. 2017. "Quality of Care in Performance-Based Financing: How It Is Incorporated in 32 Programs across 28 Countries." *Global Health: Science and Practice* 5 (1): 90–107.

Grover, D., S. Bauhoff, and J. Friedman. 2019. "Using Supervised Learning to Select Audit Targets in Performance-Based Financing in Health: An Example from Zambia." *PloS One* 14 (1): e0211262.

Hernández-Díaz, S., M. M. Werler, A. M. Walker, and A. A. Mitchell. 2000. "Folic Acid Antagonists during Pregnancy and the Risk of Birth Defects." *New England Journal of Medicine* 343 (22): 1608–14.

Ibnat, F., K. L. Leonard, L. Bawo, and R. L. Mohammed-Roberts. 2019. "The Three-Gap Model of Health Worker Performance." Policy Research Working Paper 8782, World Bank, Washington, DC.

IHME (Institute for Health Metrics and Evaluation). 2020. *GBD Compare Data Visualization.* Seattle, WA: IHME, University of Washington. http://vizhub.healthdata.org/gbd-compare.

Kassebaum, N., A. Bertozzi-Villa, M. Coggeshall, K. A. Shackelford, C. Steiner, K. R. Heuton, D. Gonzalez-Medina, et al. 2014. "Global, Regional, and National Levels and Causes of Maternal Mortality during 1990–2013: A Systematic Analysis for the Global Burden of Disease Study 2013." *The Lancet* 384 (9947): 980–1004.

Khanna, M., B. Loevinsohn, E. Pradhan, O. Fadeyibi, K. McGee, O. Odutolu, G. Fritsche, et al. 2021. "Decentralized Facility Financing versus Performance-Based Payments in Primary Health Care: A Large-Scale Randomized

Controlled Trial in Nigeria." *BMC Medicine* 19: Article 224. https://doi
.org/10.1186/s12916-021-02092-4.

Kruk, M. E., A. D. Gage, N. T. Joseph, G. Danaei, S. García-Saisó, and
J. A. Salomon. 2018. "Mortality Due to Low-Quality Health Systems in the
Universal Health Coverage Era: A Systematic Analysis of Amenable Deaths
in 137 Countries." *The Lancet* 392 (10160): 2203–12. https://doi.org/10.1016
/S0140-6736(18)31668-4.

Kwan, A., B. Daniels, S. Bergkvist, V. Das, M. Pai, and J. Das. 2019. "Use of
Standardised Patients for Healthcare Quality Research in Low- and Middle-
Income Countries." *BMJ Global Health* 4 (5): e001669. https://doi
.org/10.1136/bmjgh-2019-001669.

Lopez, C., A. Sautmann, and S. Schaner. 2022. "Does Patient Demand Contribute
to the Overuse of Prescription Drugs?" *American Economic Journal: Applied
Economics* 14 (1): 225–60.

Mills, A. 2014. "Health Care Systems in Low- and Middle-Income Countries."
New England Journal of Medicine 370 (6): 552–57.

Neelsen, S., D. de Walque, J. Friedman, and A. Wagstaff. 2021. "Financial
Incentives to Increase Utilization of Reproductive, Maternal and Child Health
Services in Low- and Middle-Income Countries: A Systematic Review and
Meta-Analysis." Policy Research Working Paper 9793, World Bank,
Washington, DC.

Peters, P. J., M. C. Thigpen, M. E. Parise, and R. D. Newman. 2007. "Safety and
Toxicity of Sulfadoxine/Pyrimethamine: Implications for Malaria Prevention
in Pregnancy Using Intermittent Preventive Treatment." *Drug Safety* 30 (6):
481–501.

Piatti-Fünfkirchen, M., S. Hadley, and B. Mathivet. 2021. "Alignment of
Performance-Based Financing in Health with the Government Budget:
A Principle Based Approach." Health, Nutrition, and Population Discussion
Paper, World Bank, Washington, DC.

Shepard D., W. Zeng, R. Mutasa, A. Das, C. Sisimayi, S. Shamu, S. Banda, and
J. Friedman. 2020. "Cost-Effectiveness of Results-Based Financing of
Maternal and Child Health Services in Zimbabwe: A controlled Pre-Post
Study." *Journal of Hospital Management and Health Policy* 4 (32). https://doi.
org/10.21037/jhmhp-20-84.

Wagstaff, A., C. Bredenkamp, and L. R. Buisman. 2014. "Progress on Global
Health Goals: Are the Poor Being Left Behind?" *World Bank Research Observer*
29 (2): 137–62.

WHO (World Health Organization). 2020. *Improving Child Survival and
Mortality.* Geneva: WHO. https://www.who.int/news-room/fact-sheets
/detail/children-reducing-mortality.

Zeng, W., D. Shepard, H. Nguyen, C. Chansa, A Das, J. Qamruddin, and J.
Friedman. 2018. "Cost-Effectiveness of Results-Based Financing, Zambia:
A Cluster Randomized Trial." *Bulletin of the World Health Organization*
96 (11), 760.

Zeng, W., E. Pradhan, M. Khanna, O. Fadeyibi, G. Fritsche, and O. Odutolu.
2021. "Cost-Effectiveness Analysis of the Decentralized Facility Financing
and Performance-Based Financing Program in Nigeria." *Journal of Hospital
Management and Health Policy.* doi:10.21037/jhmhp-20-82.

Abbreviations

ACT	artemisinin-based combination therapy
ANC	antenatal care
ARI	acute respiratory infection
ARV	antiretroviral
BP	blood pressure
CCT	conditional cash transfer
CHW	community health worker
DFF	direct facility financing
DHS	Demographic and Health Survey
DSC	district steering committee
EC	effective coverage
FDA	US Food and Drug Administration
HIV/AIDS	human immunodeficiency virus/acquired immunodeficiency syndrome
HRITF	Health Results Innovation Trust Fund
IHME	Institute for Health Metrics and Evaluation
INRUD	International Network for the Rational Use of Drugs
IPT	intermittent preventive treatment
ITN	insecticide-treated bed net
IV	intravenous
JSY	Janani Suraksha Yojana (CCT program in India)
LMICs	low- and middle-income countries
MCH	maternal and child health
MICS	Multiple Indicator Cluster Surveys
mmHg	millimeters of mercury
MMR	maternal mortality ratio
MO	medical officer

ORS	oral rehydration salts
PBF	performance-based financing
PETS	Public Expenditure Tracking System
PFM	public financial management
PMI	US President's Malaria Initiative
PNC	postnatal care
QSC	quantitative supervisory checklist
RBF	results-based financing
RCR	retroactive consultation review
RDT	rapid detection test
RMCH	reproductive, maternal, and child health
SHI	social health insurance
TB	tuberculosis
UCTs	unconditional cash transfers
UNFPA	United Nations Population Fund
UNICEF	United Nations Children's Fund
WHO	World Health Organization
WHO STEPS	World Health Organization STEPwise Approach to NCD Risk Factor Surveillance

CHAPTER 1

Introduction

Introduction

The ultimate goal of development efforts in health is the production of better health in low- and middle-income country (LMIC) populations. Such investment is still much needed because all over the developing world, coverage for health services remains low, especially among the poor, notwithstanding the progress made during the push toward the Millennium Development Goals (Wagstaff, Bredenkamp, and Buisman 2014). For example, equitable access to affordable health care is not a reality for many women, children, and adolescents in the developing world, resulting in more than six million deaths from preventable causes each year (WHO 2019, 2020). This is true both for basic services, such as maternal and child health, as well as for services aimed at preventing and treating the emerging threat of noncommunicable diseases.

This assessment is even starker if, beyond access to medical services, effective coverage is considered, that is, coverage with effective or quality services. Effective coverage can be decomposed into the product of coverage (those in need getting care) and quality (correct or successful treatment among those getting care). The estimates of effective coverage and its two components for six conditions (pregnancy, child malaria, child diarrhea, hypertension, tuberculosis, and HIV) suggest that it is currently still shockingly poor for many health conditions in many environments. The estimates further show that whether it is coverage or quality that is the bottleneck in achieving better effective coverage varies by condition and country. The results using the example of HIV treatment also indicate substantial variations by wealth quintiles and whether the poor have made substantial progress in effective coverage. Often over the past decades, greater progress has been achieved among the poor than the better off, although the coverage levels remain too low and important gaps in quality translate into stark inequity in effective coverage.

Substantial evidence suggests that the quality of care in many LMICs is low, especially for the poor. This is because public sector health workers often provide low standards of care in many developing countries: health conditions are misdiagnosed, and even when they are well diagnosed, the correct treatment or interventions might not be prescribed or implemented (Das, Hammer, and Leonard 2008). In other words, even when care is accessed, the quality of the care received can be poor. A well-known example of this dichotomy is the case of the Indian *Janani Suraksha Yojana* (safe motherhood intervention), which led to large increases in institutional deliveries but no changes in maternal or neonatal survival (Kruk et al. 2018). Overall, limited access to quality health care can be due to bottlenecks on the demand side, if the population does not seek care, or on the supply side. On the supply side, low effective coverage might be due to poorly trained staff (knowledge gap), lack of equipment (know-can gap), lack of effort from the providers (can-do gap) (Ibnat et al. 2019), or even the different treatment of patients depending on their socioeconomic status (Fink, Kandpal, and Shapira 2022).

Due to frustrations with this status quo of sustained progress in service utilization but limited gains in health outcomes, especially among the poor, the idea of performance-based financing (PBF) has gained prominence. PBF is a financing mechanism through which facilities receive payments for performance on specific predetermined indicators, as opposed to low-powered incentives like flat salaries and fixed facility budgets. The payments typically include performance pay for health workers as well as performance-linked direct financing for facilities. For instance, in Nigeria, a PBF pilot disbursed US$12 per institutional delivery, US$1.20 for an antenatal care visit, and US$0.80 for child immunization. In this instance, up to half of the finances received through such PBF payments could be used for worker incentives, while the rest could be used for facility infrastructure, responding to equipment breakdowns or shortages in drugs and supplies. The logic is straightforward: the better a facility and its workers perform on key measures, the more financing they receive, so if poor worker effort or facility performance is the barrier to improving health outcomes, then the explicit linkage between health financing and worker and facility performance should increase the supply or quality of health services provided. Indeed, the evidence from high-income countries (Doran and Roland 2011) and even some early evidence from low-income countries (Basinga et al. 2011; Falisse et al. 2014) indicates that PBF improves primary health service delivery. An influential early study, which is reviewed in box 1.1, showed that performance pay contracts improved

Box 1.1 In Focus: A short history of performance-based financing and the related evaluation agenda

Performance pay contracts have been implemented extensively in high-income health systems. Evidence from those settings, such as in the United Kingdom (Doran and Roland 2011) and the United States (Mendelson et al. 2017), suggests that remunerating health staff based on their performance can lead to improvements in the quantity and quality of primary care provided.

In parallel, performance-based financing (PBF)—incorporating performance pay in a wider package of interventions with an aim toward linking health financing to results and improving facility autonomy and management—was developed in low- and middle-income countries (LMICs) and linked to early experimentation with the introduction of market forces in primary health care. After early experiences in Afghanistan, Cambodia, Haiti, and Zambia, PBF was piloted on a larger scale in Rwanda and Burundi (Meessen et al. 2006; Fritsche, Soeters, and Meessen 2014). The impact evaluation of the Rwandan pilot was influential in suggesting that PBF could improve the delivery of maternal and child health services (Basinga et al. 2011). This evidence led to large donor investments in PBF pilots around the world and indeed may even have crowded in donor funding into health financing. A key player in this space has been the World Bank's Health Results Innovation Trust Fund (HRITF), which supported and evaluated LMIC governments in paying providers based on their results in the provision of maternal, newborn, and child health care. At its peak, the PBF portfolio comprised 36 projects that spanned 28 countries in the Africa, East Asia and Pacific, Europe and Central Asia, Latin America and the Caribbean, Middle East and North Africa, and Southeast Asia regions, the majority of which are in Sub-Saharan Africa. PBF projects represent more than

US$2.5 billion in World Bank funding. As of June 2017, 32 of 46 Sub-Saharan African countries had piloted or expanded PBF interventions (Gautier, Allegri, and Ridde 2019).

Commentators have criticized this large and rapid extension of external support as a "donor-driven fad" relying on limited context-relevant evidence and imposing a unified model that abstracts from local context and long-term consequences (Paul et al. 2018). A central critique has been that by linking performance to payments, these interventions replace health workers' intrinsic motivation and prosocial drive with extrinsic motivation. Such a replacement in turn erodes the quality of the health system after the donor financing tied to this instrument has run out. Chapter 5 in this report discusses the evidence base behind this claim and brings to bear rigorous new analysis on the topic. PBF practitioners from Africa responded to this critique by stressing the catalyzing role played and the systemwide effects brought by PBF programs in their countries and highlighting the role of local authorities and actors in adapting the design of PBF to local health systems, proposing innovations that are responsive to local needs, and integrating the PBF mechanisms in a sustainable way within their countries' health architecture (Mayaka Ma-Nitu et al. 2018).

Irrespective of the debate on the role of donors, what cannot be denied is that the HRITF explicitly adopted a learning-by-doing approach, since 29 of the 36 pilots it funded were accompanied by impact evaluations. In large part, the evidence in this report comes from this unique effort at systematically learning about the impact of PBF and performance pay approaches in low-income country health systems. In 2008, at the onset of the first trust fund, HRITF, which funded the PBF pilots and impact

(Continued)

Box 1.1 *continued*

evaluations, there were many unanswered questions about the use of PBF to improve effective coverage in LMICs. As this report demonstrates, the large number of pilot projects and impact evaluations funded by HRITF have led to substantial learning about where, when, and why PBF approaches might work and how they can be strengthened.

These pilots and the accompanying impact evaluations also demonstrate the value of "expensive" randomized controlled trials. The rigorous design of the impact evaluations and the resulting high-quality evidence have been an irreplaceable resource for the team of researchers writing this policy research report.

health service delivery in Rwanda (Basinga et al. 2011). The contracts led to large investments in PBF for primary health service delivery, including performance-linked financing for health facilities and performance pay for health workers, in the hopes that tying remuneration to performance would lead to improved health outcomes.

A large literature documents the lack of worker effort and has even culminated in a Lancet Commission report on high-quality health systems (Kruk et al. 2018). Poor quality of care sometimes stems from providers not having the necessary knowledge of clinical protocols, but it can also arise from providers applying insufficient effort (Das, Hammer, and Leonard 2008). However, in many developing countries, poor worker effort is not the only or even the most important constraint to the provision of high-quality care. For instance, in much of Sub-Saharan Africa, publicly owned health facilities generally do not have an operating budget under their control. As illustrated in figure 1.1, staff are typically centrally recruited, and salaries are paid directly by the Ministry of Health or the central administration. While the salaries paid are part of the extrinsic motivation of health workers, the incentive structure is relatively flat: pay scales are formulaic and tied to seniority and position, and wages are compressed. The intrinsic motivation of saving lives and improving the health of patients also motivates health workers, and it is generally recognized that the health sector might attract a different type of worker, who is more drawn to the mission of public health than to pecuniary motives (Besley and Ghatak 2005).

The central administration also procures all drugs and equipment and the provincial or district hospital then typically disburses to the primary-level health facilities a set of drugs and supplies at theoretically regular intervals.

Figure 1.1   Lay of the land in centralized health systems

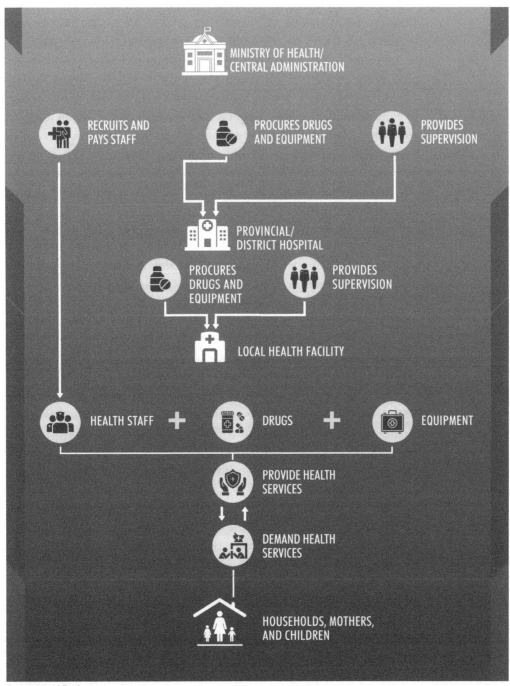

The types and quantity of drugs provided by the provincial hospital are usually based on the size of the primary health facility and the services they are supposed to provide. If a piece of equipment breaks, the facility must request repair from a centralized government agency, for instance, a district health team. The repair process, from submitting the request to when the piece of equipment is repaired, can take weeks or months. There is limited supervision, but to the extent that there is any, it is provided intermittently by the provincial or district hospital. These supervisory visits can often be audit-like in nature and perceived as punitive and evidence does not suggest that they are particularly useful in improving performance (Clements, Streefland, and Malau 2007). It is in this fiduciary and managerial context that the local health facility provides health services to the local population in its catchment area.

On the demand side, households seek curative care when they are sick and preventive care to avoid becoming ill. For example, a pregnant woman or mother of a young child is motivated to seek care at the health facility because she is intrinsically motivated to have a safe pregnancy or a healthy child. However, she may encounter barriers to obtaining care because of resource, time, or information constraints: she might not have enough money to pay for potential user fees or transportation to the health facility, might lack time for a preventive visit, or might not know which services are appropriate and needed and where and how to receive them.

A large set of interventions has been proposed and implemented to address the twin issues of low quality of care and worse access to high-quality care by poor populations. Many of these interventions rely on demand and supply incentives (figure 1.2), while others use mechanisms like quality improvement interventions, population-level education, or insurance programs.

One such intervention is cash transfer programs that support vulnerable populations by distributing transfers to low-income households to prevent shocks, protecting the chronically poor, and promoting capabilities and opportunities for vulnerable households (Glassman, Duran, and Koblinsky 2013; Barrientos and DeJong 2006; de Janvry and Sadoulet 2006; Devereux and Sabates-Wheeler 2004). The economic rationale for those programs is that they can be an equitable and efficient approach to address market failures and reach the most vulnerable populations (Fiszbein and Schady 2009).

Evidence from the economics literature suggests that contracts that tie payments to performance can be used to elicit greater effort in settings with

Figure 1.2   Lay of the land in health systems with the addition of demand- and supply-side incentives

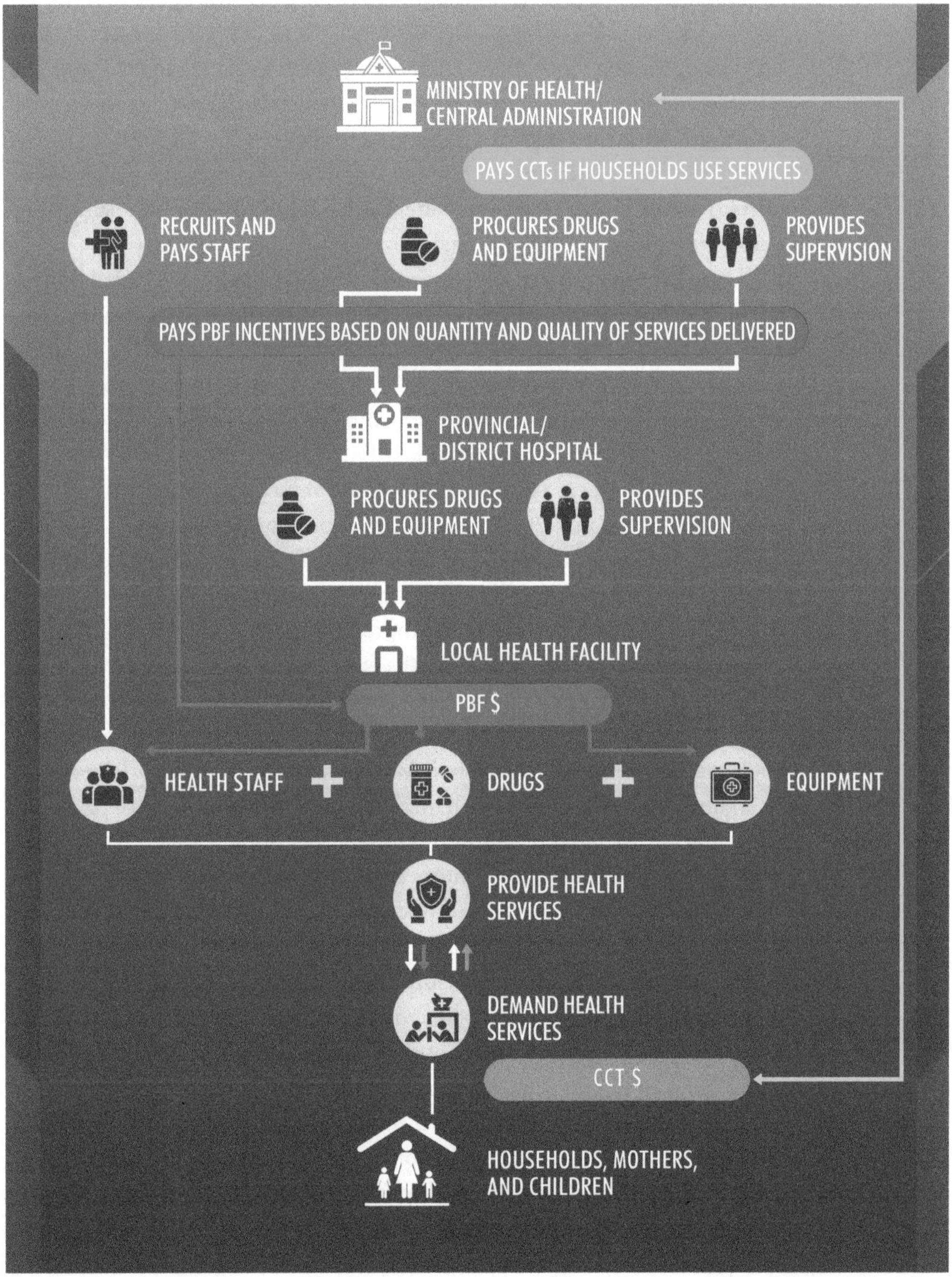

MINISTRY OF HEALTH/
CENTRAL ADMINISTRATION

PAYS CCTs IF HOUSEHOLDS USE SERVICES

RECRUITS AND
PAYS STAFF

PROCURES DRUGS
AND EQUIPMENT

PROVIDES
SUPERVISION

PAYS PBF INCENTIVES BASED ON QUANTITY AND QUALITY OF SERVICES DELIVERED

PROVINCIAL/
DISTRICT HOSPITAL

PROCURES DRUGS
AND EQUIPMENT

PROVIDES
SUPERVISION

LOCAL HEALTH FACILITY

PBF $

HEALTH STAFF + DRUGS + EQUIPMENT

PROVIDE HEALTH
SERVICES

DEMAND HEALTH
SERVICES

CCT $

HOUSEHOLDS, MOTHERS,
AND CHILDREN

Source: World Bank.

Note: CCTs = conditional cash transfers; PBF = performance-based financing.

principal-agent problems (Prendergast 1999; Lazear 2000; Duflo, Hanna, and Ryan 2012). Such contracts provide workers or the facilities in which they work a checklist of incentivized outputs and the price of each output. In theory, linking worker remuneration to performance targets aligns the interests of employers and workers. This is essentially a fee-for-service approach, with the checklist additionally signaling the importance of the purchased tasks. Such interventions may broadly be described as financial incentives for health service providers and facility management staff, conditional on the quantity and quality of services they provide.

These types of pay-for-performance contracts have been widely implemented in high-income health systems. Evidence from high-income contexts, including the United Kingdom (Doran and Roland 2011) and the United States (Mendelson et al. 2017), suggests that remunerating health workers for their performance can lead to improvements in the quantity and quality of primary care provided. Further, recent lab-in-the-field evidence from Nigeria (Bauhoff and Kandpal 2021) and South Africa (Lagarde and Blaauw 2021) suggests that pay-for-performance interventions may succeed in improving the quality of care in primary health care settings in LMICs. Thus, at least in concept, performance pay may be a viable and attractive approach for improving effective coverage in LMICs.

However, in low-income country health sectors, both the initial lay of the land and the PBF interventions considered in this report can differ dramatically from the simple fee-for-service approach implemented successfully in high-income countries. Often, in low-income country contexts, PBF is used as an umbrella term for the mechanism that includes performance payments made directly by the central authority to the health facility based on verified increases in the quantity and improvements in the quality of the health services it delivers, but also other components like facility autonomy, accountability reform, community oversight or engagement in facility administration, public financial management reform, and supportive supervision for the frontlines. Thus, performance-linked contracts are one component of the PBF intervention package, but not the entirety.

Further, unlike in high-income country experiences with performance pay, in PBF reforms, the additional funds are paid to the facility and then divided between bonus payments for health workers and drug and equipment purchases, following preestablished guidelines but leaving a degree of managerial autonomy to the facility. Indeed, the term PBF can be associated with a profusion of other terms. Some proponents also use the term "results-based financing" to capture everything from conditional cash transfers to a fee-for-service intervention for a minimum package of services. Perhaps unsurprisingly, such diversity of usage has led to debate and even confusion over the definition of what constitutes PBF (Renmans et al. 2017).

Thus, an important clarification of definitions is needed: although many versions of performance pay programs exist around the world, this report uses the term PBF to refer to a package including checklist-driven interventions that tie certain services to payments that are paid by the Ministry of Health to a health facility. These performance payments are usually in addition to the existing salary payments to health workers and the normal provision of drugs and equipment. The package also includes accountability, transparency, and more autonomy at the facility level. Indeed, the health facility typically has some autonomy, within some overall guidelines, in dividing the bonus payments between health workers and drug and equipment purchases. Another common feature of these programs is that they typically purchase the provision of maternal and child health services.

Conclusions

Around two-thirds of the International Development Association portfolio in dollar terms in the health, nutrition, and population sector at the World Bank now have a PBF component. PBF programs may be appealing to donors and countries because they link financing to performance, provide incentives at the margin that a health worker can control, and might have a broader place under health financing. This report aims to examine the totality of the evidence of the impact of PBF on primary health service delivery. It does so through careful reviews of the literature in high- and middle-income countries and primary evidence from the portfolio of World Bank–supported PBF pilots in primary health care in low-income countries. The evidence shows that PBF has led to gains in service delivery in many contexts, but much scope for improvement remains, especially in the most under-resourced settings.

The evidence also raises questions about the efficacy and effectiveness of PBF compared with two key policy alternatives, demand-side financial incentives (conditional cash transfers) and direct facility financing (DFF). The report discusses the sustainability of these various health financing approaches. The comparison of PBF and DFF disentangles the impacts of performance pay from those of the allied interventions. Both PBF and DFF packages typically include decentralized financing, autonomy, public financial management reform, supportive supervision, and community oversight, but only PBF includes performance pay for health facilities and workers. The analysis also highlights the many ways—the pricing of services, the selection of services to target through strategic purchasing, and the role of operating budgets and facility autonomy—in which health financing reforms in low-income countries could be bolstered. The report concludes by taking a step back from this evidence and asking how policy makers and task team leaders can design health system–strengthening approaches that account for all that has been learned from the implementation of previous financing interventions, particularly the PBF pilots.

References

Barrientos, A., and J. DeJong. 2006. "Reducing Child Poverty with Cash Transfers: A Sure Thing?" *Development Policy Review* 24 (5): 537–52.

Basinga, P., P. J. Gertler, A. Binagwaho, A. L. Soucat, J. Sturdy, and C. M. Vermeersch. 2011. "Effect on Maternal and Child Health Services in Rwanda of Payment to Primary Health-Care Providers for Performance: An Impact Evaluation." *The Lancet* 377 (9775): 1421–28.

Bauhoff, S., and E. Kandpal. 2021. "Information, Loss Framing, and Spillovers in Pay-for-Performance Contracts." Policy Research Working Paper 9687, World Bank, Washington, DC.

Besley, T., and M. Ghatak. 2005. "Competition and Incentives with Motivated Agents." *American Economic Review* 95 (3): 616–36.

Clements, C. J., P. H. Streefland, and C. Malau. 2007. "Supervision in Primary Health Care: Can It Be Carried Out Effectively in Developing Countries?" *Current Drug Safety* 2 (1): 19–23.

Das, J., J. Hammer, and K. Leonard. 2008. "The Quality of Medical Advice in Low-Income Countries." *Journal of Economic Perspectives* 22 (2): 93–114.

de Janvry, A., and E. Sadoulet. 2006. "Making Conditional Cash Transfer Programs More Efficient: Designing for Maximum Effect of the Conditionality." *World Bank Economic Review* 20 (1): 1–29.

Devereux, S., and R. Sabates-Wheeler. 2004. "Transformative Social Protection." IDS Working Paper 232, Institute of Development Studies, Brighton, UK.

Doran, T., and M. Roland. 2011. "Lessons from Major Initiatives to Improve Primary Care in the United Kingdom." *Health Affairs* 29 (5): 1023–29.

Duflo, E., R. Hanna, and S. P. Ryan. 2012. "Incentives Work: Getting Teachers to Come to School." *American Economic Review* 102 (4): 1241–78.

Falisse, J.-B., J. Ndayishimiye, V. Kamenyero, and M. Bossuyt. 2014. "Performance-Based Financing in the Context of Selective Free Health-Care: An Evaluation of Its Effects on the Use of Primary Health-Care Services in Burundi Using Routine Data." *Health Policy and Planning* 30: 1251–60.

Fink, G., E. Kandpal, and G. Shapira. 2022. "Inequality in the Quality of Health Services: Wealth, Content of Care, and the Price of Antenatal Consultations in the Democratic Republic of Congo." *Economic Development and Cultural Change*. https://doi.org/10.1086/713941.

Fiszbein, A., and N. Schady. 2009. *Conditional Cash Transfers: Reducing Present and Future Poverty*. Washington, DC: World Bank.

Fritsche, G.-B., R. Soeters, and B. Meessen. 2014. *Performance-Based Financing Toolkit*. Washington, DC: World Bank.

Gautier, L., M. De Allegri, and V. Ridde. 2019. "How Is the Discourse of Performance-Based Financing Shaped at the Global Level? A Poststructural Analysis." *Globalization and Health* 15 (1): 1–21.

Glassman, A., D. Duran, and M. Koblinsky. 2013. "Impact of Conditional Cash Transfers on Maternal and Newborn Health." *Journal of Health, Population, and Nutrition* 31 (4, Suppl 2): S48–S66.

Ibnat, F., K. L. Leonard, L. Bawo, and R. L. Mohammed-Roberts. 2019. "The Three-Gap Model of Health Worker Performance." Policy Research Working Paper 8782, World Bank, Washington, DC.

Kruk, M. E., A. D. Gage, N. T. Joseph, G. Danaei, S. García-Saisó, and J. A. Salomon. 2018. "Mortality Due to Low-Quality Health Systems in the Universal Health Coverage Era: A Systematic Analysis of Amenable Deaths in 137 Countries." *The Lancet* 392 (10160): 2203–12. https://doi.org/10.1016/S0140-6736(18)31668-4.

Lagarde, M., and D. Blaauw. 2021. "Effects of Incentive Framing on Performance and Effort: Evidence from a Medically Framed Experiment." *Journal of the Economic Science Association* 7 (1): 33–48.

Lazear, E. P. 2000. "Performance Pay and Productivity." *American Economic Review* 90 (5): 1346–61.

Mayaka Ma-Nitu, S., L. Tembey, E. Bigirimana, C. Y. Dossouvi, O. Baenya, E. Mago, P. M. Salongo, A. Zongo, and F. Verinumbe. 2018. "Towards Constructive Rethinking of PBF: Perspectives of Implementers in Sub-Saharan Africa." *BMJ Global Health* 3: e001036. https://doi.org/10.1136/bmjgh-2018-001036.

Meessen, B., L. Musango, J. P. Kashala, and J. Lemlin. 2006. "Reviewing Institutions of Rural Health Centres: The Performance Initiative in Butare, Rwanda." *Tropical Medicine & International Health* 11 (8): 1303–17.

Mendelson, A., K. Kondo, C. Damberg, A. Low, M. Motúapuaka, M. Freeman, M. O'Neil, R. Relevo, and D. Kansagara. 2017. "The Effects of Pay-for-Performance Programs on Health, Health Care Use, and Processes of Care: A Systematic Review." *Annals of Internal Medicine* 166 (5): 341–53.

Paul, E., L. Albert, B. N. Bisala, O. Bodson, E. Bonnet, P. Bossyus, S. Colombo, et al. 2018. "Performance-Based Financing in Low-Income and Middle-Income Countries: Isn't It Time for a Rethink?" *BMJ Global Health* 3: e000664.

Prendergast, C. 1999. "The Provision of Incentives in Firms." *Journal of Economic Literature* 37 (1): 7–63.

Renmans, D., N. Holvoet, B. Criel, and B. Meessen. 2017. "Performance-Based Financing: The Same Is Different." *Health Policy and Planning* 32 (6): 860–68.

Wagstaff, A., C. Bredenkamp, and L. R. Buisman. 2014. "Progress on Global Health Goals: Are the Poor Being Left Behind?" *World Bank Research Observer* 29 (2): 137–62.

World Health Organization. 2019. "Maternal Mortality: Evidence Brief." WHO/RHR/19.20, WHO, Geneva.

World Health Organization. 2020. "Newborns: Improving Survival and Well-Being." WHO, Geneva. https://www.who.int/news-room/fact-sheets/detail/newborns-reducing-mortality.

CHAPTER 2

Effective Coverage: A Framework Linking Coverage and Quality

Introduction

For a long time, large international initiatives like the Millennium Development Goals focused on increasing health service coverage, defined as the rate of people in need of medical care who obtain treatment from a formal health care provider. This approach is increasingly questioned because it ignores the quality of care, which is often very low, especially for the poor. There is growing evidence that health conditions are often misdiagnosed and even when the diagnosis is correct, the appropriate treatment or interventions might not be prescribed or implemented (Das, Hammer, and Leonard 2008). This chapter focuses on how the concept of effective coverage aims at providing a bridge between health coverage and quality of care, requiring that persons in need get the treatment that maximally improves their health.

The chapter shows how effective coverage can be decomposed into the product of coverage (those in need getting care) and quality (correct or successful treatment among those getting care). It also presents estimates of effective coverage and its two components for six common medical conditions (pregnancy, child malaria, child diarrhea, hypertension, tuberculosis [TB], and HIV), using household survey data. These examples illustrate the roles of coverage and quality as bottlenecks to better effective coverage and the degree to which their importance varies by medical condition and country. Finally, the chapter discusses the benefits and disadvantages of household and facility survey data in measuring effective coverage and how facility-based data could be used to expand the set of effective coverage measures.

Coverage, quality, and effective coverage

The concept of effective coverage in health was introduced by Shengelia et al. (2005). A recent scoping review identified 18 studies applying the concept, mainly in the domains of maternal and child health and chronic conditions (Jannati, Sadeghi, and Imani 2018). Effective coverage requires that everyone in need of a particular health service receives it in a timely manner and at the quality necessary to obtain the desired effect and potential health gains, as illustrated in figure 2.1. The term is used in the public health community, and it brings utilization and quality of care into one framework. As such, it is distinct from concepts like health service access, use/utilization, and coverage. Access is a necessary, but not sufficient, condition for use of services—people can have access to services but not use them. Use, in turn, does not capture need, while coverage captures need but not quality. Effective coverage captures both need and quality and is hence the most demanding and comprehensive of the four concepts.

Effective coverage is often illustrated in the form of a "care cascade" that has three elements: a population in need, coverage (among those in need), and quality of care (among those covered and in need) (figure 2.2) (Shengelia et al. 2005). Among the population in need, effective coverage is the product of the coverage rate (the fraction of the population in need receiving care) and quality (the fraction of those receiving care who receive the correct or recommended interventions, or the fraction of those receiving care whose care is successful). Effective coverage thus indicates the fraction of the population in need that receives the recommended interventions for their condition or, more ambitiously, the fraction that receives care that is successful in managing or treating the condition.

Figure 2.1   Utilization, coverage, and effective coverage

Utilization
- % population using a service
- E.g. % children taken to a health provider
- But does everyone need a consultation?

Coverage
- % population *in need* using a service
- E.g. % children with acute respiratory infection (ARI) taken to a health provider
- But do children get the correct treatment?

Effective coverage
- % population *in need* using a service *and getting the optimal treatment*
- E.g. % children with ARI taken to a provider and getting amoxicillin

Source: World Bank.

Figure 2.2 Coverage, quality, effective coverage, and the care cascade

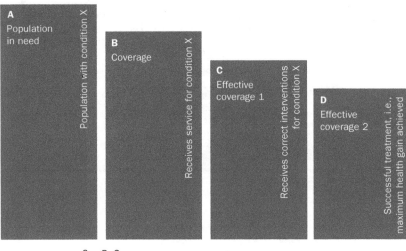

$$EC1 = \frac{C}{A} = \frac{B}{A} \cdot \frac{C}{B} = \text{Coverage rate} \cdot \text{Correct treatment rate (Quality 1)}$$

$$EC2 = \frac{D}{A} = \frac{B}{A} \cdot \frac{D}{B} = \text{Coverage rate} \cdot \text{Successful treatment rate (Quality 2)}$$

Source: World Bank.

Effective coverage tree

Figure 2.3 further illustrates the components of effective coverage by looking at different scenarios at each step of the interactions between patients and health care providers: consultation, diagnosis, and treatment. At the end of each branch of the tree, the green color symbolizes a desirable outcome, while the orange color denotes undesirable outcomes. For any medical condition, the population (A) is divided between those in need of care (B) and those not in need. Among those in need of care, a fraction (C) consults, while the rest does not and thus will not receive care. Among the fraction (C) that consults, some patients will be correctly diagnosed, while others might be incorrectly diagnosed and will thus receive irrelevant care.

Among those correctly diagnosed, relevant care will be provided to a fraction (D), but the rest might receive no care or irrelevant care despite a correct diagnosis. Going one step further than correct diagnosis and aiming at measuring successful treatment, the fraction (D) that received correct treatment can be further divided into a fraction (E) that was correctly treated and benefited from the maximum health gain, a fraction (F) that received some relevant care but for whom the maximum health gain is not realized, and a fraction (G) that received a mix of relevant and irrelevant care for whom the maximum health gain is not realized.

15

Figure 2.3   Effective coverage tree and its decomposition

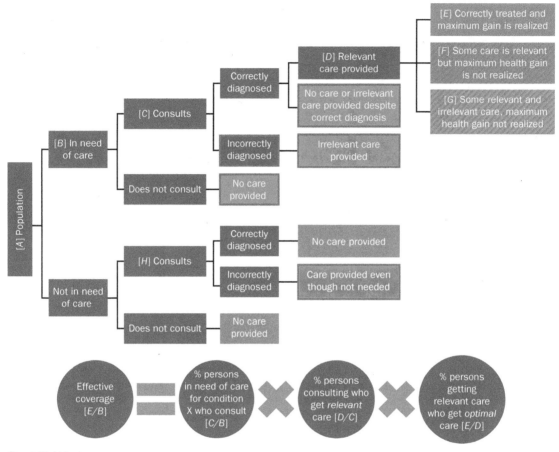

Source: World Bank.

Note: At the end of each branch of the tree, the green color denotes a desirable outcome, and orange denotes an undesirable outcome. Purple border around box indicates irrelevant care that uses scarce resources without health benefits or even causing harm.

The lower part of the tree in figure 2.3 comprises the part of the population not in need of care for the medical condition considered. When that group does not consult, no care is provided, which is the desired outcome. Similarly, if that group nevertheless consults but is correctly diagnosed as not suffering from that condition, no care will be provided. However, if the diagnosis is incorrect, that group will receive care even though it is not needed. Indeed, a problem that grows in importance as countries grow in income is the need to minimize the number of people consulting who do not need care[1] or get irrelevant care because of an incorrect diagnosis or despite a correct one.

The bottom row in figure 2.3 further illustrates how effective coverage can be measured as the product of the percentage of persons in need of care for a specific condition who consult, multiplied by the percentage consulting who get relevant care. For a more demanding definition of effective coverage, this product is further multiplied by the percentage of people getting relevant care who obtained optimal care and were successfully treated. This decomposition of effective coverage is illustrated mathematically in figure 2.4.

Quality and coverage

Graphically, effective coverage and its two components can be represented on an "effective coverage contour," as in figure 2.5, with the measure of quality on the vertical axis and the measure of coverage on the horizontal axis. Each of the three isocurves in the graph represents different combinations of quality and coverage that yield the same level of effective coverage. The closer an isocurve is to the upper right corner of the graph, the higher is the effective coverage rate for a condition.

Figure 2.6 uses the examples of antenatal care (ANC) and child pneumonia to show in detail how effective coverage can be decomposed into

Figure 2.4 Effective coverage and its decomposition as the product of coverage and quality

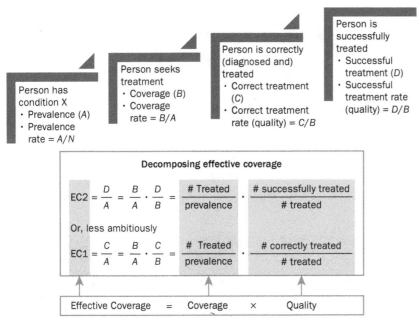

Source: World Bank.

Note: N = population.

Figure 2.5 Effective coverage contours and isocurves

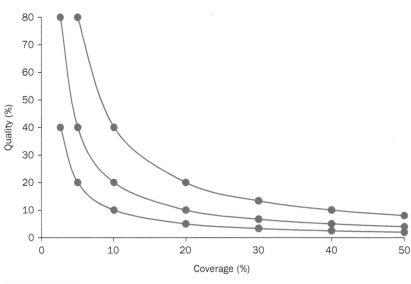

Source: World Bank.

Figure 2.6 Effective coverage and its decomposition: Antenatal care and pneumonia

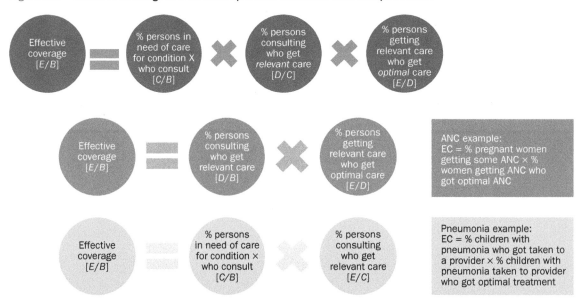

Source: World Bank.

Note: ANC = antenatal care; EC = effective coverage.

two components, coverage and quality, and illustrates how the measure of effective coverage requires information on both components.

Empirical applications

This section demonstrates the concept of effective coverage empirically using three maternal, newborn, and child health conditions and three adult conditions (table 2.1). The examples also include communicable and non-communicable diseases and preventive and curative care. In all cases, there has been extensive discussion in the literature about identifying the population in need and measuring coverage and quality. Further, in all cases, all three elements of effective coverage can, with varying degrees of accuracy, be established using data from household surveys: for four of the indicators (malaria, TB, HIV, and hypertension), the surveys involve testing, while for ANC and diarrhea, the medical conditions are relatively easy to observe by patients and caregivers.

The analysis is restricted to household survey data (1) to allow disaggregated analysis across the socioeconomic spectrum and (2) because of the challenges associated with mixed-data effective coverage studies that use household surveys to capture the population in need and coverage and facility data to capture the quality of services (Amouzou et al. 2019; Larson et al. 2016; Nguhiu, Barasa, and Chuma 2017; Leslie et al. 2017; Fink, Kandpal, and Shapira 2022). The following section discusses the advantages and disadvantages of using household and facility data to measure effective coverage and how facility data could be used to expand the set of effective coverage measures.

Antenatal care

Figure 2.7 shows the effective coverage contours, with its components, coverage and quality, for ANC for a large set of low- and middle-income countries, using data from the Multiple Indicator Cluster Surveys. Each dot represents a survey, with the abbreviated name of the country[2] and the survey year. Coverage, on the horizontal axis, is measured as the percentage of women giving birth who had at least one ANC visit. Quality is defined as the proportion among them who had at least four ANC visits, with at least one of those visits with a skilled provider, and for whom, during their ANC visits, blood pressure as well as blood and urine samples were taken. Many countries are situated in the upper right corner of figure 2.7,

Table 2.1 Definition and measurement of effective coverage for six common medical conditions

Condition	Population in need/prevalence [A]	Receives service for condition X (coverage/crude coverage) [B]	Receives correct interventions for condition X (quality 1/effective coverage 1/quality-adjusted coverage) [C]	Successful treatment: maximum health gain achieved (quality 2/effective coverage 2/outcome-adjusted coverage) [D]	Data for coverage and quality
Antenatal care	Woman age 18–49 and was pregnant during the specified period (past 2 years)	Woman received some antenatal care during pregnancy: 1+ visits. Alternative coverage indicator used in sensitivity analyses: 4+ ANC visits	Had 4+ visits, at least 1 with skilled health worker and received the following recommended interventions: blood pressure taken as well as blood and urine samples		DHS and MICS microdata
Childhood diarrhea	Caregiver reports under-5 child had diarrhea in the past 2 weeks (but not symptoms of severe dehydration and not dysentery)	Child received some treatment for diarrhea (ORS packet, pre-packaged ORS fluid, recommended homemade fluid, increased fluids, continued feeding, zinc, or antibiotics) and/or had a consultation with a formal provider	Child given ORS packet		DHS and MICS microdata
Childhood malaria	Child under-5 tests positive for malaria	Child received a medicine for malaria and/or saw a formal provider	Child received *any* antimalarial		DHS-Malaria Indicator Surveys microdata
HIV (adult)	Adult tests positive for HIV or is on HIV treatment	Received some form of HIV treatment	On antiretroviral therapy	Viral load suppressed when tested	DHS-HIV Indicator Survey microdata (Mozambique)
Tuberculosis (adult)	Adult tests positive for TB	Sought care for TB symptoms from clinic or hospital	On TB treatment		TB Prevalence Surveys online reports
Hypertension (adult)	High blood pressure (systolic 140 mmHg or diastolic 90 mmHg) or on some form of treatment for hypertension in the past 2 weeks	Has taken some form of hypertension treatment in the past 2 weeks		BP is normal when tested (systolic < 140 mmHg and diastolic < 90 mmHg) and adult is currently on treatment	WHO STEPS (mix of microdata and online reports and fact sheets); WB Health Survey and DHS microdata

Source: World Bank.

Note: ANC = antenatal care; BP = blood pressure; DHS = Demographic and Health Survey; MICS = Multiple Indicator Cluster Surveys; mmHg = millimeters of mercury; ORS = oral rehydration salts; TB = tuberculosis; WB = World Bank; WHO STEPS = World Health Organization STEPwise Approach to NCD Risk Factor Surveillance.

indicating both high coverage and high quality and thus high effective coverage. However, for the group of countries in the lower right side of figure 2.7, coverage is high but quality is low (20 to 60 percent). In a smaller group of countries, including Afghanistan, Chad, Somalia, and South Sudan, coverage is low (under 60 percent) and quality is very low (under 20 percent).

Hypertension treatment

Figure 2.8 displays the effective coverage contours for hypertension treatment among adults, using mainly the World Health Organization STEPwise Approach to NCD Risk Factor Surveillance surveys. Coverage is defined as the percentage of hypertensive individuals who received treatment, while quality is

Figure 2.7   Effective coverage contours for antenatal care

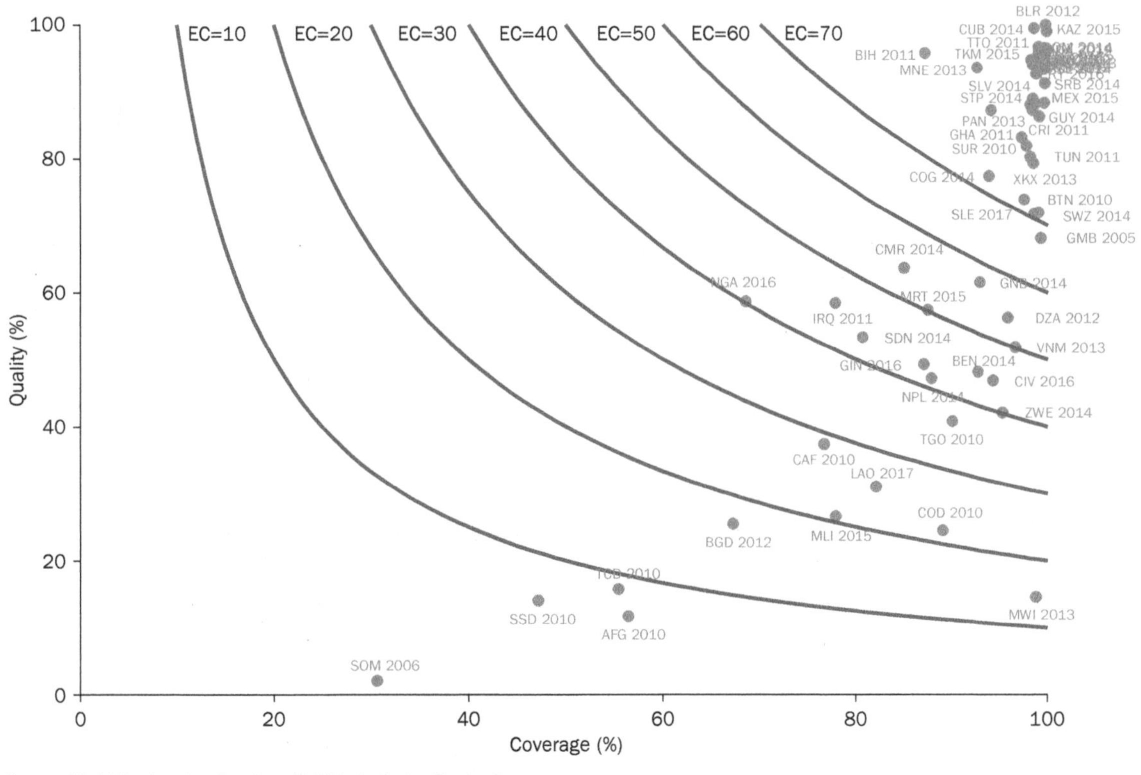

Source: World Bank, using data from Multiple Indicator Cluster Surveys.

Note: Coverage: percent of women giving birth who had 1+ antenatal care visits. Quality: of those covered, the percent who had 4+ visits, 1+ visits with a skilled provider, blood pressure taken, and blood and urine samples taken (correct treatment). EC = effective coverage. ISO 3166-1 alpha-3 codes are used for the country abbreviations (https://unstats.un.org/wiki/display/comtrade/Country+codes+in+ISO+3166).

Figure 2.8 Effective coverage contours for hypertension treatment

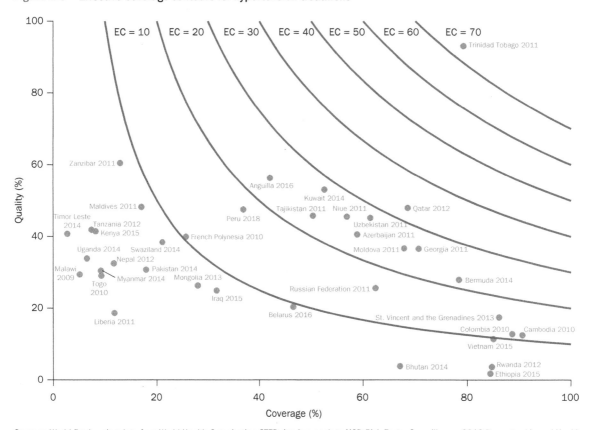

Sources: World Bank, using data from World Health Organization STEPwise Approach to NCD Risk Factor Surveillance; 2018 Demographic and Health Survey (Peru); 2011 World Bank Health Survey (Azerbaijan, Georgia, Moldova, Russian Federation, Tajikistan, and Uzbekistan).

Note: Coverage: percent of hypertensive individuals who received treatment. Quality: of those covered, the percent who have hypertension under control (successful treatment). EC = effective coverage.

measured as the percentage among those who received treatment who have their hypertension under control, that is, for whom treatment has been success-ful. The picture is quite different from that for ANC, with wide variations in the coverage levels on the horizontal axis, indicating that in many countries, people suffering from hypertension do not receive any treatment, potentially because they are not diagnosed. Quality, that is, successful treatment, is also generally low, under 60 percent but with somewhat less variation.

The hypertension example highlights how an important part of the picture can be missed by focusing only on coverage (for instance, Ethiopia and Rwanda in the lower right corner, where coverage is high and quality very low) or only on quality of care (for instance, Kenya and Tanzania on the middle left with relatively high quality but very low coverage). The example also highlights the source of the effective coverage deficit and where the payoff from action would be greatest. For example, Belarus is on the same effective coverage isocurve (EC = 10) as Vietnam and Colombia: in Belarus, that level is obtained with coverage lower than 50 percent and quality around 20 percent, while in Vietnam and Colombia, coverage is above 80 percent, but successful treatment is even lower.

Tuberculosis treatment

Figure 2.9 turns the attention to treatment for TB, using a smaller set of National Tuberculosis Prevalence Surveys. Coverage is measured as the

Figure 2.9 Effective coverage contours for tuberculosis treatment

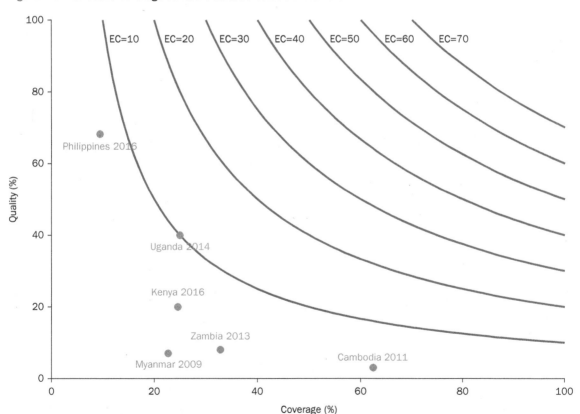

Source: World Bank, using data from National Tuberculosis Prevalence Survey online reports.

Note: Coverage: percent of bacteriologically confirmed TB cases seeking care. Quality: of those covered, percent who are on TB treatment (correct treatment). EC = effective coverage; TB = tuberculosis.

percentage of bacteriologically confirmed TB cases seeking care and quality as the percentage among them who are on TB treatment. It is important to note that while for hypertension figure 2.8 used the more demanding definition of quality, successful treatment (hypertension under control), for TB, figure 2.9 is limited to the less ambitious definition of quality (correct treatment) because of the data available in the surveys. Again, while the levels of effective coverage are quite low (equal to or below EC = 10) in all six countries, there are large variations in both coverage and quality. For example, Cambodia has the highest coverage (above 60 percent), but quality is below 10 percent, while the Philippines has substantially higher treatment quality (close to 70 percent), but coverage is only around 10 percent.

HIV/AIDS treatment

The case of HIV treatment in figure 2.10 allows a more direct comparison between the results obtained when using correct versus successful treatment as a measure of quality. In figure 2.10, the data are only from the Mozambique 2015 AIDS Indicator Survey, which includes rich data on HIV-positive individuals. In addition to the results of HIV tests, which are now common in many Demographic and Health Surveys, especially in Africa, the Mozambican survey includes indicators that allow for measuring whether HIV-positive individuals are on an antiretroviral (ARV) treatment. The correct treatment is shown in purple, and among those who are on an ARV treatment, those who are virally suppressed (undetectable viral load), that is, those who have had successful treatment, are shown in green.

Since such detailed data are available for only one country, figure 2.10 proposes a comparison across five wealth quintiles, illustrating the level of equity in coverage and quality. Coverage—the fraction of HIV-positive people who sought HIV treatment—increases with wealth as it varies between 20 percent for the poorest quintile (Q1) and around 50 percent for the richest quintile (Q5). These differences might reflect lower access to HIV care facilities and thus lower testing rates among poorer population groups, but also higher levels of discrimination and stigmatization. The measure of quality reflecting correct treatment (purple) is high, above 80 percent, and does not vary much by wealth level: once HIV-positive individuals have been diagnosed and sought care, most of them receive ARV treatment.

Figure 2.10   **Effective coverage contours for HIV/AIDS treatment in Mozambique, by wealth quintile, 2015**

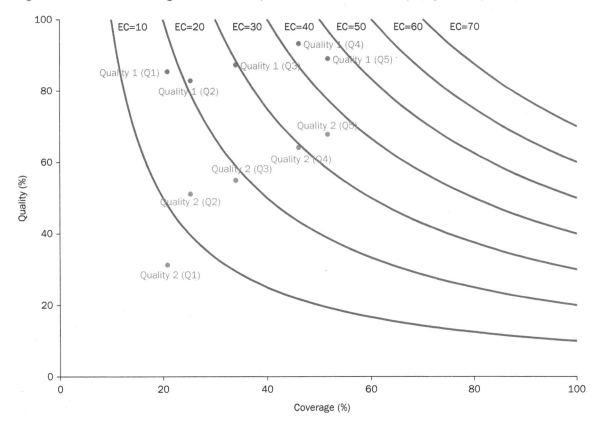

Source: World Bank, using data from the Mozambique 2015 AIDS Indicator Survey.

Note: Coverage: percent of HIV+ cases who sought treatment for HIV. Quality: (1) of those covered, the percent who are on ARV (correct treatment) in purple, and (2) of those on ARV, the percent virally suppressed (successful treatment) in green. Quintile Q1 is the poorest and Q5 is the richest. ARV = antiretroviral; EC = effective coverage.

The situation is different considering successful treatment (in green), that is, whether the patient's viral load has become undetectable. The levels of quality are lower, ranging from around 30 percent to slightly under 70 percent but with a clear wealth gradient: successful treatment is more common among the richer quintiles. This might be explained by several factors, stemming from patient and provider characteristics and including the timeliness of treatment initiation, quality of counseling, support and treatment supervision offered, and patients' adherence to their treatment regimen. While the role of the patients' characteristics and behaviors, including adherence to treatment, is most visible in the analysis of AIDS treatment, it is an important factor in the analysis of effective coverage for most medical conditions (Ng et al. 2014; Marsh et al. 2020).

Child malaria and diarrhea treatment

Figure 2.11 shows the effective coverage contours for two medical conditions that affect many children in low- and middle-income countries, malaria and diarrhea. These examples illustrate how two different approaches to defining coverage might affect the results. Indeed, for these two common childhood conditions, self-medication by well-informed parents, without consulting a formal provider, can sometimes be sufficient. The correct treatment for childhood diarrhea is taking oral rehydration salts (ORS), which can be administered by parents. Self-medication can also be correct for malaria treatment.

The effective coverage contours in panels a and b in figure 2.11 display the results for malaria treatment. Panel a displays effective coverage when coverage is defined as the percentage testing positive for malaria among children who saw a formal health care provider and/or took a medicine. Quality is defined as the percentage among those who got the correct medicine, that is, the correct treatment. Panel b uses the same measure of quality, but the definition of coverage is more restrictive as it only considers the percentage of children testing positive for malaria who saw a formal health care provider. As the definition of coverage is more restrictive in the lower quadrant, the estimates of effective coverage for each country/survey are lower and graphically shift to the left.

The effective coverage contours in panels c and d in figure 2.11 display the results for diarrhea treatment. Panel c displays effective coverage when coverage is defined as the percentage of children with diarrhea who had a consultation or received treatment, and quality is defined as the percentage among those who got ORS, that is, the correct treatment. Panel d uses the same measure of quality, but the definition of coverage is more restrictive as it only considers the percentage of children with diarrhea who saw a formal health care provider. As the definition of coverage is more restrictive in panel d, the estimates of effective coverage for each country/survey are lower and graphically shift to the left.

Figure 2.12 sums up the results for the six selected medical conditions by averaging the effective coverage numbers across countries (the number of countries included is indicated in parentheses) to arrive at one estimate for each condition. There are limitations to this exercise: the number, dates,

Figure 2.11 Effective coverage contours for child malaria and diarrhea treatment

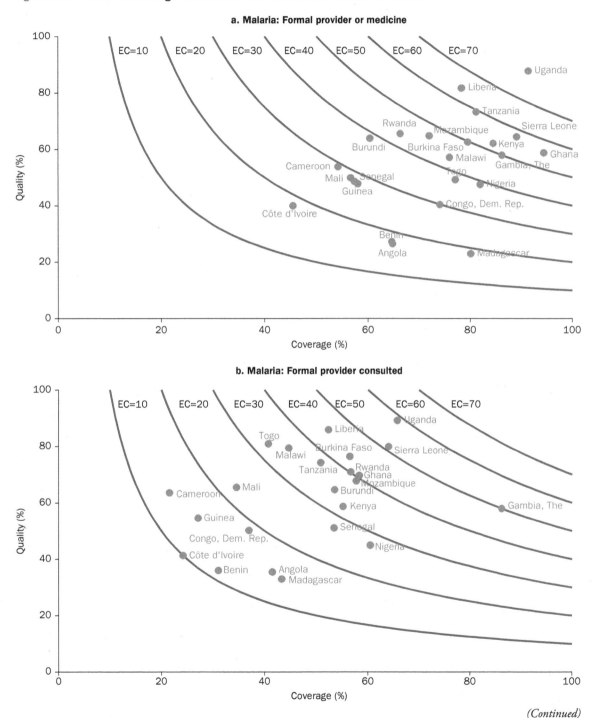

(Continued)

Figure 2.11 *continued*

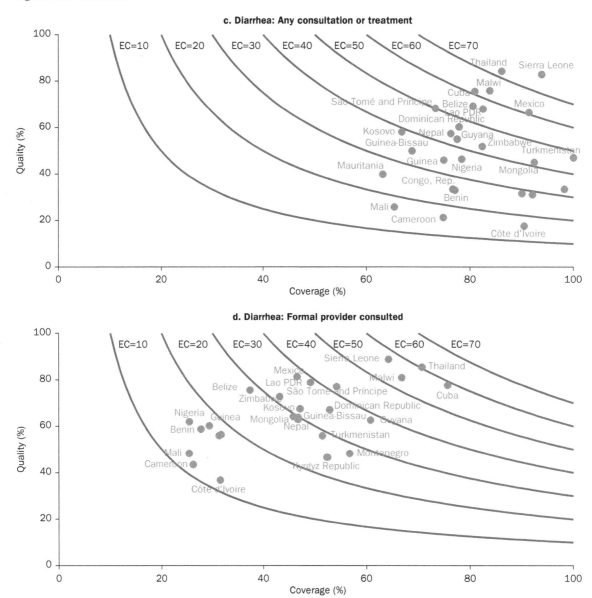

c. Diarrhea: Any consultation or treatment

d. Diarrhea: Formal provider consulted

Sources: World Bank, using data from Demographic and Health Surveys; Malaria Indicator Survey; AIDS Indicator Survey; Multiple Indicator Cluster Surveys.

Note: Coverage in panel a: percent of children testing positive for malaria who saw a formal provider and/or took medicine; quality in panel a: of those covered, the percent who got the correct medicine (correct treatment). Coverage in panel b: percent of children testing positive for malaria who saw a formal provider; quality in panel b: of those covered, the percent who got the correct medicine (correct treatment). Coverage in panel c: percent of children with diarrhea who had a consultation or received treatment; quality in panel c: of those covered, the percent who got oral rehydration treatment (correct treatment). Coverage in panel d: percent of children with diarrhea who saw a formal provider; quality in panel d: of those covered, the percent who got oral rehydration treatment (correct treatment). EC = effective coverage.

Figure 2.12 Effective coverage contours for various medical conditions

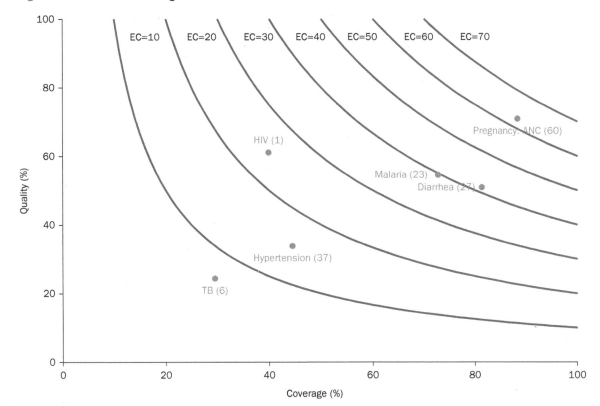

Sources: World Bank, using data from household surveys.

Note: Coverage: percent of persons with condition X getting treatment. Quality: of those covered, the percent whose treatment was correct or (for hypertension and HIV) successful. The number of countries is in parentheses. ANC = antenatal care; EC = effective coverage; TB = tuberculosis.

and composition of the set of countries vary, and for some conditions, the definition of quality is successful treatment, like for hypertension and HIV/ AIDS, while for the others it is correct treatment. Further, moving from one isocurve to another (horizontally or vertically) might entail different investment efforts for different conditions. For a given condition, moving from EC10 to EC50 might require different investments compared with moving from EC80 to full effective coverage.

Nevertheless, figure 2.12 conveys two important points. First, effective coverage varies substantially across medical conditions: it is highest for ANC and lowest for hypertension and TB. Such comparisons can indicate to policy makers where additional investments in expanding coverage and improving quality of care should be made. Second, both coverage and quality of care are necessary to achieve a high level of effective coverage.

The examples in this chapter have illustrated that the bottleneck, whether coverage or quality, to better effective coverage varies by medical condition and country.

Expanding the work on effective coverage by using data collected in health facilities

The measures of effective coverage included in this chapter so far have all relied on household survey data. However, as further discussed in chapter 3, substantial efforts are made to measure quality of care at the health facility level. Figure 2.13 shows the different potential data sources available that could be used to measure effective coverage. For quality of care, facility data sources include a review of the typical practice of a health facility or a mix of its practice and readiness to provide specific interventions, exit interviews of patients, direct observation of patient-provider interactions, and standardized patients (Daniels et al. 2017).

The different data sources have advantages and disadvantages, which are summarized in table 2.2. An important benefit of household survey data is that they generally rely on a representative sample of the population, allowing for calculating of population-level estimates of disease prevalence and treatment coverage. By definition, health facility data can only be collected from a selected group of individuals who seek care at health facilities. Household survey data have the additional advantage of collecting information from real-life treatment episodes, but their disadvantage is that they

Figure 2.13   Potential data sources for measuring effective coverage

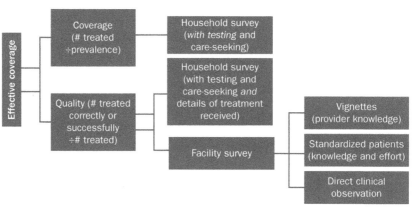

Source: World Bank.

Table 2.2 **Advantages and disadvantages of the data sources for measuring effective coverage**

	Household survey	Vignettes	Standardized patients	Direct clinical observation
Advantages	Representative sample of the entire population Real-life treatment episodes	Capture provider knowledge	Capture effort	Real-life treatment episodes
Disadvantages	Patient/caregiver recall	Hypothetical treatment episodes	Realistic but fictitious treatment episodes	Hard to establish patient's true condition; Hawthorne effects

Source: World Bank.

rely on the recall of disease and treatment episodes that occurred in the past. In addition, especially if the information is based on patient (or child caregiver) recall, the understanding of the medical conditions and procedures experienced might be imperfect.

Facility-based assessments of quality have several attractions: with the information being collected at the time of the interaction, the assessments are not (or, at least, less) subject to patient or caregiver recall bias. The information comes from trained enumerators with a medical background and therefore may be more accurate than information provided by a patient or caregiver. In addition, the information collected may cover more angles than is feasible in questions posed to a caregiver sometime after the event (Fink, Kandpal, and Shapira 2022).

Facility-based quality assessments have disadvantages, however. The patients are typically different from the interviewees in a household survey, which poses a challenge in terms of population representativeness: even if the data are linked only at the national level, it is not always straightforward (and sometimes impossible because facility assessments are limited to just a few facilities; see Kruk et al. 2017) to make the facility data representative of the (typically national) population in need. Even if the household survey data and facility data refer to the same individuals, the household survey will typically cover the full history of visits with respect to a health event, such as a pregnancy, while an exit interview or a direct observation will typically cover just one visit (Fink, Kandpal, and Shapira 2022).

Facility-based quality assessments pose other challenges. Health care provider vignettes are designed to capture provider knowledge when presented with specific medical cases, but they are based on hypothetical treatment episodes and do not measure real-life effort. Standardized patients, that is, when a trained actor comes to health facility and pretends to suffer from a specific condition to observe the provider's actions, capture not only knowledge, but also the provider's effort and are based on a realistic, but still fictitious, treatment episode. However, direct observation and standardized patient exercises are amenable to some conditions and interventions but are less suited to others, such as pregnancy or childhood diseases (Wiseman et al. 2019). Further, direct observation is potentially subject to Hawthorne effects when health care providers are aware that they are being observed and adapt their behaviors accordingly (Leonard and Masatu 2010).

Of course, not all conditions and interventions lend themselves to obtaining a measure of quality from household survey data. For example, the analysis in the chapter excluded childhood pneumonia in light of evidence that acute respiratory infection is a poor predictor of pneumonia (Bryce et al. 2013), making it impossible in household survey data to isolate genuine cases of pneumonia and establish whether the treatment given was correct.

Conclusions

This chapter has underscored that to measure whether those in need receive appropriate medical care, it is important to go beyond health coverage and also consider quality of care. Thus, effective coverage is a useful concept as it combines coverage and quality, requiring that everyone in need of a particular health service is getting it in a timely manner and at a level of quality necessary to obtain the desired effect and potential health gains. Using household survey data for six common medical conditions related to pregnancy, child, and adult health, the chapter showed how effective coverage varies by country, wealth, and medical conditions. Across medical conditions, effective coverage is highest for ANC and lowest for hypertension and TB. Overall, effective coverage remains low for many conditions in many settings, highlighting the importance of considering coverage and quality of care jointly.

The hypertension, TB, and HIV examples illustrated how the definition of quality used (correct treatment versus successful treatment) affects the measure of effective coverage. The child malaria and diarrhea examples, for which direct treatment by the caregiver is a common option, showed that how coverage is defined also matters. Moreover, these examples highlighted that patient and caregiver behaviors in seeking and adhering to treatment are an important factor in increasing effective behavior.

Finally, the chapter discussed the potential use of facility survey data and its benefits and disadvantages. The next two chapters focus on the quality of care, using examples from the World Bank's performance-based financing impact evaluation portfolio. The data are from household and facility surveys that have been conducted in the same location, facilitating the link between household- and facility-level information. The issues of irrelevant care and overuse are further explored in chapter 7. Building on the concept of effective coverage, chapter 7 introduces an indicator that measures the efficiency of care in effective coverage, or equivalently the share of expenditure that goes toward appropriate care. This measure accounts for the potential waste of resources.

Notes

1. For basic care for pregnancy, this fraction should, by definition, be zero, but in many other cases it is not zero and can be economically significant. Indeed, even in low-income countries, that fraction can be important, for example, if all cases of fever were treated as malaria. Chapter 7 investigates these issues in greater depth.
2. ISO 3166-1 alpha-3 codes are used for the country abbreviations (https://unstats.un.org/wiki/display/comtrade/Country+codes+in+ISO+3166).

References

Amouzou A., H. H. Leslie, M. Ram, M. Fox, S. S. Jiwani, J. Requejo, T. Marchant, et al. 2019. "Advances in the Measurement of Coverage for RMNCH and Nutrition: From Contact to Effective Coverage." *BMJ Global Health* 4 (Suppl 4): e001297.

Bryce, J., F. Arnold, A. Blanc, A. Hancioglu, H. Newby, J. Requejo, and T. Wardlaw. 2013. "Measuring Coverage in MNCH: New Findings, New Strategies, and Recommendations for Action." *PLoS Medicine* 10 (5): e1001423.

Daniels, B., A. Dolinger, G. Bedoya, K. Rogo, A. Goicoechea, J. Coarasa, F. Wafula, et al. 2017. "Use of Standardised Patients to Assess Quality of Healthcare in Nairobi, Kenya: A Pilot, Cross-Sectional Study with International Comparisons." *BMJ Global Health* 2 (2): e000333.

Das, J., J. Hammer, and K. Leonard. 2008. "The Quality of Medical Advice in Low Income Countries." *Journal of Economic Perspectives* 22 (2): 93–114.

Fink, G., E. Kandpal, and G. Shapira. 2022. "Inequality in the Quality of Health Services: Wealth, Content of Care, and Price of Antenatal Consultations in the Democratic Republic of Congo." *Economic Development and Cultural Change*. https://doi.org/10.1086/713941.

Jannati, A., V. Sadeghi, and A. Imani. 2018. "Effective Coverage as a New Approach to Health System Performance Assessment: A Scoping Review."

BMC Health Services Research 18: 886. https://doi.org/10.1186/s12913-018-3692-7.

Kruk, M. E., E. Kelley, S. B. Syed, F. Tarp, T. Addison, and Y. Akachi. 2017. "Measuring Quality of Health-Care Services: What Is Known and Where Are the Gaps?" *Bulletin of the World Health Organization* 95 (6): 389.

Larson, E., D. Vail, G. M. Mbaruku, R. Mbatia, and M. E. Kruk. 2016. "Beyond Utilization: Measuring Effective Coverage of Obstetric Care along the Quality Cascade." *International Journal for Quality in Health Care* 29 (1): 104–10.

Leonard, K. L., and M. C. Masatu. 2010. "Professionalism and the Know-Do Gap: Exploring Intrinsic Motivation among Health Workers in Tanzania." *Health Economics* 19 (12) : 1461–77.

Leslie, H. H., A. Malata, Y. Ndiaye, and M. E. Kruk. 2017. "Effective Coverage of Primary Care Services in Eight High-Mortality Countries." *BMJ Global Health* 2 (3): e000424.

Marsh, A. D., M. Muzigaba, T. Diaz, J. Requejo, D. Jackson, D. Chou, J. A. Cresswell, et al. 2020. "Effective Coverage Measurement in Maternal, Newborn, Child, and Adolescent Health and Nutrition: Progress, Future Prospects, and Implications for Quality Health Systems." *Lancet Global Health* 8 (5): e730–e736. doi:10.1016/S2214-109X(20)30104-2.

Ng, M., N. Fullman, J. L. Dieleman, A. D. Flaxman, C. J. L. Murray, and S. S. Lim. 2014. "Effective Coverage: A Metric for Monitoring Universal Health Coverage." *PLoS Medicine* 11 (9): e1001730. https://doi.org/10.1371/journal.pmed.1001730.

Nguhiu, P. K., E. W. Barasa, and J. Chuma. 2017. "Determining the Effective Coverage of Maternal and Child Health Services in Kenya, Using Demographic and Health Survey Data Sets: Tracking Progress towards Universal Health Coverage." *Tropical Medicine and International Health* 22 (4): 442–53.

Shengelia, B., A. Tandon, O. B. Adams, and C. J. L. Murray. 2005. "Access, Utilization, Quality, and Effective Coverage: An Integrated Conceptual Framework and Measurement Strategy." *Social Science & Medicine* 61 (1): 97–109.

Wiseman, V., M. Lagarde, R. Kovacs, L. P. L. Wulandari, T. Powell-Jackson, J. King, C. Goodman, et al. 2019. "Using Unannounced Standardised Patients to Obtain Data on Quality of Care in Low-Income and Middle-Income Countries: Key Challenges and Opportunities." *BMJ Global Health* 4 (5): e001908.

CHAPTER 3

Quality of Care: A Framework for Measurement

Introduction

Effective coverage has two components: the first is the coverage rate for a given service, and the second is the quality of care provided as part of the provision of that service. This chapter delves into the second component, quality of care, and the role that it plays in driving health outcomes in low- and middle-income countries (LMICs). Specific to the effective coverage framework introduced in the previous chapter, this chapter unpacks the relationship between the correct treatment rate and the quality of care. Increasing access to health services may not translate into better health outcomes if the quality of the services delivered is poor. Indeed, despite gains in coverage, health outcomes remain strikingly poor in most LMICs (Kruk et al. 2018; Benova et al. 2018; Das, Hammer, and Leonard 2008). A study of maternal deaths in 137 LMICs found that of an estimated 207,000 excess deaths in 2016, 57,000 were likely due to the receipt of poor quality of care, whereas an estimated 47,000 deaths were attributed to lack of access to care (Kruk et al. 2018).

Poor quality of care is often related to poor adherence to protocol by health workers (Das, Hammer, and Leonard 2008), but as this chapter discusses, low health worker effort is only one reason for poor quality. Disentangling the contribution of the various constraints to quality is important for understanding why quality is poor and whether an intervention, say performance pay for health workers, would have the scope to make a significant improvement in clinical quality and thus effective coverage. If poor effort only constitutes a minor constraint to quality and most such constraints are outside the locus of control of the health worker, then performance pay–type interventions may have limited impact on effective coverage.

This chapter discusses how poor clinical quality may arise for at least three reasons. First, structural constraints may continue to be a limiting factor, preventing health workers from providing adequate care. Second, inadequate training may result in health workers not knowing what they should do when presented with a patient. Third, health workers may not put their knowledge to use in their clinical practice; that is, they may not apply sufficient effort. Ibnat et al. (2019) cast these three constraints into a three-gap framework, where poor health outcomes can be the consequence of a *can-do* gap, a *know-do* gap, and a *know-can-do* gap or idle capacity. Although there may be other barriers to the provision of high-quality care, including absenteeism, the decomposition of these three constraints is important because it helps in understanding the need for financial incentives as a policy lever. For instance, pay for performance might motivate health workers, but if the constraints are primarily structural, then infrastructure investments might be the more effective instrument. Similarly, if inadequate medical training leads to poor provider knowledge, performance-based incentives may have a limited impact on outcomes. Chapter 4 further illustrates this point by providing an empirical example, using data on antenatal care consultations in five Sub-Saharan African countries.

Given the importance of a systematic assessment of clinical quality for both research and policy, this chapter summarizes various approaches to measuring quality of care that are used in academic research. Collecting health care quality data in a comprehensive, cost-effective, and unbiased manner is a well-documented and persistent challenge. The chapter highlights measurement methods that can distinguish provider effort from provider knowledge or competence. For instance, the purpose of the financial incentives on which this report focuses is to increase provider effort, whereas knowledge gaps may be best addressed with training. The report also argues for collecting basic cost measures as a complement. Chapter 7 returns to the question of quality measurement and discusses how to integrate quality metrics into health system reform and the design of effective performance incentives.

While many of the examples in this report focus on the provision of high-quality antenatal care, the patterns discussed here are not unique to antenatal care provision. A study that evaluated the quality of care in 25 LMICs found that 58 percent of febrile children under age five who were seen as patients received poor quality of care for suspected malaria (Macarayan, Papanicolas, and Jha 2020). Similarly, a cross-sectional study of nationally representative surveys in 28 LMICs found that health system performance for management of diabetes showed large losses to care at the stage of being tested and low rates of diabetes control (Manne-Goehler et al. 2019). Tuberculosis contributes significantly to the disease and mortality burden in LMICs (Reid et al. 2019). In a pilot study conducted in Delhi, India, researchers used standardized patients—fake patients trained to present with certain symptoms of disease to the health worker—and found that only 21 percent of the tuberculosis cases were correctly managed (Das et al. 2015). Thus, the delivery of poor-quality health care is pervasive across types of services in LMICs.

Theoretical framework for assessing quality of care

Three aspects of quality: Structure, process, and outcomes

Consistent with the model of quality of care proposed by Donabedian (2003), this chapter distinguishes between three aspects of quality: structure, process, and outcomes. Structural quality refers to the context in which care is provided. This may be the physical health center; the equipment, supplies, and drugs; as well as aspects of human resources and organization, such as training and payment methods. Process quality refers to the actions taken by the care provider in providing the service. Outcomes refer to the end health outcomes, such as maternal mortality and morbidity. Distinguishing these three components of quality allows for understanding what constrains the delivery of high-quality health care. Such an understanding is the first step in determining what the appropriate policy levers are. For instance, if effective coverage is primarily constrained by poor infrastructure, then the policy response would be to invest in infrastructure. In contrast, poor process quality may highlight lacunae in health worker training or effort, which cannot be addressed by infrastructure improvements.

Tying the evidence on poor quality to end outcomes, the recent Lancet Global Health Commission on High Quality Health Systems in the Sustainable Development Goals Era establishes that poor quality of health care is one of the major drivers of excess mortality in LMICs (Kruk et al. 2018). This report also notes that universal health coverage will not lead to sustained improvements in mortality or other intermediate health outcomes unless LMIC health systems can consistently deliver high-quality services. Thus, a growing consensus highlights the role of poor quality of care in stagnating health outcomes in LMICs and suggests that simply increasing utilization will not improve health outcomes.

It has been well documented that LMIC health systems suffer from poor structural quality (Smith and Hanson 2011; Kruk et al. 2018). In response, since the 1978 Alma Ata Declaration, sustained investments have been made in health care infrastructure in LMICs. In the past few decades, access to health care centers and more sophisticated medical services has expanded across Sub-Saharan African countries (Jamison et al. 2006). Historically, LMICs have had little to no access to the new technological growth in the health sector. However, this is changing as the trends suggest an increase in the supply of such medical technology in LMICs (Howitt et al. 2012). Since 1978, the number of health care professionals has increased significantly, including a growing workforce of community health workers across the world, including in LMICs (Perry, Zulliger, and Rogers 2014). While there is still a long way to go to ensuring universal health coverage, by many measures, these investments may have succeeded. A large body of literature suggests that the availability of health services is no longer the concern it used to be, including in many Sub-Saharan African countries (Leslie et al. 2018; Di Giorgio et al. 2020).

At the same time, the disparity between high coverage rates and poor health outcomes is perhaps clearest in the case of maternal and neonatal health, where sustained gains in health infrastructure have significantly improved access to prenatal care around the world but have had limited impact on birth and delivery outcomes as well as maternal and neonatal mortality (Chou, Walker, and Kanyangarara 2019). A 2013 report found that 75 LMICs account for 95 percent of maternal and child deaths (WHO 2013). High maternal and child deaths in LMICs are taking place despite a greater proportion of births occurring in health facilities (Montagu et al. 2017). A set of researchers constructed deterministic models to project health outcomes if quality of care was improved in a representative sample of 81 LMICs. They found that improving quality of care (in antenatal, intrapartum, and postnatal care) would produce substantial benefits at current levels of utilization, with an estimated decline in the mortality rate of about 21 to 32 percent (Chou, Walker, and Kanyangarara 2019).

Further, consumers of health care in LMICs react strongly to both structural and process quality. For instance, evidence from the Democratic

Republic of Congo shows that consumers whose local public health facility is better provisioned in terms of equipment and consumables are less likely to bypass the local facility (Fink, Kandpal, and Shapira 2022). Similarly, a study in India found that a majority of patients bypassed the local primary health care centers when seeking treatment even though doing so cost them almost twice as much out of pocket (Rao and Sheffel 2018). However, such bypassing decreased with the increase in the competence of the health care provider (Rao and Sheffel 2018). The study found that compared with nonpoor patients, poor patients were less likely to seek treatment by bypassing the local primary health care centers. Therefore, in LMICs, where health systems often face shortages of supplies (Adair-Rohani et al. 2013) and personnel (Chaudhury et al. 2006), there are great gains to be made by ensuring a basic quality of care (Akachi and Kruk 2017).

An aspect of poor process quality that this chapter does not touch upon is health worker absenteeism. Historically, the absence of health care workers has been thought of as a major hurdle in improving quality of care in LMICs (Belita, Mbindyo, and English 2013). A recent study in Uganda finds that absenteeism can drive patients seeking care away from the public sector, in turn leading to an increase in out-of-pocket expenditures by patients (Zhang, Fink, and Cohen 2021). However, another recent quality of care study in 10 African countries finds that reducing absenteeism would only have a modest impact on average care readiness (Di Giorgio et al. 2020). The study shows that health care workers in LMICs needed to be more knowledgeable to achieve greater care readiness (Di Giorgio et al. 2020). Among other factors, studies have previously documented a significant lack of basic knowledge among health care workers across several African countries on how to diagnose and manage common diseases (Pakenham-Walsh and Bukachi 2009). In addition, health care workers in LMICs often find themselves dealing with complex health issues with limited support and training, which, among other factors, can lead to ineffective quality of care (Vasan et al. 2017). To decompose observed quality of care, this chapter uses a framework that studies the quality of care when the worker is present. On the one hand, absenteeism may reflect an extreme example of mis-adherence to protocol, implying that such estimates of idle capacity present an upper bound on the quality of care available. On the other hand, it may also be the case that poor structural capacity or insufficient knowledge demotivates workers and keeps them away from the facility.

Three-gap framework

Clinical quality influences health outcomes through at least three channels. First, despite investments in physical infrastructure, structural constraints may limit provider performance, particularly in primary health care in developing countries. Second, inadequate knowledge of protocols may mean that doctors do not know what they should do. Third, doctors may simply not put their knowledge to use; this may happen because they are shirking or not exerting sufficient effort. Ibnat et al. (2019) cast these three constraints into a three-gap framework, where poor health outcomes can be the consequence of a structural gap, a knowledge gap, or an effort gap. This framework thus decomposes the notion of "process quality" into its determinants—or conversely, its constraints. This framework also permits a discussion of the different methods of accurately measuring clinical quality in addition to describing how patient characteristics interact with the quality of care they receive.

The three-gap model benchmarks actual or observed performance against target performance. For the resultant shortfall, the model distinguishes between items that the health worker has the structural capacity to perform and the knowledge to perform. This in turn allows for the definitions of the three gaps, which are summarized in table 3.1, for each instance of observed care: the gap between target performance and what the worker has the knowledge to perform (called the "know gap"); the gap between knowledge and the structural capacity, that is, the equipment, supplies, and drugs (the "can-do gap"); and the gap between capacity and knowledge and what is actually done (the "know-can-do gap"). This last gap is referred to as "idle capacity" because the health worker has all the knowledge and structural capacity to perform the relevant action but does not use that available capacity.

Table 3.1 Summarizing the three gaps

Gap	Definition
Knowledge gap or "know gap"	The share of the protocol that the health worker lacks the knowledge to perform
Structural gap or "can-do gap"	The share of the protocol that the health worker lacks the structural capacity (equipment and supplies) to perform
Idle capacity, "effort gap," or "know-can-do gap"	Target performance minus observed performance minus the know gap minus the can-do gap

Source: World Bank, based on Ibnat et al. 2019.

Measuring quality of care for research and policy

To make progress on research as well as policies aimed at improving the quality of care, robust methods are needed to measure and evaluate the quality of care provided. This section summarizes the methods used in quality-of-care research and discusses their potential use in policy contexts.

The measurement methods in the literature take several different approaches. The approach of the World Health Organization (WHO) and the International Network for the Rational Use of Drugs (INRUD) relies on aggregate numbers of medicine use, without necessarily evaluating the quality of an individual provider-patient interaction. This method can be useful when working with existing administrative data such as insurance claims.

Other approaches almost always require dedicated data collection and measurement. *Standardized patient visits*—in which data collectors visit the provider "undercover" and are trained to present a certain illness profile— can measure the provider's response to specific patient complaints. Researchers can also use *direct observation* of the doctor-patient interaction or conduct *exit interviews*, potentially combined with *re-diagnosing* the patient to assess the accuracy of the provider's diagnosis and prescription, as in the malaria case study referred to in box 3.1 and covered in more detail in chapter 7. Last, *representative surveys* can measure outcomes such as long-term health or patient satisfaction at the population level.

Box 3.1   In Focus: Identifying misuse of care: A case study of malaria treatment in Mali

One of the challenges of identifying the misuse of care and its causes is that an outside observer often cannot verify a given patient's health care needs and consequently whether the patient received appropriate care. However, in some cases, an outside diagnosis for verification is possible. For example, malaria rapid detection tests (RDTs) can be easily and quickly administered with minimal training and detect parasite antigens even after treatment has started. Researchers took advantage of this in data collected for a randomized experimental study of malaria treatment at community health clinics in Bamako, Mali, in 2016. The study team carried out at-home follow-up and conducted a malaria RDT with a subset of primary care patients who had been previously interviewed at the clinic (Lopez, Sautmann, and Schaner 2022). This approach makes it possible to measure treatment received conditional on true malaria status. The study conducted several randomized information and training interventions to understand the role of patient demand in the misuse of malaria treatment and to improve adherence to malaria test results. This chapter briefly refers to the data from this study; chapter 7 provides a more extensive discussion.

The first part of this section describes the various methods used in the literature to measure the quality of care delivered in clinical practice and their advantages and disadvantages. This is a brief summary of common methods rather than a comprehensive review; for more information, see Kwan, Daniels, et al. (2019) as well as chapter 2. Many studies combine quality of care measurements with measures of provider knowledge to isolate provider effort. A focus of this report is the impact of pay-for-performance schemes on the quality of care delivered (delved into in Chapters 5 through 8). Measuring provider effort is particularly important in the context of pay-for-performance schemes: on the one hand, short-term improvements in response to incentives are constrained by the provider's level of knowledge, while on the other hand, the right incentives might motivate providers in the longer term to improve their skill set to increase the quality of care they can provide. Therefore, the second part of this section summarizes a range of methods used for measuring health worker knowledge.

As part of the methods summary, box 3.2 discusses approaches to measuring quality of care and provider effort in antenatal care. Antenatal care is a focal application where the international community has made significant investments in pay-for-performance schemes. Quality measurement in antenatal care encounters some specific measurement challenges that the latest research has been able to overcome. The third part of this section discusses the integration of quality measurement into policy, including health management information systems, and in particular their use in pay-for-performance schemes. It argues that an important component of measuring quality of care and efficiency of effective coverage is to measure the cost of providing different levels of care.

Measuring the quality of clinical practice

The international health community has long been concerned about the quality of care provided in LMIC contexts. In 1985, the WHO convened a conference of experts on the "rational use of medicines," which set a high standard by defining rational use as follows: "Patients receive medications appropriate to their clinical needs, in doses that meet their own individual requirements, for an adequate period of time, and at the lowest cost to them and their community" (WHO 1985, 73). This initiative generated a wealth of resources, including a list of issues that constitute "irrational use." The list cites polypharmacy (the use of too many medicines for the same condition); inappropriate use of antimicrobials, including inadequate dosage; overuse of injections when an oral formulation can be given; and

Box 3.2 In Focus: Measuring quality of care and provider effort in antenatal and maternal care

While standardized patients are often referred to as the "gold standard" in measuring quality of care, they are difficult to implement in studies of maternal care seeking, from both ethical and logistical standpoints. For example, an antenatal care (ANC) study would have to recruit and train pregnant women to receive care at the sampled facility. ANC can also involve invasive procedures and tests. Direct clinical observation may be similarly difficult and relatively expensive to implement, and health facilities in rural areas may schedule ANC services only one or two days of the week, complicating logistics. Further, observing labor and delivery, particularly in primary health care settings, can be unpredictable and yield small sample sizes. The method may in particular struggle to capture performance during birth complications, which are relatively rare. At the same time, in maternal care, where the physical examination and the provider's conduct toward the patient are important aspects of quality, written vignettes or knowledge tests are relatively far removed from actual practice. For all these reasons, researchers have piloted the use of new technologies to simulate patient-provider interactions and assess provider effort, knowledge, and skill.

In recent work in Burkina Faso, researchers developed video vignettes of patients presenting maternal or early childhood symptoms (Banuri et al. 2018). These vignettes were locally developed and featured a local actor, who described complications like pre-term labor or mastitis. A video can represent the patient's socioeconomic status more realistically. In the Burkina Faso experiment, vignettes for nonpoor patients were one minute long, whereas vignettes that portrayed poorer patients were longer (100 seconds) and the actress dressed differently, used more "rambling" language, and appeared to be less educated. The authors find that the video vignettes captured a range of performance by the health workers, including lower performance on the longer vignettes. They conclude that video vignettes can capture health worker effort, including its interaction with the patient's socioeconomic status.

Health worker performance during birth complications that endanger the well-being of the mother or newborn may be the most important dimension of quality in maternal care, but capturing it is difficult. For such rare complications, training with portable and cost-effective anatomical models, like MamaNatalie and NeoNatalie, has been shown to improve provider knowledge and skill (DeStephano et al. 2015; Al-beity et al. 2019). The impact evaluation of the Kyrgyz Republic performance-based financing (PBF) pilot (see box 6.1, in chapter 6) used these anatomical models to measure the management of postpartum hemorrhage and birth asphyxia. The evaluation found that performance on anatomical models was significantly and positively correlated with performance during direct clinical observation (Friedman and Kandpal 2021). The pilot also tied payments to these assessments of provider skill and found that PBF directly improved observed provider performance during labor and delivery as well as birth outcomes for mother and child, suggesting that anatomical models can be useful for both measurement and as a training tool to improve provider practice.

Future research on quality of care in ANC will also have to address the question of nonindicated care. This is particularly important because PBF interventions can potentially increase the overprovision of incentivized preventive services (see chapter 7). There are many aspects of overtreatment that the data currently do not capture. The ANC checklists were designed to measure compliance with World Health Organization protocol rather than to record all actions, whether necessary or not, performed by the health care provider. Moreover, in many cases, nonindicated drugs or procedures can be identified only by matching the observed care with gestational age. At a minimum, maternal care PBF programs should track nonindicated care or overprescription in ANC for incentivized services—even if the service in question is preventive in nature, it may not be indicated for every individual case.

failure to prescribe in accordance with clinical guidelines (WHO 2002), among other problems.

In this context, the set of measures cited most often for assessing rational medicine use are the INRUD indicators (WHO 1993). The INRUD core indicators represent a minimum set of indicators that the WHO recommends for studies on medication use and prescription practices. However, they mostly measure *levels* of care but not *appropriateness* of care and therefore cannot assess many aspects of high-quality of care. Table 3.2 shows medication use statistics from the Mali case study borrowed from the INRUD list. Most of the indicators do not relate actual use to optimal use of a treatment (although some studies attempt to define whether better use is represented by an indicator's increase or decrease, for example, Holloway et al. 2020). This issue has limited the literature. For example, a systematic review of studies on irrational medicine use in China and Vietnam, based on the WHO framework, notes that "[n]o eligible studies were found to assess whether or not unnecessary or expensive drugs were prescribed, and whether or not the prescription was in accordance with clinical guidelines" (Mao et al. 2015, 9).

The most relevant but less used INRUD indicator is from the list of complementary indicators: "prescription in accordance with treatment guidelines." As the WHO guidelines note, this measure can be highly effective for well-defined conditions with clear treatment guidelines, but problems exist in terms of defining health problems, in defining what is acceptable treatment, and in obtaining enough encounters with specific problems during the course of a drug use survey. These few lines point to the many challenges that arise when measuring appropriate care and identifying insufficient care as well as nonindicated care. At the core is the

Table 3.2 Rational use of medicines consultation indicators: Mali case study

Indicator	Mean
Prescribed antibiotics (%)	63
Received injection or IV (%)	40
Medications prescribed (average)	3.8
Medications bought (average)	2.5

Sources: World Bank, using data from the INRUD/WHO Indicators in the Mali case study; Lopez, Sautmann, and Schaner 2022.

Note: The indicators were created from data collected for an experimental study on malaria treatment in Mali, which had 627 patient observations in the control group (see box 3.1). All patients with acute symptoms were approached for clinic entry and exit interviews. INRUD indicators cannot directly assess whether a given treatment was appropriate, although the documented levels of antibiotics and injection use and the rate of polypharmacy (multiple medications for a single condition) in this sample are very high. INRUD = International Network for the Rational Use of Drugs; IV = intravenous; WHO = World Health Organization.

problem that quality depends not only on what *is* provided, but also on what *should* be provided.[1]

In recent years, a new generation of studies in the health economics literature has developed several methods that tackle this issue to assess quality of care. The first of these methods, often declared the "gold standard" (Dupas and Miguel 2017), is so-called *audit* or *standardized patient* studies, which have been used in multiple research studies across many LMICs.[2] Akin to mystery shoppers, standardized patients are trained to present with a specific illness profile and visit the provider incognito, and they are later debriefed about the consultation. Kwan, Bergkvist, et al. (2019) provide an introduction on how to use the method for research, accompanied by a toolkit and manual, and King et al. (2019) provide practical implementation guidance.

The standardized patient method has several benefits. Most importantly, of course, providers do not know who among their patients are audit cases,[3] making it likely that the visit records are representative of the provider's behavior in day-to-day patient interactions. Because the "true" underlying condition is known to the researcher by design, the provider's behavior can be benchmarked against recommended clinical practice, and their conclusions can be compared with the correct diagnosis. Each component of the consultation can be recorded, from the number of questions asked to the diagnosis and length of time spent with the patient. The method also allows the researcher to vary patient behavior or characteristics systematically to understand provider responses, for example, to identify gender or ethnic discrimination (Borkhoff et al. 2009; Planas et al. 2015) or to measure how providers treat patients with different levels of medical knowledge (Currie, Lin, and Meng 2014). For these purposes, it is particularly useful that several standardized patients can visit the same provider and record their behavior in multiple cases, and conversely, the same individual trained as a standardized patient can present with different illness profiles, different ways of behaving and dressing, and so on.

A disadvantage is that the types of conditions presented, or the scripted behavior and responses by the standardized patients, may not be representative of the actual patient population. Real patients may also have a history of illness or clinical records with which the physician is familiar. In addition, standardized patient studies share with "mystery shopper" and audit research designs in other contexts the problem that they are often not double-blinded, that is, the person assessing quality knows (or infers) the objectives of the study. This may lead the assessor to change their behavior subconsciously to elicit a specific response, causing confirmatory bias (Bertrand and Duflo 2017).

Another method of quality measurement is direct observation. Here, a trained clinician—for instance, a physician, nurse/midwife, or medical student—sits in on the visit and takes notes on various aspects of the consultation. Usually, these observation data are collected using a structured checklist, which reflects established protocols for that type of service (WHO guidelines, national health policy, or other accepted medical protocols). A study in Tanzania shows that the responses in the direct observation checklist correspond closely with patient recall in a "retroactive consultation review" (RCR) (Leonard and Masatu 2006). Moreover, despite an initial Hawthorne effect—that is, the observed physician responding to being observed by increasing their effort—the quality of care recorded in the observed interactions is similar to that in unobserved interactions (as measured by an RCR) after the first approximately 10 consultations (Leonard and Masatu 2010). To the extent that *patients* do not change their behavior under observation, this approach is closest to "real life" in the sense that the conditions and persons observed are a representative sample of the relevant patient population. However, it may be difficult to construct a checklist that is detailed enough yet covers all the possible cases the physician encounters, especially in a generalist practice.

In some situations, the best way to measure quality is by conducting a patient interview after the consultation with the physician, as in an RCR. Leonard and Masatu (2006) report high agreement between direct physician observation and patient reports when the RCR occurs shortly after the consultation. This is particularly useful when the interview can be combined with a re-evaluation of the patient's diagnosis. For example, in the malaria case study described in box 3.1, enumerators conducted exit interviews at the clinic as well as follow-up interviews and a malaria test at home the next day. This method uses real patients and may avoid observation bias in physician behavior at least to some degree—but there are disadvantages too. First, patients often cannot accurately report what tests were conducted. Second, Lopez, Sautmann, and Schaner (2022) find that there is selection bias in home malaria testing: only patients with more serious symptoms agree to the rapid diagnostic test (RDT), which involves a finger prick to take blood. The authors therefore construct a malaria risk index from the home test, using predicted malaria probability based on symptom reports and patient demographics to extend the analysis to all patients at the clinic.

To illustrate, figure 3.1 shows the share of patients who received antimalarial prescriptions by predicted malaria risk, by providers who did and did

Figure 3.1   Prescriptions for antimalarials in the malaria case study

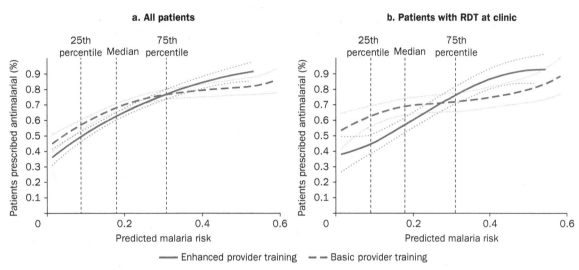

Source: World Bank, using data from Lopez, Sautmann, and Schaner 2022.

Note: Prescriptions for antimalarials are from the malaria case study (box 3.1), by predicted malaria risk based on malaria test results of the home sample and by treatment group (enhanced versus basic provider training). The figure shows all patients in panel a and only patients who received an RDT at the clinic in panel b. It demonstrates that training on the sensitivity and specificity of RDT tests for malaria reduces prescription rates for low-risk patients but increases them for high-risk patients, improving overall match rates. The use of predicted risk for the full sample overcomes issues of selection into home malaria testing. The dotted lines represent 95% confidence intervals. RDT = rapid detection test.

not receive an in-depth training module on the accuracy of malaria testing (the control group only received basic practical training on RDT use). In clinics where providers had additional training, patients with low malaria risk received fewer prescriptions and patients with high risk received more prescriptions. This method of re-diagnosing a subset of the sample and predicting illness risk for the remaining patients may be useful in other settings as well.

The measures of quality of care used in chapter 2 were not taken at the provider level but instead relied on representative population surveys. Researchers use representative surveys to measure health outcomes such as vaccination rates, birth rates, morbidity, mortality, or anthropometrics (for example, child stunting and weight) or patient satisfaction and recall of medical procedures performed. This approach has the benefit of measuring the *outcomes* of any care received as the ultimate objects of interest. Chapter 2 discusses the advantages and disadvantages of measuring health care quality at the population versus the provider level in more detail; this chapter only notes that in population surveys it is typically not possible to link outcomes directly to the actions of individual providers, although patient populations may be associated with local health facilities. The method also typically requires large samples.

Assessing health worker knowledge

To benchmark clinical practice and understand provider effort, many studies separately assess the individual provider's level of knowledge. One method for assessing knowledge is vignettes: a vignette presents a hypothetical case or patient, and the provider's behavior, proposed course of action, and diagnosis in this staged "consultation" are observed or recorded. Vignettes can be done in different formats, such as in writing, as an interview, or as a fully simulated interaction. For example, an interviewer may describe a list of symptoms to the health worker, and the health worker is asked to describe how they would proceed under real-life circumstances, including asking questions about the history of the illness, listing necessary examinations, prescribing medication, or diagnostic tests. Vignettes have been used in a variety of contexts and studies, including in LMICs (Peabody et al. 2000; Das and Hammer 2005; Das, Hammer, and Leonard 2008), and are the most common form of measuring provider knowledge in the standardized patient studies cited above. An advantage is that the provider's knowledge can be tested for the same conditions that are also simulated during the standardized patient visit.

As an alternative approach, Leonard and Masatu (2010) propose taking advantage of the Hawthorne effect. They show that physicians provide distinctly higher quality of care when they are under observation by a trained clinician during the first approximately 10–15 patient visits; afterward, diagnostic inputs and accuracy drop by 20 percent and an estimated 38 percent, respectively (Leonard and Masatu 2010). It must be assumed that physicians are "on their best behavior" during the early visits and their conduct therefore represents their true capacity and knowledge. The researcher can then compare the provider's highest possible performance—from observing up to 10 visits—with their day-to-day performance, measured in later observed visits or with one of the other methods. This way of assessing knowledge has similar advantages and disadvantages as the observational method of quality measurement: the data are representative and come from real patient interactions, but the visits observed in the different observation phases may be for different illnesses or cases, making it difficult to compare them. Further, the researcher may be unable to observe rare conditions.

Measuring efficiency of care

An important piece of information on the provision of care is the *efficiency* of delivering a given level of quality of care, which requires measuring: (1) the actual cost of health care, (2) the share of patients who do or do not receive the correct care, and (3) the cost of providing the optimal level of care.

Chapter 7 returns to the concept of the efficiency of effective coverage in more detail. The first task can be accomplished using administrative data such as a health management information system or patient survey data, although any administrative data need to be detailed enough to be able to attribute cost to specific provider-patient interactions. For example, this requires measuring the time different staff spend on a given consultation and attributing the materials used to specific cases.

The second and third tasks are more difficult because they require estimating the cost of the provider's effort and time to deliver the desired quality of care. While the cost of the optimal treatment may be *lower* in terms of material costs than the treatment that is actually received, due to the frequent provision of nonindicated care, the health worker's effort will almost always be *higher* when the optimal level of care is provided. Studies that use knowledge and skill tests (for example, vignettes or observed patient visits when the Hawthorne effect is still present), as well as impact evaluations that use financial incentives to increase provider effort, could be important sources of data for estimating the cost of the "optimal" provision of care in terms of time and effort spent. Standardized patient and other quality of care studies can serve to estimate the share of patients receiving the appropriate care. Understanding the efficiency of care and how it is affected by financial incentives could be a fruitful area for future research.

Conclusions

Understanding the extent to which various constraints restrict the provision of high-quality care helps inform policies aimed at improving the quality of health services and health outcomes. For instance, an approach to improving provider effort might be explicitly linking facility or provider payments to results. So-called performance-based financing programs typically pay for quality directly, by paying for specific indicators of process quality, or indirectly, adjusting the total payment according to a broader measure of quality.

However, limited analysis has attempted to quantify the size of structural gaps relative to knowledge or effort gaps. Without knowing what the binding constraints are to improving clinical quality, it is difficult to gauge the effectiveness of these investments. For example, addressing low effort provision by providers requires a different toolkit than does addressing poor knowledge or a shortage of supplies. Quantifying these relative sizes may thus aid policy makers in deciding how much to invest where.

By highlighting that there may be multiple causes of observed poor clinical quality, not just poor worker effort, the framework presented here also underlines the need for a variety of approaches to improve the provision of care. For instance, evidence of structural constraints—a lack of essential equipment, drugs, and supplies for providing basic antenatal care—would suggest the continued need for investments in health facility infrastructure. In addition, if the investigation finds evidence of idle capacity—or a lack of effort by health workers—this would, in turn, suggest the continued need for interventions that motivate health workers, including pay-for-performance or other financial incentive–driven approaches.

Notes

1. The problem of an outside observer is the same as that of the patient: they must rely on the provider to accurately diagnose the patient's health care needs. Assessing whether the provider's recommendations are accurate essentially requires another equally qualified physician. This classical "informed expert" problem—where the seller of a service is also the expert who helps the customer determine their own needs—is at the root of many of the problems related to the provision of low quality of care (Wolinsky 1993).
2. Researchers have used standardized patients in Benin, China, India, Kenya, Peru, South Africa, and Tanzania to study provider behavior when patients consulted for angina, asthma, diarrhea, family planning, respiratory infection, tuberculosis, STDs, etc. (Banerjee et al. 2020; Christian et al. 2018; Currie, Lin, and Meng 2014; Currie, Lin, and Zhang 2011; Daniels et al. 2017; Das, Chowdhury, et al. 2016; Das et al. 2012; Das, Holla, et al. 2016; Kohler et al. 2017; Kwan et al. 2018; Planas et al. 2015; Sylvia et al. 2015, 2017).
3. For ethical reasons, they typically know and must agree to be visited by standardized patients in principle but do not know who it is.

References

Adair-Rohani, H., K. Zukor, S. Bonjour, S. Wilburn, A. C. Kuesel, R. Hebert, and E. R. Fletcher. 2013. "Limited Electricity Access in Health Facilities of

Sub-Saharan Africa: A Systematic Review of Data on Electricity Access, Sources, and Reliability." *Global Health Science and Practice* 1 (2): 249–61. https://doi.org/10.9745/GHSP-D-13-00037.

Akachi, Y., and M. E. Kruk. 2017. "Quality of Care: Measuring a Neglected Driver of Improved Health." *Bulletin of the World Health Organization* 95 (6): 465–72. https://doi.org/10.2471/BLT.16.180190.

Al-beity, F. A., A. Pembe, A. Hirose, J. Morris, S. Leshabari, G. Marrone, and C. Hanson. 2019. "Effect of the Competency-Based *Helping Mothers Survive Bleeding after Birth* (HMS BAB) Training on Maternal Morbidity: A Cluster-Randomised Trial in 20 Districts in Tanzania." *BMJ Global Health* 4 (2): e001214. https://doi.org/10.1136/bmjgh-2018-001214.

Banerjee, A., J. Das, J. Hammer, R. Hussam, and A. Mohpal. 2020. "The Market for Healthcare in Low-Income Countries." Working Paper. Harvard Business School, Cambridge, MA.

Banuri, S., D. de Walque, P. Keefer, O. D. Haidara, P. J. Robyn, and M. Ye. 2018. "The Use of Video Vignettes to Measure Health Worker Knowledge: Evidence from Burkina Faso." *Social Science & Medicine* 213: 173–80.

Belita, A., P. Mbindyo, and M. English. 2013. "Absenteeism amongst Health Workers—Developing a Typology to Support Empiric Work in Low-Income Countries and Characterizing Reported Associations." *Human Resources for Health* 11 (1): 34. https://doi.org/10.1186/1478-4491-11-34.

Benova, L., Ö. Tunçalp, A. C. Moran, and O. M. Campbell. 2018. "Not Just a Number: Examining Coverage and Content of Antenatal Care in Low-Income and Middle-Income Countries." *BMJ Global Health* 3 (2): e000779.

Bertrand, M., and E. Duflo. 2017. "Field Experiments on Discrimination." In *Handbook of Economic Field Experiments*, vol. 1, edited by E. Duflo and A. Banerjee, 309–93. Amsterdam, Netherlands: Elsevier.

Borkhoff, C. M., G. A. Hawker, H. J. Kreder, R. H. Glazier, N. N. Mahomed, and J. G. Wright. 2009. "Patients' Gender Affected Physicians' Clinical Decisions When Presented with Standardized Patients but Not for Matching Paper Patients." *Journal of Clinical Epidemiology* 62 (5): 527–41. https://doi.org/10.1016/j.jclinepi.2008.03.009.

Chaudhury, N., J. Hammer, M. Kremer, K. Muralidharan, and F. H. Rogers. 2006. "Missing in Action: Teacher and Health Worker Absence in Developing Countries." *Journal of Economic Perspectives* 20 (1): 91–116. https://doi.org/10.1257/089533006776526058.

Chou, V. B., N. Walker, and M. Kanyangarara. 2019. "Estimating the Global Impact of Poor Quality of Care on Maternal and Neonatal Outcomes in 81 Low- and Middle-Income Countries: A Modeling Study." *PLoS Medicine* 16 (12): e1002990. https://doi.org/10.1371/journal.pmed.1002990.

Christian, C. S., U.-G. Gerdtham, D. Hompashe, A. Smith, and R. Burger. 2018. "Measuring Quality Gaps in TB Screening in South Africa Using Standardised Patient Analysis." *International Journal of Environmental Research and Public Health* 15 (4): 729. https://doi.org/10.3390/ijerph15040729.

Currie, J., W. Lin, and J. Meng. 2014. "Addressing Antibiotic Abuse in China: An Experimental Audit Study." *Journal of Development Economics* 110: 39–51. https://doi.org/10.1016/j.jdeveco.2014.05.006.

Currie, J., W. Lin, and W. Zhang. 2011. "Patient Knowledge and Antibiotic Abuse: Evidence from an Audit Study in China." *Journal of Health Economics* 30 (5): 933–49. https://doi.org/10.1016/j.jhealeco.2011.05.009.

Daniels, B., A. Dolinger, G. Bedoya, K. Rogo, A. Goicoechea, J. Coarasa, F. Wafula, et al. 2017. "Use of Standardised Patients to Assess Quality of Healthcare in Nairobi, Kenya: A Pilot, Cross-Sectional Study with International Comparisons." *BMJ Global Health* 2 (2): e000333. https://doi.org/10.1136/bmjgh-2017-000333.

Das, J., A. Chowdhury, R. Hussam, and A. V. Banerjee. 2016. "The Impact of Training Informal Health Care Providers in India: A Randomized Controlled Trial." *Science* 354 (6308): aaf7384. https://doi.org/10.1126/science.aaf7384.

Das, J., and J. Hammer. 2005. "Which Doctor? Combining Vignettes and Item Response to Measure Clinical Competence." *Journal of Development Economics* 78 (2): 348–83.

Das, J., J. Hammer, and K. Leonard. 2008. "The Quality of Medical Advice in Low-Income Countries." *Journal of Economic Perspectives* 22 (2): 93–114.

Das, J., A. Holla, V. Das, M. Mohanan, D. Tabak, and B. Chan. 2012. "In Urban and Rural India, a Standardized Patient Study Showed Low Levels of Provider Training and Huge Quality Gaps." *Health Affairs* 31 (12): 2774–84.

Das, J., A. Holla, A. Mohpal, and K. Muralidharan. 2016. "Quality and Accountability in Health Care Delivery: Audit-Study Evidence from Primary Care in India." *American Economic Review* 106 (12): 3765–99. https://doi.org/10.1257/aer.20151138.

Das, J., A. Kwan, B. Daniels, S. Satyanarayana, R. Subbaraman, S. Bergkvist, R. K. Das, et al. 2015. "Use of Standardised Patients to Assess Quality of Tuberculosis Care: A Pilot, Cross-Sectional Study." *The Lancet Infectious Diseases* 15 (11): 1305–13.

DeStephano, C. C., B. Chou, S. Patel, S. Slattery, and N. Hueppchen. 2015. "A Randomized Controlled Trial of Birth Simulation for Medical Students." *American Journal of Obstetrics and Gynecology* 213 (1): 91.e1–91.e7. https://doi.org/10.1016/j.ajog.2015.03.024.

Di Giorgio, L., D. K. Evans, M. Lindelow, S. N. Nguyen, J. Svensson, W. Wane, and A. Welander Tärneberg. 2020. "Analysis of Clinical Knowledge, Absenteeism and Availability of Resources for Maternal and Child Health: A Cross-Sectional Quality of Care Study in 10 African Countries." *BMJ Global Health* 5 (12): e003377. https://doi.org/10.1136/bmjgh-2020-003377.

Donabedian, A. 2003. *An Introduction to Quality Assurance in Health Care.* Oxford University Press. http://ebookcentral.proquest.com/lib/londonschoolecons/detail.action?docID=3053650.

Dupas, P., and E. Miguel. 2017. "Impacts and Determinants of Health Levels in Low-Income Countries." In *Handbook of Economic Field Experiments, vol. 2,* edited by E. Duflo and A. Banerjee, 3–93. Amsterdam, Netherlands: Elsevier.

Fink, G., E. Kandpal, and G. Shapira. 2022. "Inequality in the Quality of Health Services: Wealth, Content of Care, and Price of Antenatal Consultations in the Democratic Republic of Congo." *Economic Development and Cultural Change.* https://doi.org/10.1086/713941.

Friedman J., and E. Kandpal. 2021. "The Roles of Financial Incentives and Performance Monitoring in Improving the Quality of Health Care: Evidence from a National Pay-for-Performance Trial in the Kyrgyz Republic." World Bank, Washington, DC.

Holloway, K. A., V. Ivanovska, S. Manikandan, M. Jayanthi, A. Mohan, G. Forte, and D. Henry. 2020. "Identifying the Most Effective Essential Medicines Policies for Quality Use of Medicines: A Replicability Study Using Three World Health Organisation Data-Sets." *PLoS One* 15 (2): e0228201. https://doi.org/10.1371/journal.pone.0228201.

Howitt, P., A. Darzi, G.-Z. Yang, H. Ashrafian, R. Atun, J. Barlow, A. Blakemore, et al. 2012. "Technologies for Global Health." *The Lancet (British Edition)* 380 (9840): 507–35. https://doi.org/10.1016/S0140-6736(12)61127-1.

Ibnat, F., K. L. Leonard, L. Bawo, and R. L. Mohammed-Roberts. 2019. "The Three-Gap Model of Health Worker Performance." Policy Research Working Paper 8782, World Bank, Washington, DC.

Jamison, D. T., J. G. Breman, A. R. Measham, G. Alleyne, M. Claeson, D. B. Evans, et al., and World Bank, eds. 2006. *Disease Control Priorities in Developing Countries* (second ed.). Disease Control Priorities Project. New York: Oxford University Press.

King, J. J. C., J. Das, A. Kwan, B. Daniels, T. Powell-Jackson, C. Makungu, and C. Goodman. 2019. "How to Do (or Not to Do) … Using the Standardized Patient Method to Measure Clinical Quality of Care in LMIC Health Facilities." *Health Policy and Planning* 34 (8): 625–34. https://doi.org/10.1093/heapol/czz078.

Kohler, P. K., E. Marumo, S. L. Jed, G. Mema, S. Galagan, K. Tapia, E. Pillay, J. DeKadt, E. Naidoo, J. C. Dombrowski, and K. K. Holmes (2017). "A National Evaluation Using Standardised Patient Actors to Assess STI Services in Public Sector Clinical Sentinel Surveillance Facilities in South Africa." *Sexually Transmitted Infections*, 93 (4): 247–52. https://doi.org/10.1136/sextrans-2016-052930.

Kruk, M. E., A. D. Gage, N. T. Joseph, G. Danaei, S. García-Saisó, and J. A. Salomon. 2018. "Mortality Due to Low-Quality Health Systems in the Universal Health Coverage Era: A Systematic Analysis of Amenable Deaths in 137 Countries." *The Lancet* 392 (10160): 2203–12. https://doi.org/10.1016/S0140-6736(18)31668-4.

Kwan, A., S. Bergkvist, B. Daniels, J. Das, V. Das, and M. Pai. 2019. "Using Standardized Patients to Measure Health Care Quality: A Manual and Toolkit for Projects in Low- and Middle-Income Countries." Working Paper. https://github.com/qutubproject/using-standardized-patients.

Kwan, A., B. Daniels, S. Bergkvist, V. Das, M. Pai, and J. Das. 2019. "Use of Standardised Patients for Healthcare Quality Research in Low- and Middle-Income Countries." *BMJ Global Health* 4 (5): e001669. https://doi.org/10.1136/bmjgh-2019-001669.

Kwan, A., B. Daniels, V. Saria, S. Satyanarayana, R. Subbaraman, A. McDowell, S. Bergkvist, R. K. Das, V. Das, J. Das, and M. Pai. 2018. "Variations in the Quality of Tuberculosis Care in Urban India: A Cross-Sectional, Standardized Patient Study in Two Cities." *PLOS Medicine* 15 (11): e1002653. https://doi.org/10.1371/journal.pmed.1002653.

Leonard, K., and M. C. Masatu. 2006. "Outpatient Process Quality Evaluation and the Hawthorne Effect." *Social Science & Medicine* 63 (9): 2330–40.

Leonard, K., and M. C. Masatu. 2010. "Professionalism and the Know-Do Gap: Exploring Intrinsic Motivation among Health Workers in Tanzania." *Health Economics* 19 (12): 1461–77.

Leslie, H. H., L. R. Hirschhorn, T. Marchant, S. V. Doubova, O. Gureje, and M. E. Kruk. 2018. "Health Systems Thinking: A New Generation of Research to Improve Healthcare Quality." *PLoS Medicine* 15 (10): e1002682. https://doi.org/10.1371/journal.pmed.1002682.

Lopez, C., A. Sautmann, and S. Schaner. 2022. "Does Patient Demand Contribute to the Overuse of Prescription Drugs?" *American Economic Journal: Applied Economics* 14 (1): 225–60. https://doi.org/10.1257/app.20190722.

Macarayan, E. K., I. Papanicolas, and A. K. Jha. 2020. "The Quality of Malaria Care in 25 Low-Income and Middle-Income Countries." *BMJ Global Health* 5 (2): e002023. https://doi.org/10.1136%2Fbmjgh-2019-002023.

Manne-Goehler, J., P. Geldsetzer, K. Agoudavi, G. Andall-Brereton, K. K. Aryal, B. W. Bicaba, P. Bovet, et al. 2019. "Health System Performance for People with Diabetes in 28 Low- and Middle-Income Countries: A Cross-Sectional Study of Nationally Representative Surveys." *PLoS Medicine* 16 (3): e1002751. https://doi.org/10.1371/journal.pmed.1002751.

Mao, W., H. Vu, Z. Xie, W. Chen, and S. Tang. 2015. "Systematic Review on Irrational Use of Medicines in China and Vietnam." *PLoS One* 10 (3): e0117710. https://doi.org/10.1371/journal.pone.0117710.

Montagu, D., M. Sudhinaraset, N. Diamond-Smith, O. Campbell, S. Gabrysch, L. Freedman, M. E. Kruk, and F. Donnay. 2017. "Where Women Go to Deliver: Understanding the Changing Landscape of Childbirth in Africa and Asia." *Health Policy and Planning* 32 (8): 1146–52. https://doi.org/10.1093/heapol/czx060.

Pakenham-Walsh, N., and F. Bukachi. 2009. "Information Needs of Health Care Workers in Developing Countries: A Literature Review with a Focus on Africa." *Human Resources for Health* 7: article 30. https://doi.org/10.1186/1478-4491-7-30.

Peabody, J. W., J. Luck, P. Glassman, T. R. Dresselhaus, and M. Lee. 2000. "Comparison of Vignettes, Standardized Patients, and Chart Abstraction: A Prospective Validation Study of 3 Methods for Measuring Quality." *JAMA* 283 (13): 1715–22.

Perry, H. B., R. Zulliger, and M. M. Rogers. 2014. "Community Health Workers in Low-, Middle-, and High-Income Countries: An Overview of Their History, Recent Evolution, and Current Effectiveness." *Annual Review of Public Health* 35 (1): 399–421. https://doi.org/10.1146/annurev-publhealth-032013-182354.

Planas, M. E., P. J. Garcia, M. Bustelo, C. P. Carcamo, S. Martinez, H. Nopo, J. Rodriguez, M. F. Merino, and A. Morrison. 2015. "Effects of Ethnic Attributes on the Quality of Family Planning Services in Lima, Peru: A Randomized Crossover Trial." *PLoS One* 10 (2): e0115274. https://doi.org/10.1371/journal.pone.0115274.

Rao, K. D., and A. Sheffel. 2018. "Quality of Clinical Care and Bypassing of Primary Health Centers in India." *Social Science & Medicine* 207: 80–88. https://doi.org/10.1016/j.socscimed.2018.04.040.

Reid, M. J. A., N. Arinaminpathy, A. Bloom, B. R. Bloom, C. Boehme, R. Chaisson, D. P. Chin, et al. 2019. "Building a Tuberculosis-Free World: The Lancet Commission on Tuberculosis." *The Lancet (British Edition)* 393 (10178): 1331–84. https://doi.org/10.1016/S0140-6736(19)30024-8.

Smith, R. D., and K. Hanson. 2011. *Health Systems in Low- and Middle-Income Countries: An Economic and Policy Perspective.* Oxford University Press. https://doi.org/10.1093/acprof:oso/9780199566761.001.0001.

Sylvia, S., Y. Shi, H. Xue, X. Tian, H. Wang, Q. Liu, A. Medina, and S. Rozelle. 2015. "Survey Using Incognito Standardized Patients Shows Poor Quality Care in China's Rural Clinics." *Health Policy and Planning* 30: 322–33. https://doi.org/10.1093/heapol/czu014.

Sylvia, S., H. Xue, C. Zhou, Y. Shi, H. Yi, H. Zhou, S. Rozelle, M. Pai, and J. Das. 2017. "Tuberculosis Detection and the Challenges of Integrated Care in Rural China: A Cross-Sectional Standardized Patient Study." *PLoS Medicine* 14 (10): e1002405. https://doi.org/10.1371/journal.pmed.1002405.

Vasan, A., D. C. Mabey, S. Chaudhri, H.-A. Brown Epstein, and S. D. Lawn. 2017. "Support and Performance Improvement for Primary Health Care Workers in Low- and Middle-Income Countries: A Scoping Review of Intervention Design and Methods." *Health Policy and Planning* 32 (3): 437–52. https://doi.org/10.1093/heapol/czw144.

World Health Organization. 1985. "The Rational Use of Drugs: Review of Major Issues." Report of the Conference of Experts. Geneva: WHO. https://apps.who.int/iris/handle/10665/62311.

World Health Organization. 1993. *How to Investigate Drug Use in Health Facilities: Selected Drug Use Indicators.* Geneva: WHO.

World Health Organization. 2002. *Promoting Rational Use of Medicines: Core Components.* WHO/EDM/2002.3. Geneva: WHO.

World Health Organization. 2013. *World Health Statistics 2013: A Wealth of Information on Global Public Health.* WHO/HIS/HSI/13.1. Geneva: WHO.

Wolinsky, A. 1993. "Competition in a Market for Informed Experts' Services." *RAND Journal of Economics* 24 (3): 380–98. https://doi.org/10.2307/2555964.

Zhang, H., G. Fink, and J. Cohen. 2021. "The Impact of Health Worker Absenteeism on Patient Health Care Seeking Behavior, Testing and Treatment: A Longitudinal Analysis in Uganda." *PloS One* 16 (8): e0256437. https://doi.org/10.1371/journal.pone.0256437.

CHAPTER 4

Decomposing the Constraints to Quality of Care Using Data on Antenatal Care Consultations from Five Sub-Saharan African Countries

Introduction

This chapter first provides the motivation for the use of antenatal care (ANC) consultations for assessment of the quality of care and explains the three-gap framework in detail. Then, the chapter presents the data and describes how the various components are used to assess the three gaps. Next, it discusses the findings on the three gaps. The chapter concludes with a discussion of the policy implications of the results and ties them to the rest of this report, in particular chapter 5.

ANC consultations are used to examine the extent to which clinical quality is constrained by (1) the competency of health care providers, (2) the availability of equipment and consumables, and (3) the effort gap. That is, for different components of ANC, the chapter assesses the share of consultations in which the providers know they should perform an action, have the equipment and supplies needed, and yet do not perform the action. Then, the analysis explores the characteristics of facilities, providers, and patients that correlate with the different gaps in the provision of high-quality care. This analysis is novel for several reasons. Many previous assessments of health facility quality used physical infrastructure and supplies (Gatti et al. 2021), which this report terms structural quality, or health worker knowledge (Das, Hammer, and Leonard 2008) as proxies for clinical quality. However, as this report shows, provider practice often diverges notably from what providers are trained to do. While this analysis is not the first to show this divergence between knowledge and practice (Kabongo et al. 2017; Lange, Mwisongo, and Mæstad 2014; Mohanan et al. 2015), it quantifies the extent to which idle capacity explains poor quality of care. That is, what portion of unperformed, essential care could have been provided had the health worker simply chosen to do so? Further, the data contain detailed information on facility, provider, and patient characteristics. As such, the analysis not only quantifies idle capacity relative to structural and knowledge gaps, but also explores whether any such correlates systematically explain such underperformance. Finding meaningful signals of correlation would identify clear places for interventions aimed at improving health worker effort.

As figure 4.1 demonstrates, there is a consistent—and often large—gap between coverage and effective coverage in ANC in the five countries studied in this chapter—Cameroon, the Central African Republic, the

Figure 4.1 **Effective antenatal care coverage in five Sub-Saharan African countries**

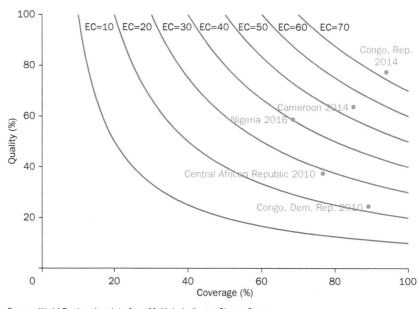

Source: World Bank, using data from Multiple Indicator Cluster Surveys.

Note: Coverage: percent of women giving birth who had 1+ ANC visits. Quality: of those with coverage, the percent who had 4+ ANC visits with a skilled provider, blood pressure taken, and blood and urine samples taken (correct treatment). ANC = antenatal care; EC = effective coverage.

Democratic Republic of Congo, Nigeria, and the Republic of Congo. For the best performer, the Republic of Congo, coverage is near universal, but effective coverage is below 80 percent. For the worst performer in terms of effective coverage, the Democratic Republic of Congo, the gap is 4.5-fold: approximately 90 percent of all women receive ANC, but only about 20 percent receive effective ANC. As noted in chapter 3, this decomposition tries to understand why the rate of successful or correct treatment, as defined in the effective coverage framework provided in chapter 2, might be less than 100 percent. These trends highlight the poor content of care in these settings and motivate the need for a decomposition aimed at unpacking the various drivers of such shortfalls.

Why antenatal care?

This chapter focuses on ANC consultations for the assessment of quality of care. Although there are many other aspects of care provision that could form the basis of such analysis—curative care, for instance—maternal and neonatal diseases, along with communicable and nutritional diseases, contribute about a third of the global burden of disease (IHME 2018). Poor maternal and neonatal health outcomes, in the form of high morbidity and mortality, are pervasive across low- and middle-income countries (LMICs) but particularly so in Sub-Saharan Africa. While maternal mortality (deaths attributed to pregnancy or birth-related complications) declined by 38 percent from 2000 to 2017, the maternal mortality ratio (MMR) remains high (300–499 per 100,000 live births), very high (500–999), or extremely high (>1,000) in much of Sub-Saharan Africa (IHME 2018). Map 4.1 illustrates that maternal mortality rates are the highest in the world in Sub-Saharan Africa and Afghanistan. Sub-Saharan Africa accounts for two-thirds of all maternal deaths worldwide, with an MMR of 533 maternal deaths per 100,000 live births. Indirect causes (chiefly including anemia, malaria, and heart disease), hemorrhage, and hypertension are the three leading causes of maternal deaths. Similarly, while globally the number of neonatal deaths declined by more than half from 1990 to 2019, Sub-Saharan Africa has the highest neonatal mortality rate in the world, at 27 deaths per 1,000 live births (WHO 2020). Preterm birth, birth asphyxia, and infections and birth defects are the leading causes of neonatal mortality.

ANC visits are promoted by the World Health Organization (WHO) as reducing maternal and neonatal mortality. For this to be the case, there must

Map 4.1   Maternal mortality rates around the world, 2017

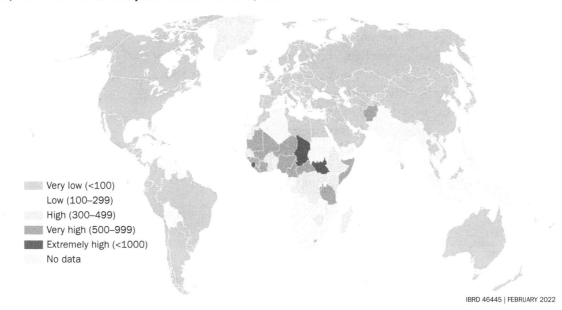

Very low (<100)
Low (100–299)
High (300–499)
Very high (500–999)
Extremely high (<1000)
No data

IBRD 46445 | FEBRUARY 2022

Source: World Bank.

Note: Maternal mortality rate = deaths per 100,000 live births.

be a link between birth outcomes and ANC visits. In its guidelines for ANC, released in November 2016, the WHO recommended tracking ANC coverage among pregnant women in LMICs using two indicators of the number of visits (the proportion of women receiving at least one visit and those receiving at least four visits) and whether the first visit was during the first trimester of pregnancy. However, a review of the evidence of ANC and maternal mortality and morbidity found no link between simple service utilization and the number of ANC visits or whether a midwife, general practitioner, or gynecologist provided care (Carroli, Rooney, and Villar 2001).

In contrast, the same review found that the detection and prevention of anemia—through routine supplementation with iron and folate as well as through malaria chemoprophylaxis—significantly reduced the percentage of women who became anemic in pregnancy. Similarly, the detection and treatment of hypertension and proteinuria, which is indicative of preeclampsia, a potentially life threatening pregnancy complication characterized by high blood pressure, kidney or liver damage, reduced case fatality. On neonatal mortality risks, the review found that routine screening for and prevention of infection during ANC consultations reduced fetal loss and maternal and infant morbidity. This review thus highlights the importance of considering the content or quality of ANC in addition to its simple coverage—in other words, the effective coverage of ANC. Studying the effective coverage of ANC is important from a health outcomes standpoint.

In addition, while the literature on provider effort largely focuses on curative care as a driver of mortality and morbidity (Mohanan et al. 2015; Das et al. 2012; Rethans et al. 2007; Peabody et al. 2000), ANC is also linked to reductions in maternal and neonatal mortality (Carroli, Rooney, and Villar 2001; Adam et al. 2005; Hollowell et al. 2011). From an analytical standpoint, ANC provides a particularly useful set of outcomes for four reasons. First, the WHO has established globally standardized and well-known guidelines that can be used to benchmark clinical quality. These guidelines can be linked to specific actions—and associated equipment, drugs, supplies, and knowledge—recorded in the data, including for the sort of cross-country comparisons conducted here (WHO 2016). Table 4.1 maps the WHO recommendations to the indicators and proxies used in this chapter. Second, ANC requires all three actions—physical inputs, knowledge, and effort—allowing for gauging the various constraints to performance. Third, since ANC consultations are relatively common, the sample sizes are large enough to provide sufficient power. In other words, ANC also provides a relatively large sample of pregnant women with a similar "condition," which may help uncover even relatively fine patterns in the data. Fourth, although the coverage of antenatal consultations has increased globally, there remains variation in the quality of care as measured by the content of the consultations (Hodgins and D'Agostino 2014). This chapter decomposes the observed gaps in clinical quality into (1) structural constraints, (2) knowledge constraints, and (3) an effort gap, by linking data from three different sources: facility assessments, interviews with health care providers, and direct observations of prenatal consultations.

This chapter thus assesses the quality of care in maternal health using data from primary health centers in five of the countries that have the highest MMRs: Cameroon, the Central African Republic, the Democratic Republic of Congo, Nigeria, and the Republic of Congo. The number of maternal deaths per 100,000 live births in 2017 is estimated at 917 in Nigeria, 829 in the Central African Republic, 529 in Cameroon, 472 in the Democratic Republic of Congo, and 378 in the Republic of Congo (WHO 2019). The countries are also characterized by high fertility, with total fertility rates of 5.8 in the Democratic Republic of Congo, 5.3 in Nigeria, 4.6 in the Central African Republic, 4.5 in Cameroon, and 4.4 in the Republic of Congo (United Nations Population Division 2019). Together, the five countries account for 18 percent of the global maternal

Table 4.1   WHO essential protocol for antenatal care consultations

Category of action	Interventions outlined in the clinical guidelines	Indicators and proxies used in the analysis
History	Assess significant symptoms. Take medical and obstetric history. Confirm pregnancy and calculate estimated due date.	HIV status
		Blood group/rhesus
		Current pregnancy danger signs
		Previous tetanus vaccination
		Last menstrual period
Examination	Complete general and obstetrical examination.	Weight
		Blood pressure
		Uterine height
		Fetal heartbeat
		Check for edema
Screening and tests	HIV	HIV test
	Syphilis	Syphilis
	Hemoglobin	Hemoglobin/blood test
	Proteinuria	Urine
Preventive measures		Insecticide-treated bed net
	Iron and folate	Iron/folic pills
		Antimalarials
	Tetanus toxoid	Tetanus toxoid injection
Health education	Nutrition	Nutrition
	Emergency plan	Danger signs

Sources: World Bank; WHO 2016.

mortality burden and 37 percent of the maternal mortality burden in Sub-Saharan Africa (Kassebaum et al. 2014).

Data

The chapter analyzes data from baseline surveys collected between 2012 and 2015 for impact evaluations of results-based financing pilots financially supported by the World Bank and the Health Results Innovation Trust Fund. All the studies were a part of an impact evaluation portfolio aimed at creating a global database on the effectiveness of incentive-based payments in health systems. As a result, the surveys all followed a similar sampling methodology and used the same basic set of survey instruments. Every sampled facility and health worker in the database is supposed to provide ANC. The sample largely consists of nurses, midwives, and community health workers providing care in primary health settings. At the health facilities, the surveys included health facility assessments measuring facility-level management, funding, and drug, equipment, and infrastructure availability; health provider interviews including vignettes on the provision of ANC; patient exit interviews; and direct observations of ANC consultations between patients and providers. These similarities in instruments and sampling methodology allow this study to use these baseline surveys to compare the three gaps in the five countries. Annex 4B describes the harmonization process, analytical decisions, and data limitations in detail.

The next section discusses the evidence from the five countries in the data set on the relative sizes of the three gaps. It links data from three sources: interviews and knowledge tests of health care providers, structural assessments of health facilities, and direct clinical observations of ANC consultations. Structural assessments of health facilities provide the data on the physical constraints faced by the facilities: what equipment, supplies, and drugs do they have relative to what they need? Health worker interviews provide information on what providers know to do when presented with a hypothetical scenario, and direct observations allow measuring what providers actually do in consultations with patients. Therefore, comparing what providers *can* do given equipment and drug availability with what they *know* how to do and comparing that with what they actually *do* allows measuring the relative sizes of the three gaps.

Results

This section presents the findings on the quality of care of ANC consultations in Cameroon, the Central African Republic, the Democratic Republic of Congo, Nigeria, and the Republic of Congo.

Health worker knowledge, physical capacity, and practice

This subsection describes the results on health worker knowledge, the availability of equipment and supplies, and what is in fact done, without linking the different elements.

Health worker knowledge

The first gap in the three-gap model is the know gap, which estimates gaps in health worker knowledge—what is it that the health workers simply do not know? Thus, the assessment turns to health worker knowledge of the WHO essential protocol for ANC. There are two key aspects of this analysis. First, these are health workers whose job description includes the provision of ANC. Second, a key methodological difference between the implementation of the knowledge test and the vignette in the Democratic Republic of Congo may result in different assessments of the levels of health worker knowledge. As is discussed below, health workers in the Democratic Republic of Congo were presented with several care options and had to select the relevant ones, while in the other countries, providers had to list from memory all relevant care to be provided. As such, the assessment does not compare knowledge levels between the other four countries with that in the Democratic Republic of Congo.

Table 4.2 presents the results of the knowledge tests. The highest levels of knowledge are related to physical examinations. The availability of equipment and high levels of performance on these exams—weighing the pregnant woman, taking her blood pressure, measuring the size of her uterus, and listening to the fetal heartbeat—suggest that they may be relatively salient in these contexts. However, apart from listening to the fetal heartbeat, none of these actions have clear links to maternal or neonatal health outcomes (Carroli, Rooney, and Villar 2001). The salience of knowledge of actions that are less well linked to end outcomes may in fact crowd out the performance of actions that may be less salient but in fact have a clearer link to mortality and morbidity.

However, beyond the basic physical examinations, there is significant variation within and across the five countries studied. Broadly, the results for health worker knowledge suggest a few patterns, particularly in the provision of preventive care. While some basic aspects of ANC are well known, knowledge of protocol is far from universal, with stark differences across countries, but also within countries, with particularly low levels of knowledge of preventive care and counseling.

Physical capacity

The second gap discussed in the three-gap model is the know-can gap, which refers to deficiencies in physical infrastructure, drugs, and supplies that keep health workers from providing all the care they know to provide. Thus, this subsection examines the structural capacity of the health facilities in the data. Figure 4.2 and table 4A.1, in annex 4A, present the availability of equipment and consumables used for ANC at the health facilities where observations of first prenatal consultations were observed. The results highlight several striking patterns. Consistent with the high levels of knowledge of basic physical examinations in all the countries studied, permanent equipment—scales,

Table 4.2   Health worker knowledge tests on the WHO antenatal care protocol, using vignettes

Protocol items mentioned by providers in the clinical vignette	Cameroon		Central African Republic		Democratic Republic of Congo		Nigeria		Republic of Congo	
	%	N	%	N	%	N	%	N	%	N
History-taking										
HIV status	23	64	59	32	73	182	33	270	10	41
Blood group and rhesus	9	64	34	32	70	182	—	—	10	49
Tetanus immunizations	17	64	31	32	82	182	42	268	22	49
Last menstrual date	95	64	94	32	96	182	89	270	92	49
Physical examination										
Body weight	73	64	91	32	97	182	88	270	90	50
Blood pressure	72	64	81	32	93	182	88	269	92	50
Measure uterine height	89	64	84	32	95	182	51	270	84	50
Listen to fetal heartbeat	88	64	78	32	95	182	66	269	70	50
Check for edema/swelling	92	64	66	32	92	182	63	270	74	50
Diagnostic tests										
HIV test	92	64	81	32	73	182	63	270	53	51
STI test: Syphilis and/or gonorrhea	94	64	88	32	70	182	25	270	49	51
Hemoglobin test	86	64	47	32	92	182	71	270	55	51
Urine test	97	64	88	32	81	182	80	270	94	51
Preventive treatment										
Insecticide-treated mosquito net	17	64	25	32	93	182	69	268	42	43
Iron/folic acid supplements	98	64	81	32	98	182	89	270	70	43
Intermittent preventive treatment for malaria	94	64	72	32	94	182	62	269	51	43
Tetanus toxoid vaccine	15	62	—	—	—	—	40	270	—	—
Counseling topics										
Nutrition	94	64	75	32	86	182	80	269	73	41
Pregnancy danger signs	33	64	41	32	85	182	46	270	15	41

Source: World Bank

Note: STI = sexually transmitted infection; WHO = World Health Organization; — = not available.

blood pressure cuff, measuring tape, and obstetric stethoscope—is generally available, so basic physical capacity does not appear to be a binding constraint in most of these countries. However, even for this relatively well-provisioned category, there are some gaps: for instance, 16 percent of the facilities in the Democratic Republic of Congo did not have blood pressure cuffs. Beyond such permanent but basic equipment, there is a broad-based lack of

Figure 4.2 Availability of drugs and consumables, equipment, and other supplies for providing antenatal care

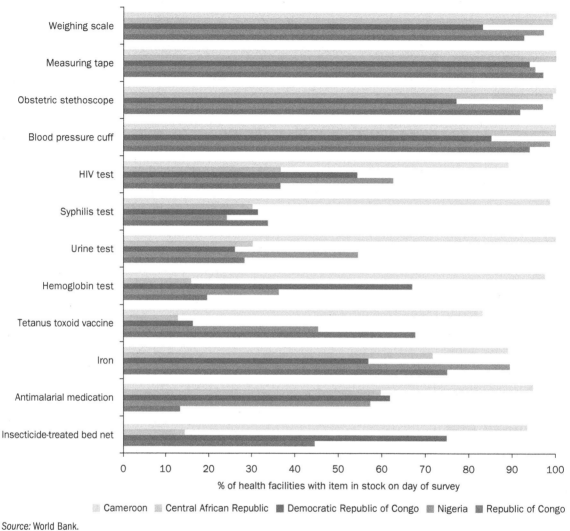

% of health facilities with item in stock on day of survey

Cameroon   Central African Republic   Democratic Republic of Congo   Nigeria   Republic of Congo

Source: World Bank.

equipment, supplies, and consumables required for providing antenatal consultations. The items least likely to be found in these facilities are also the ones necessary for providing the most impactful ANC interventions described in table 4.1: insecticide-treated bed nets, iron supplements, and diagnostic test kits for urine and sexually transmitted infections.

At the same time, there is a fair bit of variation in structural capacity within and across the countries. As with health worker knowledge, Cameroon generally has the highest levels of basic equipment, with near-universal availability of some items, but other essential drugs and supplies are only available about 90 percent of the time. Only 28 percent of the facilities in the Democratic Republic of Congo had kits for conducting urine tests, which are needed to test for protein in urea, a marker of pre-eclampsia—a life-threatening complication if left untreated. Availability of test kits is equally poor in the Republic of Congo, with only about a third of all facilities having syphilis or urine tests in stock. The data further suggest that of these five countries, the Democratic Republic of Congo and the Republic of Congo have the poorest structural capacity to provide preventive care during pregnancies. By and large, this analysis shows that the providers in the health centers in these five countries face significant physical constraints to performing actions that require consumables. It is important to keep in mind, however, that the providers could have referred the women to other facilities for testing or could have provided the women prescriptions. Nonetheless, these results highlight that despite decades of investments in infrastructure, the availability of equipment, supplies, and drugs that are necessary for the provision of basic ANC in health centers that they are supposed to provide—and in fact do provide—routinely is far from universal. This is true for each of the five countries.

Practice

Before estimating the know-can-do gap, or idle capacity, it is necessary to understand what the health workers do in actual patient-provider interactions, not just what they know or have the equipment to perform. Thus, figure 4.3 presents the content of care recorded through direct observations of first ANC consultations. The figure shows that overall, the level of performance is quite low. These are all actions in the WHO essential protocol for ANC, and yet few of them are universally provided. Performance on many actions falls well short of even 75 or 50 percent provision across the five countries studied.

In terms of specific actions, in all five countries, the same three history-taking questions were the most common: date of last menstruation, number of past pregnancies, and whether the women had experienced any interrupted pregnancy in the past. While background questions are important to date the length of a pregnancy and establish any patterns of concern in the woman's medical history, there is little good evidence tying such questions to improved health outcomes.

Perhaps unsurprisingly, given the high levels of related equipment availability and knowledge, the completion rates of physical examinations were higher than for other components of care. Elements of care like weighing the woman and taking her blood pressure were provided between

Figure 4.3 Performance in patient-provider interactions during antenatal care

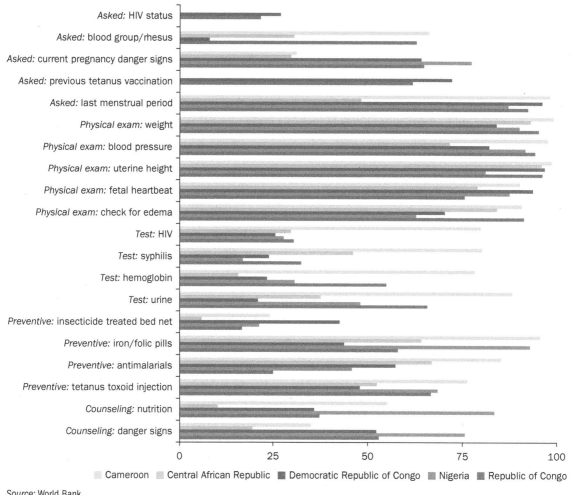

Source: World Bank.

80 percent (the Democratic Republic of Congo) and almost 100 percent of the time (Cameroon). In contrast, the levels of performance for diagnostic tests were among the lowest observed: in only 24 percent of the consultations in the Democratic Republic of Congo and 28 percent in Nigeria did the provider perform or refer a woman for an HIV test. Even for tests without any potential stigma attached to them, say those for urine and hemoglobin levels, performance was low: in the Democratic Republic of Congo, providers only performed these two tests 21 and 23 percent of the time, respectively; in Nigeria, it was 48 and 31 percent, respectively.

The WHO essential protocol also includes a set of counseling actions—screening for danger signs and optimal nutrition in pregnancy. Women in Nigeria received the most counseling during their consultations, while the lowest level was found in the Central African Republic. Box 4.1 explores whether the available data on health facility, worker, or patient characteristics help explain who provides or receives higher quality care.

Estimation of idle capacity and irrelevant treatment

Idle capacity

Using the assessed know gaps, know-can gaps, and actual performance, this subsection estimates the know-can-do gaps, or idle capacity, relative to a target of 100 percent performance of the essential WHO protocol for ANC. The subsection discusses the estimates of idle capacity in the five countries; the following subsection discusses the potential correlates or determinants of idle capacity.

Figure 4.4 and table 4A.2, in annex 4A, present the estimated idle capacity for each relevant action and highlight several patterns in the data. (Figures 4A.1 to 4A.5, in annex 4A, present the country-level findings.) The analysis highlights the presence of sizable know-can-do gaps that obstruct the provision of higher quality ANC for every action on the WHO essential protocol for ANC. That is, for every possible action, at least some of the time, providers know the action to be clinically appropriate and can

---

Box 4.1   In Focus: Exploring the drivers of variation in the content of care

Do certain types of health workers—doctors versus midwives—or health facilities—public versus private—typically provide different levels of care? Do certain types of patients—wealthier women, those with their first pregnancies—receive higher levels of care? Figure B4.1.1 shows deviations from the mean content of care index created for Cameroon, the Central African Republic, the Democratic Republic of Congo, Nigeria, and the Republic of Congo. The index is constructed with principal component analysis using all the elements presented in table 4.1. As with the knowledge index, the content of care index is normalized such that for each country, the mean equals zero and the standard deviation equals one. The figure shows that across the five settings, there are few systematic predictors of who the highest performing health workers are. For instance, in the Democratic Republic of Congo and Nigeria, doctors appear to perform at the highest levels, but in Cameroon they perform significantly worse than nurses and midwives. For most of the other examined factors, the content of care index does not vary significantly by the correlate.

(Continued)

Box 4.1 *continued*

Figure B4.1.1 Variation in content of care in patient-provider interactions in antenatal care

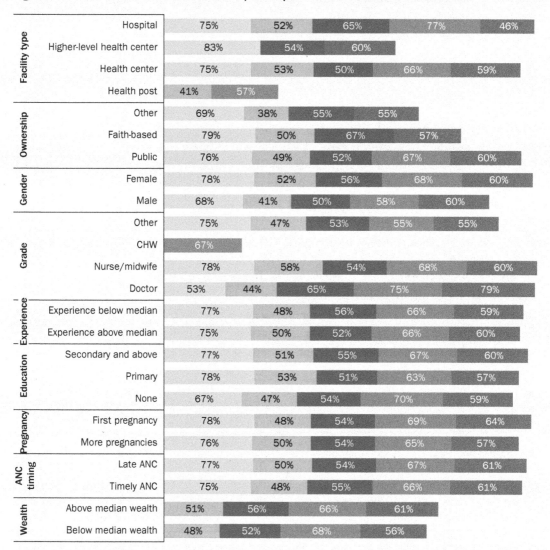

Cameroon · Central African Republic · Democratic Republic of Congo · Nigeria · Republic of Congo

Source: World Bank.

Note: ANC = antenatal care; CHW = community health worker.

Figure 4.4   Know-can-do gaps in the provision of antenatal care

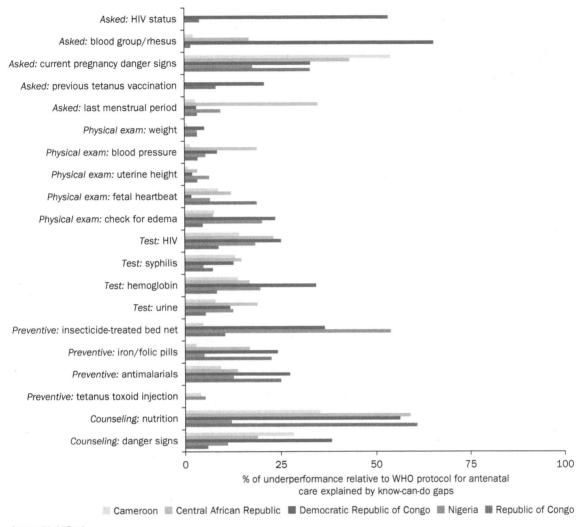

% of underperformance relative to WHO protocol for antenatal care explained by know-can-do gaps

Cameroon   Central African Republic   Democratic Republic of Congo   Nigeria   Republic of Congo

Source: World Bank.
Note: WHO = World Health Organization.

undertake it with the available supplies and equipment, but nonetheless they do not perform that action when they are observed providing ANC. This last gap is the know-can-do gap, or "idle capacity," because the health worker has all the knowledge and structural capacity to perform the relevant action but does not use that available capacity (Ibnat et al. 2019).

This gap is particularly large for diagnostic tests, screening women for salient events during past pregnancies, and counseling on danger signs. For instance, providers failed to prescribe hemoglobin tests between 8 percent (the Republic of Congo) and 34 percent (the Democratic Republic of Congo)

71

of the time and HIV tests 33 percent of the time, although during the knowledge test, they stated that they would prescribe these tests and the facility had the physical capacity and all the necessary supplies to conduct them. Large know-can-do gaps were also recorded where the provider knew the importance of an action but did not carry it out and no physical capacity was required (such as in the instance of counseling). For example, in 38 percent of the observed consultations in the Democratic Republic of Congo, 28 percent in Cameroon, and 19 percent in the Central African Republic, providers did not counsel women on danger signs—headache, blurred vision, high fever, difficulty breathing, and sudden vaginal bleeding—during a pregnancy or inform them of necessary actions in case of a danger sign. In Cameroon, where the other gaps are among the smallest estimated, health workers only ask about danger signs experienced in the current pregnancy in 54 percent of the consultations. In the Republic of Congo, health workers failed to counsel women on optimal nutrition 61 percent of the time. As these are know-can-do gaps, they are measured among all the health workers who reported during a knowledge test that this action should be performed. In general, some of the largest know-can-do gaps are observed for counseling actions, suggesting significant room for improvement in provider effort.

However, the know-can-do gap was observed not just in counseling but also in other areas of ANC consultations. While this gap is small for most of the physical examinations, in the Republic of Congo, health workers did not listen to the fetal heartbeat in 19 percent of the observed consultations, although providers stated that it should be conducted and the health center had functioning stethoscopes. In Nigeria, providers did not check for signs of edema 20 percent of the time. In the Democratic Republic of Congo, idle capacity was observed in 25 percent of the consultations with respect to HIV testing and in 13 percent of the consultations with respect to syphilis testing.

There is significant cross-country variation in the levels of quality, where the best performer, Cameroon, has an average know-can-do gap of 0.11, and the worst performer, the Democratic Republic of Congo, has an average know-can-do gap of 0.29. In other words, in Cameroon, idle capacity explains approximately 11 percent of underperformance, while in the Democratic Republic of Congo it explains 29 percent; however, this may—at least in part— be due to the different implementation of the knowledge vignettes in the Democratic Republic of Congo. In the Democratic Republic of Congo, all the possible response options were presented to the health worker, who had to select what she thought was appropriate. In contrast, in the other four countries, the workers had to list all the relevant options from memory; they were not presented with a list.

Irrelevant or inappropriate treatment and antenatal care

While much of the analysis and indeed the data are geared toward picking up underperformance, poor quality of care can also manifest in the form of irrelevant or inappropriate treatment, also called overtreatment. These terms refer to the provision of care that is at best unnecessary and at worst harmful to the patient. Such overtreatment has been shown to be significant in settings with poor quality of care (Das et al. 2016). Since the available data capture what was performed relative to the WHO protocol for necessary care, all such overtreatment cannot be captured. For instance, if health workers provided antibiotics that were not part of the WHO protocol, the questionnaires underlying the data would not have captured that action.

Nonetheless, from the data available, two indicators can be defined (presented in figure 4.5) that capture overtreatment. The first is the provision of a tetanus shot in the second or later ANC visit within the first trimester—considerably earlier than the WHO recommended period between 27 and 36 weeks of pregnancy—and without checking the records to see if the woman had received a shot in her previous visit. The fact that the assessment can rule out the provider even checking the patient's

Figure 4.5 **Overuse in antenatal care provision in five Sub-Saharan African countries**

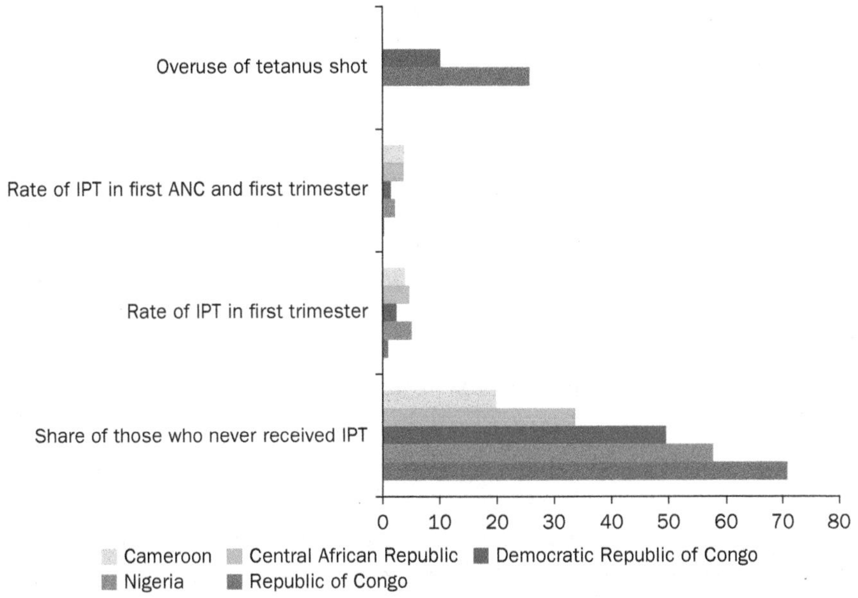

Source: World Bank.

Note: IPT refers to intermittent preventive treatment, which is the initiation of prophylactic malaria treatment using prescription sulfadoxine/pyrimethamine. ANC = antenatal care.

vaccination record card to see if she had already received a tetanus shot in this pregnancy mitigates some concerns about health workers providing care that is not strictly necessary in case the patient does not return for another antenatal visit. The data show that in the Central African Republic, Cameroon, and Nigeria, such overuse is generally not observed. However, in the Democratic Republic of Congo and the Republic of Congo, such overprescription is observed 10 and 26 percent of the time, respectively.

The second indicator is the provision of prophylactic malaria treatment, using prescription sulfadoxine/pyrimethamine, in the first trimester. When correctly timed, such preventive malaria treatment can improve neonatal birth outcomes (Carroli, Rooney, and Villar 2001), and evidence suggests that too-early initiation of such treatment may be harmful to fetal development (Peters et al. 2007; Hernández-Díaz et al. 2000). A caveat about this indicator may be that health workers may not know if the woman will return for a future visit and thus provide the treatment even at the risk of harming the developing fetus, particularly if they are not aware of the potential for harm. While the assessment cannot fully address this concern, as shown in figure 4.5, between 20 and 71 percent of all women in the data never receive preventive malaria care, suggesting that health workers often fail to provide the treatment even when given the correct opportunity for treatment. Taken together, these two indicators suggest that overtreatment exists even in the context of preventive care. Indeed, the fact that overtreatment can be captured despite the data not being geared toward picking it up may be indicative of substantial such overtreatment.

Correlates of the know-can-do gap

The previous subsection documented the presence of a sizable know-can-do gap in all the contexts studied. Effectively, this means that providers are not providing the highest level of care they can. Often that shortfall—the idle capacity—is substantial. This raises the question of why providers may not be exerting sufficient effort. The literature has identified several reasons: for instance, the providers may be busy, not paid sufficiently well, or lack motivation. They may exert greater effort for wealthier or better educated patients. This subsection exploits the richness of the data to examine the correlates of the measured know-can-do gaps using all the available data on patient, provider, and facility characteristics.

Table 4A.3 in annex 4A presents this exploratory analysis. It provides the mean know-can-do gap and the 95 percent confidence interval for each action, by country and correlate. Since the know-can-do gap represents a deficiency, a smaller value is better from a normative standpoint. As with the indexes of knowledge and practice, there are few systematic patterns in the data. The facility characteristics, including whether the facility is faith based or its level (hospital or lower), are not significantly correlated with the know-can-do gap for any of the countries studied. The one exception is that hospitals in the Democratic Republic of Congo exhibit slightly higher levels of the know-can-do gap compared with other facilities.

The provider characteristics include gender, experience, and grade—that is, whether the provider is a doctor, nurse/midwife, community health worker, or other. Again, there are few meaningful patterns for the know-can-do gap. (The results are presented in figure 4.6.) The one exception worth noting is that in three of the five countries, the Democratic Republic of Congo, Nigeria, and the Republic of Congo, doctors have lower idle capacity than other cadres, although this difference is often insignificant. However, Cameroon demonstrates the reverse, with doctors exhibiting the greatest idle capacity (although the difference is not statistically significant). In the Central African Republic, there are no doctors in the sample.

Figure 4.6 Correlation between idle capacity and provider type

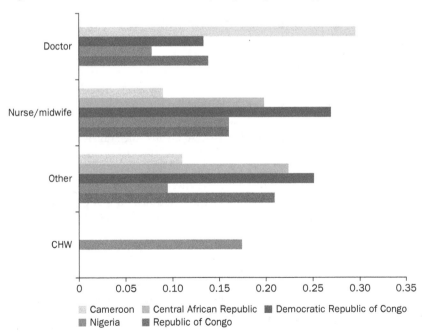

Source: World Bank.

Note: CHW = community health worker.

Otherwise, the assessment finds no significant differences in idle capacity by the provider's gender or experience.

The patient characteristics include wealth, education, and pregnancy and care-seeking history. Even these have somewhat limited explanatory power for the observed effort gap. However, in three of the five countries, there is a U-shape in how quality correlates with patient education, with the least educated and most educated patients receiving the most complete level of care. Women in their first pregnancies also appear to receive care with less idle capacity associated with it in four of the five countries. However, there is no evidence of a correlation with late versus timely ANC, which is note-worthy because often wealthier women are more likely to receive timely care, meaning that utilization itself can be a proxy for patient socioeconomic status (Das et al. 2016; Fink, Kandpal, and Shapira 2022). Box 4.2 discusses the literature on whether discrimination by the provider can lead to greater know-can-do gaps. However, a direct examination of patient wealth does not reveal a significant association with the know-can-do gap.

In addition, despite the exceptional level of detail in the data, and including everything from facility to patient characteristics, all these

Box 4.2   In Focus: Does discrimination contribute to poor effort?

This chapter shows that there is limited evidence on what drives idle capacity in health care provision but nevertheless finds that in some contexts, wealthier patients receive better care. Such differences may arise for several reasons. For one, women of different socioeconomic backgrounds might sort into different facilities. Wealthier women may live in the catchment areas of better facilities (Fink, Kandpal, and Shapira 2022), be more aware of facility quality, or be more able to pay to travel to better facilities (Akin and Hutchinson 1999; Leonard, Mliga, and Haile Mariam 2002; Kruk, Goldmann, and Galea 2009; Cohen, Lofgren, and McConnell 2017; Cronin, Guilkey, and Speizer 2019). However, recent evidence from Kenya (McCollum et al. 2018) as well as the World Bank report on Social Delivery Indicators (Gatti et al. 2021) suggest that at least in terms of infrastructure,

wealthier and poorer areas have facilities of similar quality.

Yet, a recent study by Fink, Kandpal, and Shapira (2022) highlights inequality in the provision of high-quality care, with inequality in effective antenatal care (ANC) being three times as high as inequality in simple ANC coverage, as shown figure B4.2.1. The figure presents concentration curves plotting the cumulative proportion of coverage and effective coverage against the cumulative proportion of recently pregnant women ranked by household wealth. An equal distribution of care would lie along the 45-degree line. Both concentration curves—the one for simple ANC coverage and that for effective coverage—deviate from the line of equality. However, the concentration curve for simple coverage is noticeably closer to the line of equality than the concentration curve for effective

(Continued)

Box 4.2 *continued*

Figure B4.2.1 **Inequality in the provision of ANC and effective ANC in the Democratic Republic of Congo**

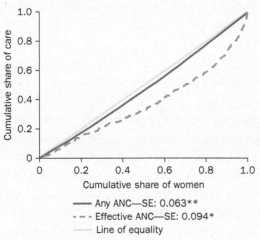

Source: Fink, Kandpal, and Shapira 2019.

Note: ANC = antenatal care; SE = standard error.

*p < .05, **p < .01.

ANC, suggesting that there is greater wealth inequality in access to high-quality care than there is in access to any care. Thus, despite the similarities in the structural quality of facilities, for some reason, wealthier women appear to get better quality of care, at least in some settings.

One reason may be that wealthier women visit the same facilities but receive better care from the same health providers than do poorer women. In this case, using facility infrastructure to assess quality is problematic as the same facility may represent very different levels of quality, depending on provider practice in interactions with wealthy and poor patients. There has been limited empirical evidence of such discriminatory behavior by providers (Das and Sohnesen 2007). However, the study on the Democratic Republic of Congo shows that even within the same facilities, wealthier women receive more complete

care, which may be indicative of discriminatory practices (Fink, Kandpal, and Shapira 2022). This finding indeed challenges the use of facility-level characteristics as a proxy for quality of care.

As the Democratic Republic of Congo study notes, however, a finding of differential quality of care within facilities does not necessarily imply discrimination: many facilities charge separately for different components of care, especially for diagnostic testing and drugs or insecticide-treated bed nets. So, wealthier women may simply be able to pay for the larger package of services or feel more empowered to ask for certain procedures. Alternatively, poorer women might choose a more limited package of services if facilities charge separately for consumables, lab tests, and drugs. Indeed, differences in the content of care might be driven by the pregnant women, and the data may not capture such underlying causes in variation. For example, it is not known whether patients or providers initiate discussions on family planning or nutrition.

Further, to the extent that wealth and education are correlated, wealthier women may be better informed about the importance of the tests and drugs and have a higher willingness to pay for them—although the Democratic Republic of Congo study controls for education. Health workers may thus skip elements of care they think the patient cannot pay for or that may require higher levels of effort—for instance, an explanation of what a particular test accomplishes—to provide to the poor. Related results from a lab-in-the-field experiment in Burkina Faso suggest that providing care to the poor requires higher levels of effort from providers because the poor might have lower health-related knowledge or present more complex health conditions (Banuri et al. 2018). However, consistent with the finding that idle capacity does not vary with patient wealth, the data suggest that idle capacity is similar across patient wealth quintiles in all the countries studied.

examined correlates explain less than 15 percent of the effort gap (table 4A.4, in annex 4A). The limited explanatory power of these rich sets of covariates thus highlights the difficulty in understanding the different drivers of idle capacity in LMIC contexts. This subsection has shown a broad-based presence of idle capacity in each of these contexts, including for actions that do not require physical equipment or supplies and for which health worker knowledge is high. However, what is driving those gaps is largely unknown.

Conclusions

This chapter built on the existing literature to provide an assessment of quality of care that decomposes constraints to quality into inadequate structural quality, that is, insufficient supplies or equipment; poor health worker knowledge; and underprovision of effort (health workers simply not doing the clinically necessary actions for which they have all needed supplies, equipment, and knowledge). The analysis focused on ANC as a key driver of the global burden of disease. Using rich data on ANC consultations, the chapter showed that poor quality, as benchmarked by the WHO protocol for ANC, is widespread. Across five Sub-Saharan African countries—Cameroon, the Central African Republic, the Democratic Republic of Congo, Nigeria, and the Republic of Congo—which are among the world's leading contributors to maternal and neonatal mortality, health workers only perform about 50 to 60 percent of the WHO essential protocol for ANC.

The results show that an important share of quality deficits can be explained by a lack of effort/provider behavior, as illustrated using a decomposition of detailed data linking health facility infrastructure to health worker knowledge, and actual provision of care in patient-provider interactions. The decomposition shows that despite decades of infrastructure investments, structural capacity constraints continue to bind in most primary health care settings in these countries. Shortfalls in the availability of basic medical equipment and supplies are widespread, even for a widely provided service like ANC in facilities that are supposed to provide this service. Indeed, in every country examined, structural capacity constraints bind for at least some of the components of a complete ANC visit. Similarly, among health workers who are supposed to provide basic ANC, knowledge of basic ANC protocol is far from complete in all the countries examined.

However, the decomposition also shows that a third of all observed mis-adherence to international protocol is explained not by structural or knowledge gaps but by idle capacity— when health workers have all the necessary structural capacity and knowledge but still fail to perform the necessary actions. Such idle capacity exists in all five countries studied in this chapter and for each component of the WHO essential protocol for ANC. Indeed, sizable know-do gaps exist even in actions like risk screening—which entails asking the patient about complications in prior pregnancies and does not require any supplies or equipment.

The WHO guidelines on the minimum number and required timing of ANC visits assume a certain minimum content of care—in other words, the implicit assumption is that a visit is inherently useful. ANC visits represent a cost to the household's time—and there are, of course, out-of-pocket costs to households to avail themselves of such care. This reliance on service utilization is despite the evidence reviewed in the chapter suggesting a tenuous link between simple coverage and health outcomes. At the same time, ANC visits may be adopted as conditions for receiving cash transfers: households receive money from the government if they expend the time. However, as the chapter has shown, shortages of supplies or inadequate equipment are often not the only binding constraint; in many cases, effort is the lowest common denominator. This begs the question of whether policies should encourage ANC visits without ensuring that the quality of care delivered is sufficiently high for its benefits to offset the cost the visits represent to the households.

The results also provide evidence of significant variation across and within countries. The within-country variation stems from differences in the quality of care provided between facilities, but also within facilities. Idle capacity is not only pervasive across actions, it is also significant in terms of size. In the five countries studied in this chapter, even if all the structural and knowledge gaps were closed, fully a third of the shortfall in adherence to the WHO essential protocol for ANC would still remain as is. Further, the estimated know-do gaps presented in this chapter are likely underestimates of the actual know-do gaps because of the Hawthorne effect in direct clinical observations (Leonard and Masatu 2006).

In addition, the chapter showed that deviations from protocol can include overprescription. This topic is covered in depth in chapter 7, but the finding of overprescription in the context of ANC is striking because the measurement of preventive care is not geared toward picking up overprescription. Notably, the finding of overprescription includes actions that may be harmful to fetal development. Most of the evidence on overuse focuses on curative care and not preventive care. This finding thus motivates the concern surrounding overuse and a more careful assessment of it, particularly in relationship to financial incentives aimed at improving quality of care, a topic to which this report will return later.

This chapter thus makes several contributions to the literature on the determinants of quality of care in primary health care settings in LMICs. First, it established that poor quality of care is pervasive in these settings. Second, it decomposed the observed level of care to show that it is driven by a combination of poor structural quality and poor health worker knowledge, but also by a lack of effort by health workers. Thus, the chapter suggested that physical and knowledge constraints are a limiting factor in many LMICs even for basic health service provision. However, the chapter also highlighted that policies must address the know-do gap. Previous literature has highlighted the important role played by financial incentives in determining provider effort (Das et al. 2016), and other studies have shown that extrinsic and intrinsic motivation are important drivers of health worker performance (Leonard and Masatu 2006, 2010; Leonard, Masatu, and Vialou 2007). Such evidence may underline the potential for tying performance to payments. Of course, interventions that bolster skills, such as hands-on training programs (Rowe et al. 2018), may be effective in improving performance and even idle capacity. This may be the case if skills and knowledge of protocol are not the same—for instance, health workers may know how to counsel a woman on proper nutrition in theory, but if they lack experience in actually counseling a patient, they may be unwilling to attempt it, particularly in front of a third-party enumerator. Thus, interventions that seek to increase effective coverage by improving the quality of care may need to leverage multiple entry points into the health system.

Finally, particularly rich data on potential explanatory factors, on facilities, health workers, and patients, allowed the chapter to explore what may explain such idle capacity. However, the decomposition of the differences in the overall performance and know-do gaps by facility and patient characteristics, with one exception, found little meaningful covariation in the measures with any set of correlates in the data. The "usual suspects," like health worker training, grade, or gender, do not explain the idle capacity.

The one exception is that there may be some patient-driven differentials in quality of care: concentration curves show that wealthier women receive better care in some of these settings. Using an example from the Democratic Republic of Congo, the chapter illustrated that wealthier women appear to receive better quality of care than poorer women, even within the same facilities. This is not necessarily indicative of discrimination as the results could be explained by differences in education, ability to pay for additional diagnostic tests or medication, or even empowerment, with wealthier women feeling more comfortable asking for certain aspects of care.

The partial explanatory power of these rich data highlights the need for further study of the drivers of effort gaps in primary health care in LMIC contexts. Chapters 5 and 6 in this report examine the impacts of two popular health financing approaches—performance-based financing and direct facility financing—on quality of care assessed through a three-gap framework. The report revisits the know-do gap framework to examine the impact of these two supply-side health financing approaches in relation to quality of care and equity.

Annex 4A: Additional tables and figures

Table 4A.1   Structural capacity

Description	CAM Mean (%)	CAM N	CAR Mean (%)	CAR N	DRC Mean (%)	DRC N	NIG Mean (%)	NIG N	ROC Mean (%)	ROC N
Scale	100	82	99	117	83	224	97	313	93	67
Measuring tape	100	82	100	129	94	227	95	290	97	68
Obstetric stethoscope	100	80	99	128	77	217	97	358	92	60
Blood pressure cuff	100	85	100	115	85	228	99	358	94	66
HIV test	89	82	37	139	54	184	63	187	37	60
Syphilis test	99	79	30	139	32	184	24	169	34	59
Urine test	100	80	30	139	26	184	54	178	28	60
Hemoglobin test	97	79	16	139	67	130	36	124	20	51
Tetanus toxoid	83	77	13	133	16	160	45	119	68	34
Iron	89	82	72	134	57	160	89	208	75	40
Antimalarial	95	77	60	134	62	160	57	164	13	30
Insecticide-treated net	93	61	14	139	75	227	—	0	45	65
Prescribed or gave tetanus toxoid injection	76	202	52	365	48	572	68	622	67	99
Lab capacity for blood typing	68	79	31	139	54	125	26	118	86	51

Source: World Bank.

Note: CAM = Cameroon; CAR = Central African Republic; DRC = Democratic Republic of Congo; NIG = Nigeria; ROC = Republic of Congo; — = not available;.

Table 4A.2 Know-can-do gaps in the provision of antenatal care

	CAM Know-can-do gap (%)	CAM N	CAR Know-can-do gap (%)	CAR N	DRC Know-can-do gap (%)	DRC N	NIG Know-can-do gap (%)	NIG N	ROC Know-can-do gap (%)	ROC N
Asked: HIV status				95	53	421	—	—	4	51
Asked: blood group/rhesus	2	139	17	95	65	423	18	423	2	62
Asked: current pregnancy danger signs	54	145	43	95	33	423	—	—	33	61
Asked: previous tetanus vaccination	—	—	—	—	21	422			8	61
Asked: last menstrual period	3	145	35	95	3	423	9	425	3	61
Physical exam: weight	1	141		78	5	407	3	375	3	61
Physical exam: blood pressure	1	145	19	74	8	413	5	425	3	59
Physical exam: uterine height	1	134	3	92	2	412	6	345	3	61
Physical exam: fetal heartbeat	9	139	12	91	2	402	7	425	19	53
Physical exam: check for edema	8	144	7	95	24	423	20	424	5	64
Test: HIV	14	142	23	95	25	315	18	201	9	57
Test: syphilis	13	138	15	95	13	316	5	187	7	55
Test: hemoglobin	14	139	17	95	34	222	20	122	8	48
Test: urine	8	140	19	95	12	315	13	199	5	56
Preventive: insecticide-treated bed net	5	129		95	36	414	54	416	10	48
Preventive: iron/folic pills	3	141	17	95	24	281	5	241	23	31
Preventive: antimalarials	9	130	14	95	27	281	13	190	25	32
Preventive: tetanus toxoid injection	4	125	—	—	—	—	5	134	—	—
Counseling: nutrition	35	145	59	95	56	423	12	423	61	51
Counseling: danger signs	28	145	19	95	38	423	11	426	6	51

Source: World Bank.

Note: CAM = Cameroon; CAR = Central African Republic; DRC = Democratic Republic of Congo; NIG = Nigeria; ROC = Republic of Congo; — = not available.

Table 4A.3 Correlates of the know-can-do gap

	Cameroon			Central African Republic			Democratic Republic of Congo			Nigeria			Republic of Congo		
	Mean	95% CI	N	Mean	95% CI	N	Mean	95% CI	N	Mean	95% CI	N	Mean	95% CI	N
Facility type															
Hospital	0.75	(0.69-0.81)	37	0.52	(0.49-0.55)	46	0.65	(0.61-0.68)	113	0.77	(0.74-0.81)	113	0.46	(0.42-0.49)	3
Higher-level health center	0.83	(0.80-0.86)	25	—	—	—	0.54	(0.49-0.58)	77	—	—	77	0.60	(0.55-0.65)	58
Health center	0.75	(0.73-0.77)	141	0.53	(0.51-0.56)	191	0.50	(0.49-0.52)	380	0.66	(0.65-0.68)	380	0.59	(0.53-0.65)	41
Health post	—	—	—	0.41	(0.39-0.44)	125	—	—	—	0.57	(0.51-0.64)	—	—	—	25
Ownership															
Public	0.76	(0.73-0.78)	139	0.49	(0.47-0.51)	324	0.52	(0.51-0.54)	463	0.67	(0.65-0.68)	463	0.60	(0.56-0.64)	74
Faith-based	0.79	(0.75-0.82)	54	0.50	(0.45-0.56)	25	0.67	(0.62-0.72)	39	—	—	—	0.57	(0.48-0.67)	17
Other	0.69	(0.59-0.78)	10	0.38	(0.29-0.47)	16	0.55	(0.50-0.60)	70	—	—	—	0.55	(0.42-0.68)	11
Provider's grade															
Doctor	0.53	(0.43-0.64)	8	0.44	—	1	0.65	(0.54-0.77)	10	0.75	(0.64-0.85)	9	0.79	—	1
Nurse/midwife	0.78	(0.76-0.81)	122	0.58	(0.53-0.62)	62	0.54	(0.52-0.55)	484	0.68	(0.66-0.71)	128	0.60	(0.56-0.64)	80
Community health worker	—	—	—	—	—	—	—	—	—	0.67	(0.65-0.68)	406	—	—	—
Other	0.75	(0.72-0.78)	73	0.47	(0.45-0.49)	302	0.53	(0.48-0.58)	78	0.55	(0.48-0.63)	30	0.55	(0.48-0.62)	21
Provider's gender															
Female	0.78	(0.76-0.80)	152	0.52	(0.50-0.54)	237	0.56	(0.54-0.58)	362	0.68	(0.67-0.70)	485	0.60	(0.56-0.64)	87
Male	0.68	(0.63-0.73)	44	0.41	(0.39-0.44)	106	0.50	(0.48-0.52)	202	0.58	(0.54-0.62)	96	0.60	(0.49-0.71)	9
Provider's experience															
Below median	0.77	(0.75-0.80)	85	0.48	(0.45-0.50)	171	0.56	(0.54-0.58)	279	0.66	(0.64-0.68)	277	0.59	(0.55-0.64)	51
Above median	0.75	(0.72-0.78)	108	0.50	(0.47-0.53)	122	0.52	(0.49-0.54)	256	0.66	(0.64-0.69)	277	0.60	(0.54-0.65)	41
Education															
Secondary and above	0.77	(0.74-0.80)	96	0.51	(0.43-0.59)	20	0.55	(0.53-0.58)	256	0.67	(0.65-0.69)	248	0.60	(0.56-0.65)	62
Primary	0.78	(0.75-0.80)	86	0.53	(0.50-0.56)	118	0.51	(0.49-0.54)	153	0.63	(0.60-0.66)	139	0.57	(0.50-0.64)	24
None	0.67	(0.60-0.74)	19	0.47	(0.45-0.49)	185	0.54	(0.51-0.57)	145	0.70	(0.68-0.73)	190	0.59	(0.46-0.71)	8

(Continued)

Table 4.3 continued

	Cameroon			Central African Republic			Democratic Republic of Congo			Nigeria			Republic of Congo		
	Mean	95% CI	N	Mean	95% CI	N	Mean	95% CI	N	Mean	95% CI	N	Mean	95% CI	N
Pregnancy rank															
First pregnancy	0.78	(0.74–0.81)	58	0.48	(0.45–0.51)	81	0.54	(0.51–0.57)	137	0.69	(0.67–0.71)	257	0.64	(0.59–0.70)	26
Higher rank	0.76	(0.73–0.78)	143	0.50	(0.48–0.52)	242	0.54	(0.52–0.55)	417	0.65	(0.63–0.67)	365	0.57	(0.53–0.62)	68
ANC timing															
Late ANC	0.77	(0.75–0.79)	142	0.50	(0.48–0.53)	201	0.54	(0.52–0.55)	488	0.67	(0.66–0.69)	392	0.61	(0.57–0.65)	62
Timely ANC	0.75	(0.71–0.79)	56	0.48	(0.45–0.52)	102	0.55	(0.50–0.60)	75	0.66	(0.64–0.69)	196	0.61	(0.54–0.67)	27
Wealth															
Above median	—	—	—	0.51	(0.48–0.53)	158	0.56	(0.54–0.59)	268	0.66	(0.64–0.68)	306	0.61	(0.56–0.66)	40
Below median	—	—	—	0.48	(0.46–0.50)	165	0.52	(0.50–0.54)	286	0.68	(0.66–0.70)	299	0.56	(0.51–0.62)	45

Source: World Bank.

Note: The sample is observed for first antenatal consultations. ANC = antenatal care; CI = confidence interval; — = not available.

Table 4A.4   Explaining the know-can-do gap using a regression framework

	CAM		CAR		DRC		NIG		ROC	
Y Mean	0.12	0.12	0.20	0.20	0.26	0.26	0.10	0.10	0.12	0.12
Provider FE	–	X	–	X	–	X	–	X	–	X
Facility ownership										
Religious	–0.04*	—	0.01	—	0.01	—	—	—	–0.02	—
	(0.02)	—	(0.05)	—	(0.04)	—	—	—	(0.04)	—
Other	–0.01	—	0.03	—	0.04	—	—	—	–0.05	—
	(0.02)	—	(0.07)	—	(0.02)	—	—	—	(0.04)	—
Facility type										
Hospital	0.00	—	0.09***	—	–0.09***	—	0.04	—	—	—
	(0.03)	—	(0.03)	—	(0.02)	—	(0.03)	—	—	—
Higher-level health center	–0.01	—	—	—	–0.03	—	—	—	–0.02	—
	(0.02)	—	—	—	(0.02)	—	—	—	(0.04)	—
Health post	—	—	0.03	—	—	—	0.07	—	—	—
	—	—	(0.05)	—	—	—	(0.05)	—	—	—
Female provider	0.02	—	0.00	—	–0.02	—	–0.09***	—	–0.04	—
	(0.02)	—	(0.03)	—	(0.02)	—	(0.02)	—	(0.06)	—
Grade										
Doctor	0.29***	—	—	—	–0.10	—	0.06	—	—	—
	(0.03)	—	—	—	(0.06)	—	(0.04)	—	—	—
CHW	—	—	—	—	—	—	0.00	—	—	—
	—	—	—	—	—	—	(0.02)	—	—	—
Other	0.01	—	0.06**	—	–0.09***	—	0.04	—	0.12**	—
	(0.02)	—	(0.03)	—	(0.03)	—	(0.03)	—	(0.06)	—
Experience										
Years	0.00	—	0.00	—	0.00***	—	0.00	—	–0.00	—
	(0.00)	—	(0.00)	—	(0.00)	—	(0.00)	—	(0.00)	—
First pregnancy	0.01	0.00	0.02	0.04	–0.00	–0.01	–0.00	0.02	–0.02	–0.10
	(0.02)	(0.01)	(0.03)	(0.02)	(0.02)	(0.01)	(0.01)	(0.02)	(0.05)	(0.10)
Late ANC	0.00	–0.00	–0.02	–0.01	–0.02	–0.03	–0.01	–0.01	–0.01	0.06
	(0.02)	(0.02)	(0.03)	(0.03)	(0.03)	(0.02)	(0.01)	(0.02)	(0.04)	(0.07)

(Continued)

Table 4A.3 continued

	CAM		CAR		DRC		NIG		ROC	
Y Mean	0.12	0.12	0.20	0.20	0.26	0.26	0.10	0.10	0.12	0.12
Provider FE	−	X	−	X	−	X	−	X	−	X
Education										
Primary	−0.07***	0.01	−0.02	0.02	0.02	−0.02**	0.04***	−0.01	−0.03	0.13
	(0.02)	(0.02)	(0.03)	(0.02)	(0.02)	(0.01)	(0.02)	(0.04)	(0.06)	(0.23)
Secondary and	−0.05**	0.01	0.01	0.03	0.01	−0.01	−0.01	−0.03	−0.00	0.14
above	(0.02)	(0.02)	(0.04)	(0.03)	(0.02)	(0.01)	(0.01)	(0.03)	(0.06)	(0.20)
Wealth										
Second	—	—	−0.07	−0.03	0.01	0.01	0.03	0.00	−0.04	−0.08
	—	—	(0.04)	(0.04)	(0.03)	(0.01)	(0.02)	(0.02)	(0.06)	(0.16)
Third	—	—	−0.01	−0.03	−0.00	0.01	0.04**	0.03	0.01	−0.10
	—	—	(0.03)	(0.04)	(0.03)	(0.01)	(0.02)	(0.03)	(0.09)	(0.09)
Fourth	—	—	−0.02	−0.05	0.00	−0.01	0.06***	0.01	0.02	−0.12
	—	—	(0.04)	(0.04)	(0.03)	(0.01)	(0.02)	(0.03)	(0.06)	(0.08)
Highest	—	—	−0.04	0.00	0.01	0.01	0.06***	−0.00	0.04	0.01
	—	—	(0.03)	(0.03)	(0.03)	(0.02)	(0.02)	(0.03)	(0.09)	(0.07)
Constant	0.14***	0.11***	0.15***	0.22***	0.25***	0.29***	0.13***	0.10***	0.19*	0.05
	(0.03)	(0.02)	(0.03)	(0.03)	(0.03)	(0.02)	(0.03)	(0.04)	(0.10)	(0.18)
aR^2	—	0.84	—	0.69	—	0.87	—	0.76	—	0.64
RMSE	0.09	0.04	0.08	0.05	0.15	0.06	0.11	0.06	0.10	0.06
F	.	0.11	.	1.65	3.29	1.39	3.78	0.90	1.41	.
N	131	131	71	71	395	395	336	336	46	46

Source: World Bank.

Note: Standard errors are in parentheses. ANC = antenatal care; aR^2 = adjusted R-squared; CAM = Cameroon; CAR = Central African Republic; CHW = community health worker; DRC = Democratic Republic of Congo; FE = fixed effects; NIG = Nigeria; ROC = Republic of Congo; RMSE = root mean square error; — = data not available.

* $p < .10$, ** $p < .05$, *** $p < .01$.

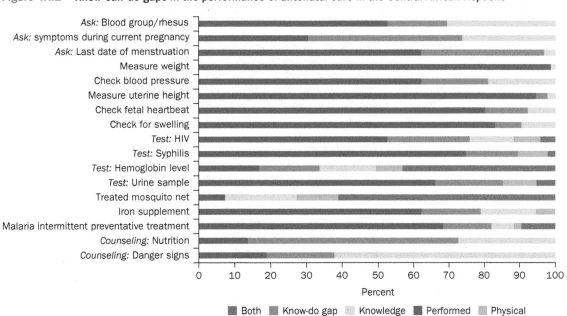

Figure 4A.1   Know-can-do gaps in the performance of antenatal care in Cameroon

Source: World Bank, using data from the 2012 baseline survey for the impact evaluation of performance-based financing pilot.

Figure 4A.2   Know-can-do gaps in the performance of antenatal care in the Central African Republic

Source: World Bank, using data from the 2012 baseline survey for the impact evaluation of performance-based financing pilot.

Figure 4A.3 **Know-can-do gaps in the performance of antenatal care in the Democratic Republic of Congo**

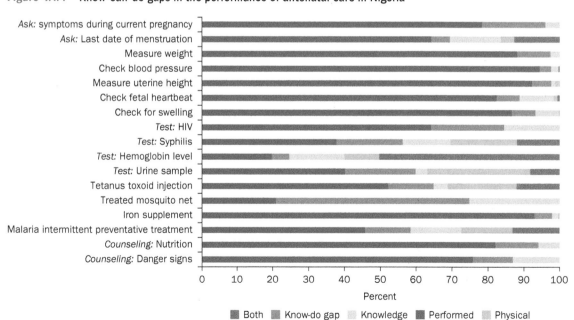

Source: World Bank, using data from the 2015 baseline survey for the impact evaluation of performance-based financing pilot.

Figure 4A.4 **Know-can-do gaps in the performance of antenatal care in Nigeria**

Source: World Bank, using data from the 2014 baseline survey for the impact evaluation of performance-based financing pilot.

Figure 4A.5 Know-can-do gaps in the performance of antenatal care in the Republic of Congo

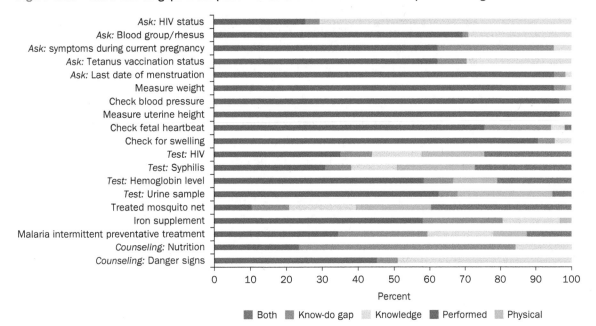

Source: World Bank, using data from the 2014 baseline survey for the impact evaluation of performance-based financing pilot.

Annex 4B: Data

All five surveys included comprehensive assessments of each sampled health facility, typically conducted in a single day, in health facilities offering primary health care. The data can thus be combined from four different survey modules collected during the facility assessments: the general facility assessment measuring availability of medical supplies and equipment through direct observations; health provider interviews, including clinical vignettes on the provision of antenatal care; direct observations of ANC consultations; and patient exit interviews. Triangulating these data elements enables linking adherence to ANC protocol with providers' knowledge and availability of supplies and equipment.

For each of the five countries—Cameroon, the Central African Republic, the Democratic Republic of Congo, Nigeria, and the Republic of Congo, there are detailed data on availability, quality, and storage of the essential equipment, drugs, and supplies needed to provide ANC. In addition, for each facility, in-depth interviews and tests of the knowledge of ANC protocol were conducted with health workers providing this service, as well as direct clinical observations of patient-provider interactions and related patient exit interviews in the context of ANC. The exit interviews also provide data on the patients' characteristics, including wealth and educational attainment. We are not aware of another data set that has so much detail on such a broad range of characteristics—for instance, even the Service Provision Assessment conducted as part of many Demographic and Health Surveys does not include direct clinical observation of actual care provision or patient exit interviews. The various instruments and richness of the covariates within each instrument allow for a comprehensive assessment of the barriers to the provision of high-quality care.

The analysis is restricted to the first consultations women had during their pregnancies. These consultations are more comparable to each other because their content does not depend on previous consultations and includes procedures that should be conducted regardless of women's medical and fertility histories. In total, we report results on 1,866 ANC consultations that took place in 803 health facilities in the five countries. We report on knowledge of 589 ANC providers; not all the observed ANC providers were interviewed, either because of their availability on the day of the assessment or given the selection protocol for each survey.

Variables and analysis

The assessment of quality of care focuses on 20 processes that can be broadly grouped into the following five categories: medical history-taking, physical examination, diagnostic tests, preventive treatment, and counseling topics. A first group of variables describes which processes can be performed in each health facility. Availability of equipment and consumables is created from the general facility assessment for the elements of care. For diagnostic tests, we report whether the facilities had the capacity to perform the different tests on the day of the assessment. A second group of variables relates to providers' knowledge of the different processes and is obtained from responses to the clinical vignettes. In all the countries, the interviewed health workers were presented with a case of a young woman arriving for a first ANC consultation. The providers had to list all the processes that they would have provided to the women in the hypothetical case. A third group of variables indicates which of the 20 processes were performed during the observed consultations.

For each of the 20 processes, the three variable groups described above are combined to create a know-do gap variable, indicating whether non-adherence cannot be explained by lack of knowledge or supplies. For example, a know-do gap in blood pressure measurement is identified if blood pressure was not measured during an observed consultation although a functioning blood pressure cuff was available at the facility and the provider stated that blood pressure needs to be measured during first consultations. For processes that do not require any equipment or consumables, such as medical history-taking and counseling, the know-do gap is defined only according to the providers' knowledge and practice.

We examine whether compliance to protocol and know-do gaps differ in facility, provider, and pregnant woman characteristics. The facility characteristics include facility type and whether facilities are public, non-for-profit faith-based, or under other type ownership. The provider characteristics include providers' grade, gender, and whether their experience is above median. Women's characteristics include education level, household wealth constructed with principal component analysis of household assets, whether it is her first pregnancy, and whether she received the first consultation during the first trimester of her pregnancy.

We used descriptive analysis to assess the frequencies of the variables by country. For protocol adherence and the know-do gap, we created summary indexes by taking the average over the 20 processes (with equal weights for all processes). That is, the adherence index represents the share of the processes performed during a consultation, and the know-do gap index represents the share of processes for which a know-do gap is identified. To assess correlates of these indexes, we present means and 95% confidence intervals for the protocol adherence by facility, provider, and client characteristics.

Data limitations

As rich as the data are, they are not without limitations. The first such limitation is potential observation bias, or the Hawthorne effect. This effect refers to a temporary increase in productivity or other performance measure by a worker in response to the act of observation itself. Indeed, the literature suggests that health workers perform at a higher level when they are observed than when they are not, and this performance is presumably not sustained in the absence of the observation (Leonard and Masatu 2006). For our analysis, the presence of a Hawthorne effect would mean that we are likely to underestimate the know-do gap, meaning that the performance level captured by our direct clinical observation of patient-provider interactions may be higher than it would be otherwise. As providers may not be able fix a broken piece of equipment or instantly procure a drug of which there is a stockout, the Hawthorne effect largely refers to actions that are within a health worker's locus of control. Thus, it likely disproportionally affects actions that might be captured under idle capacity—that is, actions that they can do but otherwise do not.

Second, although the five countries studied here by and large used harmonized instruments, there were some differences in the specific components of some instruments. By and large, these differences are small and permit us to construct harmonized variables for the analysis for all the countries. The only exception is the health worker knowledge test or clinical vignette instrument, which was administered in a significantly different way in the Democratic Republic of Congo than in the remaining four countries. In the Democratic Republic of Congo, the feasible actions were all listed to the health worker, who was simply asked to identify the relevant steps. As a result, the Democratic Republic of Congo vignette essentially primed health workers on the relevant actions and likely thus leads to a significantly higher estimate of worker knowledge than for the other four countries. In the other four countries, the health workers were not primed in this way and had to list whatever actions they could recall. As a result, for knowledge, while we compare levels of performance across the other four countries, we do not compare them with the Democratic Republic of Congo.

Third, there were some differences in the sampling processes employed by the various evaluation teams. For instance, the evaluation was nationally representative in the Republic of Congo but only representative of the states or provinces that were selected as part of the performance-based financing pilot in the other four countries. Further, our sample largely consists of public facilities with a few faith-based facilities in Cameroon and the Democratic Republic of Congo. As a result, we do not present pooled analysis and do not interpret our results as being nationally representative in every case.

References

Adam, T., S. S. Lim, S. Mehta, Z. A. Bhutta, H. Fogstad, M. Mathai, and G. L. Darmstadt. 2005. "Cost Effectiveness Analysis of Strategies for Maternal and Neonatal Health in Developing Countries." *BMJ* 331 (7525): 1107.

Akin, J. S., and P. Hutchinson. 1999. "Health-Care Facility Choice and the Phenomenon of Bypassing." *Health Policy and Planning* 14 (2): 135–51.

Banuri, S., D. de Walque, P. Keefer, O. D. Haidara, P. J. Robyn, and M. Ye. 2018. "The Use of Video Vignettes to Measure Health Worker Knowledge: Evidence from Burkina Faso." *Social Science & Medicine* 213: 173–80.

Carroli, G., C. Rooney, and J. Villar. 2001. "How Effective Is Antenatal Care in Preventing Maternal Mortality and Serious Morbidity? An Overview of the Evidence." *Paediatric and Perinatal Epidemiology* 15: 1–42.

Cohen, J., K. Lofgren, and M. McConnell. 2017. "Precommitment, Cash Transfers, and Timely Arrival for Birth: Evidence from a Randomized Controlled Trial in Nairobi Kenya." *American Economic Review* 107 (5): 501–05.

Cronin, C. J., D. K. Guilkey, and I. S. Speizer. 2019. "Measurement Error in Discrete Health Facility Choice Models: An Example from Urban Senegal." *Journal of Applied Econometrics* 34 (7): 1102–20.

Das, J., J. Hammer, and K. Leonard. 2008. "The Quality of Medical Advice in Low-Income Countries." *Journal of Economic Perspectives* 22 (2): 93–114.

Das, J., A. Holla, V. Das, M. Mohanan, D. Tabak, and B. Chan. 2012. "In Urban and Rural India, a Standardized Patient Study Showed Low Levels of Provider Training and Huge Quality Gaps." *Health Affairs* 31 (12): 2774–84.

Das, J., A. Holla, A. Mohpal, and K. Muralidharan. 2016. "Quality and Accountability in Health Care Delivery: Audit-Study Evidence from Primary Care in India." *American Economic Review* 106 (12): 3765–99.

Das, J., and T. P. Sohnesen. 2007. "Variations in Doctor Effort: Evidence from Paraguay: Doctors in Paraguay Who Expended Less Effort Appear to Have Been Paid More Than Doctors Who Expended More." *Health Affairs* 26 (Suppl2): w324–w337.

Fink, G., E. Kandpal, and G. Shapira. 2019. "Inequality in the Quality of Health Services: Wealth, Content of Care, and Price of Antenatal Consultations in the Democratic Republic of Congo." Policy Research Working Paper 8818, World Bank, Washington, DC.

Fink, G., E. Kandpal, and G. Shapira. 2022. "Inequality in the Quality of Health Services: Wealth, Content of Care, and Price of Antenatal Consultations in the Democratic Republic of Congo." *Economic Development and Cultural Change*. https://doi.org/10.1086/713941.

Gatti, R., K. Andrews, C. Avitabile, R. Conner, J. Sharma, and A. Yi Chang. 2021. "The Quality of Health and Education Systems across Africa: Insights from a Decade of Service Delivery Indicators (SDI) Surveys." World Bank, Washington, DC.

Hernández-Díaz, S., M. M. Werler, A. M. Walker, and A. A. Mitchell. 2000. "Folic Acid Antagonists during Pregnancy and the Risk of Birth Defects." *New England Journal of Medicine*. 343 (22): 1608–14.

Hodgins, S., and A. D'Agostino. 2014. "The Quality-Coverage Gap in Antenatal Care: Toward Better Measurement of Effective Coverage." *Global Health: Science and Practice* 2 (2): 173–81.

Hollowell, J., D. Puddicombe, R. Rowe, L. Linsell, P. Hardy, M. Stewart, M. Newburn, et al. 2011. "The Birthplace National Prospective Cohort Study: Perinatal and Maternal Outcomes by Planned Place of Birth Birthplace in

England Research Programme." Final Report Part 4, NIHR Service Delivery and Organisation Programme, Oxford, UK.

Ibnat, F., K. L. Leonard, L. Bawo, and R. L. Mohammed-Roberts. 2019. "The Three-Gap Model of Health Worker Performance." Policy Research Working Paper 8782, World Bank, Washington, DC.

IHME (Institute for Health Metrics and Evaluation). 2018. *Findings from the Global Burden of Disease Study 2017.* Seattle, WA: IHME.

Kabongo, L., J. Gass, B. Kivondo, N. Kara, K. Semrau, and L. R. Hirschhorn. 2017. "Implementing the WHO Safe Childbirth Checklist: Lessons Learnt on a Quality Improvement Initiative to Improve Mother and Newborn Care at Gobabis District Hospital, Namibia." *BMJ Open Quality* 6 (2): e000145.

Kassebaum, N. J., A. Bertozzi-Villa, M. S. Coggeshall, K. A. Shackelford, C. Steiner, K.R. Heuton, D. Gonzalez-Medina, et al. 2014. "Global, Regional, and National Levels and Causes of Maternal Mortality during 1990–2013: A Systematic Analysis for the Global Burden of Disease Study 2013." *The Lancet* 384 (9947): 980–1004.

Kruk, M. E., E. Goldmann, and S. Galea. 2009. "Borrowing and Selling to Pay for Health Care in Low- and Middle-Income Countries." *Health Affairs* 28 (4): 1056–66.

Lange, S., A. Mwisongo, and O. Mæstad. 2014. "Why Don't Clinicians Adhere More Consistently to Guidelines for the Integrated Management of Childhood Illness (IMCI)?" *Social Science & Medicine* 104: 56–63.

Leonard, K., and M. C. Masatu. 2006. "Outpatient Process Quality Evaluation and the Hawthorne Effect." *Social Science & Medicine* 63 (9): 2330–40.

Leonard, K., and M. C. Masatu. 2010. "Professionalism and the Know-Do Gap: Exploring Intrinsic Motivation among Health Workers in Tanzania." *Health Economics* 19 (12): 1461–77.

Leonard, K. L., M. C. Masatu, and A. Vialou. 2007. "Getting Doctors to Do Their Best: The Roles of Ability and Motivation in Health Care Quality." *Journal of Human Resources* 42 (3): 682–700.

Leonard, K. L., G. R. Mliga, and D. Haile Mariam. 2002. "Bypassing Health Centres in Tanzania: Revealed Preferences for Quality." *Journal of African Economies* 11 (4): 441–71.

McCollum, R., R. Limato, L. Otiso, S. Theobald, and M. Taegtmeyer. 2018. "Health System Governance Following Devolution: Comparing Experiences of Decentralisation in Kenya and Indonesia." *BMJ Global Health* 3 (5): e000939.

Mohanan, M., M. Vera-Hernández, V. Das, S. Giardili, J. D. Goldhaber-Fiebert, T. L. Rabin, S. S. Raj, et al. 2015. "The Know-Do Gap in Quality of Health Care for Childhood Diarrhea and Pneumonia in Rural India." *JAMA Pediatrics* 169 (4): 349–57.

Peabody, J. W., J. Luck, P. Glassman, T. R. Dresselhaus, and M. Lee. 2000. "Comparison of Vignettes, Standardized Patients, and Chart Abstraction: A Prospective Validation Study of 3 Methods for Measuring Quality." *JAMA* 283 (13): 1715–22.

Peters P. J., M. C. Thigpen, M. E. Parise, and R. D. Newman. 2007. "Safety and Toxicity of Sulfadoxine/Pyrimethamine: Implications for Malaria Prevention in Pregnancy Using Intermittent Preventive Treatment." *Drug Safety* 30 (6): 481–501.

Rethans, J. J., S. Gorter, L. Bokken, and L. Morrison. 2007. "Unannounced Standardised Patients in Real Practice: A Systematic Literature Review." *Medical Education* 41 (6): 537–49.

Rowe, A. K., S. Y. Rowe, D. H. Peters, K. A. Holloway, J. Chalker, and D. Ross-Degnan. 2018. "Effectiveness of Strategies to Improve Health-Care Provider Practices in Low-Income and Middle-Income Countries: A Systematic Review." *The Lancet Global Health* 6 (11): e1163–e1175.

United Nations Population Division. 2019. *World Population Prospects: 2019 Revision*. New York: United Nations Population Division. https://data .worldbank.org/indicator/SP.DYN.TFRT.IN.

World Health Organization. 2016. *WHO Recommendations on Antenatal Care for a Positive Pregnancy Experience*. Geneva: WHO.

World Health Organization. 2019. *Maternal Mortality: Evidence Brief*. WHO/ RHR/19.20. Geneva: WHO.

World Health Organization. 2020. "Newborns: Improving Survival and Well-Being." WHO, Geneva. https://www.who.int/news-room/fact-sheets/detail /newborns-reducing-mortality.

CHAPTER 5

Performance-Based Financing Improves Coverage of Reproductive, Maternal, and Child Health Interventions

Introduction

The goal of universal health coverage is to develop health systems that provide all people access to services without inflicting financial hardship in paying for them. This goal was stated by the World Health Organization (WHO) in 2005 and has led to sustained investments in and technical assistance to health systems in low- and middle-income countries (LMICs) (WHO 2010). Nonetheless, 17 years later, the sustainable financing of health systems remains a central challenge on the path to universal health coverage (English et al. 2016; Reich et al. 2016). Analysis by the Brookings Institution estimates that LMICs face an annual financing gap of US$370 billion to reach Sustainable Development Goal 3, ensure healthy lives and promote well-being for all at all ages. This gap is particularly acute in Sub-Saharan Africa, which accounted for 16 percent of the world's population, 3 percent of the global health force, 23 percent of the global disease burden, but only 1 percent of total global health expenditures in 2015 (Ogbuoji et al. 2019; African Union 2014). A WHO report on health financing in Africa notes that the strategies and mechanisms underpinning health financing systems can pose problems (WHO 2013). For instance, in about half of all African countries, at least 40 percent of total health expenditure is in the form of household out-of-pocket payments. Flows within existing public financial management systems can be skewed toward urban areas and specialized care even though primary health care reform has long been a focus of government and donor efforts to expand access to care (WHO 1978).

In addition, public financial management systems may not be aligned with health financing reforms, and public expenditure tracking systems can be clogged, both leading to staggering delays in salary disbursements. This can lead to detrimental effects on worker satisfaction and motivation, in turn leading to the provision of poor care (Diamond 2013). Perhaps unsurprisingly, then, an additional challenge in these contexts is the financing of *high-quality* health systems. Indeed, only relatively recently has ensuring high-quality care become a focus of donor and international organization effort (WHO 2013, 2018). Nonetheless, chapters 2 to 4 of this report highlight how LMICs, especially those in Sub-Saharan Africa, continue to face significant gaps in the provision of effective coverage, particularly high-quality health services for maternity care. Chapters 3 and 4 further suggest that while structural and knowledge gaps persist in health service delivery, the underprovision of effort by health workers explains a large portion of low quality of care. Turning to strategies to improve effective coverage and the quality of health service delivery, this chapter reviews much of the previously published evidence on how financial incentives, on both the demand and supply sides, have improved health utilization rates. The chapter focuses on a widespread approach to supply-side financial incentives in the form of performance pay. Typically, in LMICs, performance pay is incorporated into performance-based financing (PBF) approaches, which consist of performance pay and other critical features, including public financial management reform, health facility autonomy, decentralization, supportive supervision for the frontlines, and community engagement. PBF has been described as "a tool for helping create better, more inclusive, and more accessible health services" (Fritsche, Soeters, and Meessen 2014, 2). This chapter and chapter 6 assess whether performance pay and the overall PBF approach have indeed delivered "better" care, by studying their impacts on structural and process quality as well as health outcomes, care that is "more inclusive," by assessing the evidence on equity impacts, and care that is "more accessible," by examining coverage and effective coverage.

The chapter starts with an overview of performance pay and provides a theoretical framework that explains why performance pay may improve effective coverage. It then summarizes the recent evaluative evidence, including from the World Bank's investments in PBF approaches in LMICs, such as impacts on quality of care and equity. This overview of the evidence also considers the evidence on the impacts of PBF on service utilization, equity, and the quality of care, using the know-can-do gap framework described in chapter 3. The impact evaluations tied to PBF projects funded by the World Bank suggest that PBF interventions have had, at best, mixed impacts on health service coverage and clinical quality. The observed gains are not pro-poor as the relatively wealthy can better respond to improvements in facility quality and often return from the private sector to the public sector in response to investment in the public sector. In contrast, because a key criticism of performance pay is that it might erode health worker motivation (Paul et al. 2018), the chapter conducts a systematic and well-identified multi-country analysis of the impacts of PBF on health worker motivation and satisfaction.[1]

As discussed in chapter 3, two key obstacles to improving effective coverage are (1) the quality of care and (2) the staffing of facilities and provision of health services in poor and remote areas. To address the first concern, in most of the PBF pilots, facilities received an additional quality bonus based on their performance on a quality scorecard that was designed to measure performance on indicators of structural and process quality rather than simply the quantity of services provided (see, for instance, Kandpal et al. (2019) for an overview of the implementation of this quality bonus in the Nigerian PBF pilot). In addition, in many instances, facility managers were provided training twice a year on the best practices in facility management and financial administration. To address the second concern, many of the PBF interventions studied here provided an additional bonus tied to the facility's remoteness—often this bonus could be substantial, up to 40 percent of the quarterly payment before the bonus—depending on the distance from the local administrative headquarters. Finally, as part of the accountability aspect of PBF pilots, the reported levels of targeted services as well as the associated payments were published online on national PBF portals (Fritsche, Soeters, and Meessen 2014).

In addition, because the goal is efficient and equitable delivery of high-quality health services, PBF programs in LMICs often include additional components beyond performance pay. In the programs studied in this chapter, the PBF payments are also typically accompanied by additional financing for infrastructure, supplies, and consumables, which are disbursed directly to the health facility. This can be an important departure from business-as-usual in primary health care provision in LMICs. Further, as implemented in health care in LMICs, PBF interventions are generally part of a broader health system reform that includes autonomy, supervision, monitoring, and community oversight or engagement in facility management (Meessen, Soucat, and Sekabaraga 2011; Renmans et al. 2017). When these interventions were piloted in LMICs and subsequently rolled out, it was widely believed that such composite and overarching interventions were especially suited for revitalizing health system performance in low-income settings. Public health experts believed that PBF could catalyze comprehensive reforms and help address structural problems such as lack of responsiveness, inefficiency, and inequity. Performance pay for providers combined with autonomy of decision making at the individual health facility level was considered a radically different approach that could simultaneously alleviate worker absenteeism, lack of resources, and accountability (Meessen, Soucat, and Sekabaraga 2011).

However, these programs are not without criticism. A few critics have questioned the use of PBF given the complexity of implementing it relative to decentralized financing approaches. Similarly, questions have been raised about its impacts on equity and the heterogeneity in payment schemes and program design, making it difficult to extrapolate impacts and leaving the effectiveness of the intervention particularly vulnerable to implementation fidelity (Paul et al. 2018; Ridde et al. 2018; Ireland, Paul, and Dujardin 2011). Another criticism concerns the role of donor agencies in promoting PBF approaches, and it has been argued that at times donor agencies have overridden local demands or even needs to push for PBF. Critics have argued that such a "donor-driven agenda" limits the systemwide and long-term impacts of PBF programs because it essentially becomes a short-run intervention that lacks stakeholder ownership. Indeed, a central criticism of performance pay—and by extension PBF—is that it can damage health systems through detrimental impacts on worker motivation (Turcotte-Tremblay et al. 2016; Lohmann, Houlfort, and De Allegri 2016). This line of criticism posits that by paying for specific tasks, performance pay crowds out the intrinsic motivation of health workers, who should be pro-socially motivated (Paul et al. 2018; Ridde et al. 2018). The critics argue that when the donor finances run out, all the health system is left with is an unmotivated taskforce and no sustained gains to health outcomes or even service delivery.

PBF, health system performance, and health worker effort in theory

To formalize the link between PBF and effective coverage, this chapter summarizes a conceptual framework linking health worker effort, as well as broader health system considerations, to pecuniary incentives to motivate the consideration of PBF interventions as a means for improving service provision and effective coverage (this conceptual framework is presented in Friedman and Scheffler (2016)). The framework links effective coverage to incentivized health payments by assessing various channels through which incentive financing may impact effective coverage.

A standard economic framework that often serves to motivate the PBF approach is the "principal-agent" model, where the purchaser of health services (the "principal") delegates, often through a formal contract, to a provider of health services (the "agent"). Even a straightforward contractual arrangement may encounter complications if the objectives of the principal and agent are different or if the information available to the agent is not the same as that of the principal. In standard principal-agent theory, the degree of differential information between principal and agent as well as the principal's ability to monitor the agent's output and effort determine the optimal contract form. For situations when it is difficult to monitor the agent's effort but not the outputs of that effort, or when the agent may have private information on the local health production process that the principal does not have, it may be preferable to reward the agent based on performance and, especially, the achievement of prespecified outputs (see Savedoff and Partner (2010) for a general discussion of this framework).

Another relevant feature of the principal-agent contract is the degree of financial risk imposed on the agent by the chosen contract. On the one hand, if too small a share of overall compensation is made available to the agent through a performance component of the contract, it may not be sufficient to spur the necessary effort to meet the targets. On the other hand, if too large a share of overall compensation is made contingent on performance, this can introduce excessive financial risk for the agent, possibly leading to demotivation, high stress, lower performance, and staff turnover.

In addition to financial incentives, PBF programs involve additional health system reforms, such as facility autonomy and increased supervision and monitoring. All told, the new mix of services and service effectiveness produced under PBF may result in a higher or lower level of population health, depending on at least six factors: health-increasing substitution, health-decreasing substitution, provider surplus extraction, net externalities, monitoring costs, and risk premium costs. The degree to which these six factors are modified by PBF will determine the impact of the program on the effective coverage of health services. Figure 5.1 depicts these six factors in a highly stylized manner to demonstrate their potential impact on population health. This figure relates population health as a function of the share of a provider's revenue (or a health worker's wage) that is based on PBF. The y-axis measures a broad summary measure of effective health coverage, as targeted by the health system reform.

In figure 5.1, the net effect of the six factors potentially influenced by PBF is aggregated in the curve labeled "Total," with point A marking the PBF incentive level that is expected to maximize effective coverage. As the share of health provider revenue based on PBF increases, overall health increases, levels off, and then begins to decrease as the negative impact of

Figure 5.1 **Key factors of performance-based financing that influence population health: An illustration**

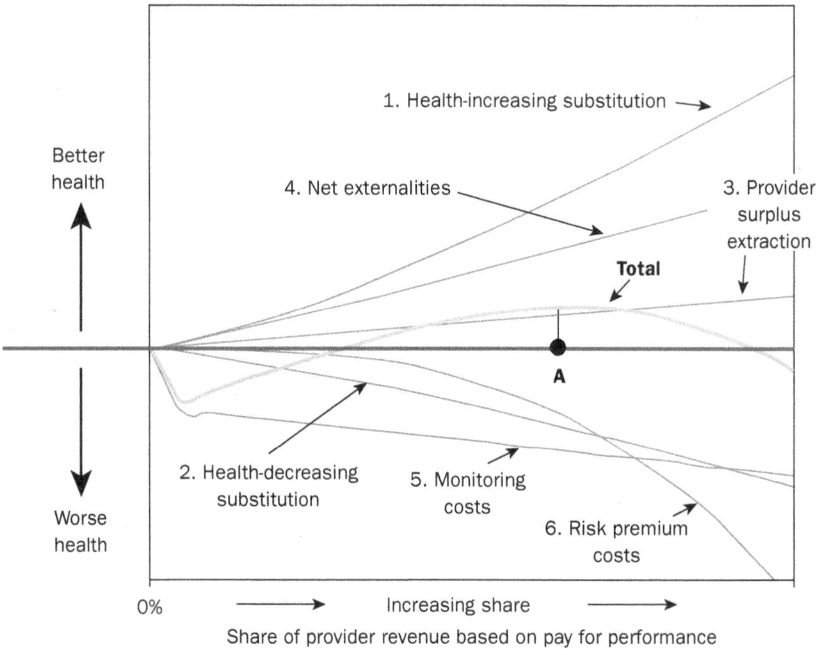

Source: Friedman and Scheffler 2016.

the risk premium cost begins to dominate. This stylistic figure decomposes, in a qualitative sense, PBF's impact on population health into the channels through which the program operates. The relative contribution and shape of each line are largely based on theoretical constructs and will certainly vary across programs and contexts; additional work will be needed for a fuller understanding of these relationships.

Most PBF programs use the additional funds introduced by the program to pay for health worker and facility bonuses, as well as increased health system monitoring. The same funds could have been spent in alternative ways. For example, the funds could have been used to increase base compensation rates, hire additional staff, accredit private providers, or build new facilities. To isolate the impact of the incentives from the overall funding increase, the health impact on the vertical axis in figure 5.1 is in reference to an unobserved counterfactual condition, that is, if those new funds were being used to increase base reimbursement under more standard supply-side approaches.

In figure 5.1, the horizontal axis is the share of provider revenue that is based on PBF, because the fraction of incentivized payment in total payment is a key PBF design issue. The share that will maximize population health depends on health system characteristics, such as the payment model, administrative controls, and the potential to increase efficiency, as well as other features of the contract, such as the monitoring level, decision-making authority, job design, and asset ownership. In most of the countries studied here, the performance payments were capped between 20 and 40 percent of worker base pay.

Factor 1: Health-increasing substitution

Health-increasing substitution occurs when more efficient services and inputs replace less efficient ones. For example, as more antenatal health screens become available, less costly delivery services will be needed if health problems are identified earlier and well managed. In figure 5.1, health-increasing substitution is assumed to begin gradually as a function of incentive size, as the incentive must exceed the marginal cost of the incentivized action for it to affect behavior. Once these thresholds are exceeded, the slope increases. While a fairly linear relation is assumed here, the actual relation may be nonlinear depending on the provider's cost function for effort to provide different services. Health-increasing substitution can also include actions that are not directly incentivized but are perhaps complementary to actions that are incentivized. Bauhoff and Kandpal (2021) provide a theoretical model and some empirical evidence of such an example.

Factor 2: Health-decreasing substitution

Health-decreasing substitution occurs when less efficient services and inputs replace more efficient ones, which can arise when an agent performs multiple tasks (Holmstrom and Milgrom 1991). In colloquial terms, incentivized tasks may "crowd-out" unincentivized ones. It is impractical to include explicit incentives for each possible task a health worker can undertake, in part because many tasks are unobserved or difficult to measure. Therefore, the health worker can substitute effort from unobserved and nonrewarded tasks (for example, counseling), which may be relatively more efficient for health production, toward the rewarded subtasks (for example, record keeping). For example, in the United Kingdom's Quality and Outcomes Framework, some providers report that the record keeping necessary under the PBF program has reduced available time to listen to patients' concerns (Maisey et al. 2008). In figure 5.1, health-decreasing substitution is assumed to mirror health-increasing substitution as the incentive for change must be greater than the cost of the incentivized action. If the PBF measures are well designed, then the magnitude of health-decreasing substitution will be less than the magnitude of health-increasing substitution, and there will be a net positive impact on health related to overall substitution effects. Few studies have looked at PBF impacts on unincentivized health activities, but those that have found little evidence of negative coverage impacts (Kandpal 2016; Diaconu et al. 2020).

Factor 3: Provider surplus extraction

Provider surplus extraction is the difference between the health worker's net utility, taking into account effort costs and time not devoted to work, under PBF when compared with the counterfactual condition. Any surplus that the principal extracts from the provider can be used to purchase additional health care services. The degree of surplus extraction will vary both due to the PBF program design as well as across provider types. On the one hand, the realized surplus should be greater from an originally inefficient provider. If the surplus extraction from these workers is large enough, it may cause inefficient providers to leave and thus result in a sorting of the health workforce over time (Lazear 2000). On the other hand, surplus extraction will be less from an efficient provider. While from the perspective of the social planner, provider surplus extraction is largely a distributional issue, from the payer's perspective, the extracted surplus is used to improve health through increased provider effort. In figure 5.1, provider surplus extraction is simply depicted as linear with respect to the provider's share of revenue based on PBF. The actual slope and magnitude of the relation will depend on the degree of preexisting provider surplus.

Factor 4: Net externalities

In addition to the direct impacts of a PBF program on incentivized health services, a PBF program may change the effective coverage of health services if it modifies health system norms and decision-making processes. Any resultant changes in effective health coverage from these modifications can be termed externalities since the changes are not directly targeted by or directly linked to the incentivized health services and related actions. For example, a positive externality may arise if PBF implementation improves general health system decision making through the analysis of data generated by the PBF program. The increased practice of data-driven decision making may have a positive effect on a wide variety of services not directly tied to incentives. Negative externalities can also arise. A PBF program may cause workers to become less team oriented or otherwise demotivated if they feel they must compete for bonuses. In figure 5.1, the net externalities example is assumed to be positive and, further, related to investments in monitoring as increased investment in monitoring systems would hopefully yield these externalities.

Factor 5: Monitoring costs

A PBF program will typically incur an initial fixed expenditure to set up a health service and health quality monitoring system and link this system to payments, and then bear ongoing monitoring and verification costs of the payment-related data. These costs reduce the budget available for the production of health care services, thus possibly resulting in worse health. In figure 5.1, the stylized monitoring cost curve includes this setup cost when PBF is introduced. Monitoring costs may continue to increase, as a function of the PBF share in revenue, to dissuade any tendency from providers to game the system and deliberately misreport for a higher payment.

Factor 6: Risk premium costs

Most health workers are assumed to be risk-averse with respect to future income uncertainty. As overall uncertainty increases with the share of total compensation due to PBF, especially if the PBF payment is partly a function of factors beyond the worker's control, such as patient care-seeking decisions, a risk-averse health worker will require a risk premium to continue in the program. This risk premium component reduces the available resources for health care provision, resulting in worse population health. The greater the share of total payment from PBF is, the greater is the uncertainty, and hence the higher is the premium necessary for a worker to participate. As such, in figure 5.1, the risk premium is assumed to increase at an increasing rate of the PBF's share of a provider's revenue. This stylization is consistent with providers being almost risk neutral with respect to small amounts of compensation, and growing more risk averse when a larger proportion of income is at stake (Rabin 2000).

Summary of the mechanisms

To summarize this conceptual overview of PBF mechanisms, two of the aforementioned channels should positively affect population health: the health-increasing substitution of health care services and inputs as well as provider surplus extraction. Three factors should negatively affect health: decreasing substitution of health care services and inputs, monitoring costs, and risk premium costs. A sixth factor, net externalities, involves possible wider impacts beyond the direct impacts on incentivized indicators, such as those brought on by linking incentive payments to a robust digital data system. Program externalities could positively or negatively affect health depending on the net benefits and costs. When a policy maker considers a PBF program design, how all six of these factors will respond in the specific health setting should be considered for a comprehensive understanding of the potential impact of the program.

The above framework accounts for one commonly stated motivation for PBF programs, namely underutilized capacity in the health system and how such underutilized capacity can be harnessed through the introduction of incentives. If such capacity exists, then gains would be expected from PBF on the margins that are most responsive to "health worker surplus extraction." However, there are several other possible barriers to effective coverage, in addition to "slackness," that respond to other types of health interventions. These challenges include (1) demand-side barriers to care that are in part financial—directly addressing these barriers may improve coverage; (2) inadequate supply-side financing that affects the availability of staff and other key inputs to the production of effective coverage; (3) ineffective health system management practices, which can be improved through goal setting, supportive feedback, and so forth, which in turn can better martial existing resources to produce effective coverage; and (4), related to (3), strategies to motivate health workers independent of financial incentives.

An effective PBF program would thus provide incentives at the margins that a health worker can control, and these programs can have a broader place under health financing. However, other constraints to improving effective coverage might be better addressed under alternative financing mechanisms or other approaches to health system reform. The conceptual framework provided here identifies several dimensions along which it may be expected that financial incentives would affect the coverage of services, quality of care, and perhaps even health equity. The next section turns to recent evidence on the impact of PBF on these dimensions in the contexts of primary health service delivery in LMICs.

Evidence of the impact of PBF on the quality and quantity of health service delivery in LMICs

An early PBF pilot that was implemented in Rwanda showed that the use of performance pay for strategic purchasing successfully increased institutional delivery rates (Basinga et al. 2011). Considering this evidence and the persistent conundrum of health system financing in LMICs, several donors and lending agencies encouraged governments in LMICs to adopt PBF approaches. The argument made in favor of these interventions was that PBF improves both the efficiency and the quality of care (Shroff, Bigdeli, and Meessen 2017; Ireland, Paul, and Dujardin 2011). The World Bank's Health Results Innovation Trust Fund (HRITF) supports and evaluates LMIC governments in paying providers based on their results in the provision of maternal, newborn, and child health care (see box 1.1, in chapter 1).

Of the completed impact evaluations in the HRITF portfolio, most of them present at least some evidence of impacts on service utilization and many on quality of care (Kandpal 2016). Most frequently, the impacts on quality are observed on structural quality, with all the studies in question reporting improvements in the availability of basic delivery and antenatal care (ANC) equipment, essential drugs, and supplies. These impacts can be sizable, as reported in the literature. Figure 5.2 illustrates the impacts of PBF on essential structural capacity for ANC in Cameroon and Nigeria—the two countries among the five Sub-Saharan African countries studied in chapter 4 for which there are complete impact evaluation data. An overall index of structural quality and an index of all drugs and supplies are reported above the dotted line in the figure. Increases in structural quality would be to the right of the zero vertical line. The figure shows significant impacts of PBF on many dimensions of structural quality in both countries, although the improvements are far from universal in either context. Indeed, in both countries, a few drugs became less available relative to business-as-usual.

At the same time, the evidence suggests there were no meaningful impacts on health worker knowledge. As discussed in the theoretical framework, PBF pilots have the potential to increase health worker knowledge, but this broad-based finding of a null impact suggests that in practice, at least in these contexts, the channels—job aids, salience, and so forth—through which PBF interventions might increase knowledge are not the binding constraints to the production of health worker knowledge.

Figure 5.2 **Impacts of performance-based financing on facility physical capacity in Cameroon and Nigeria**

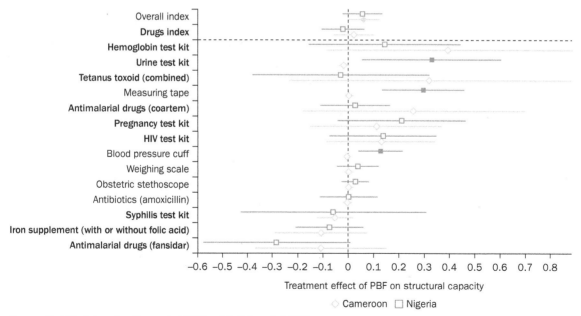

Sources: World Bank, based on Khanna et al. 2021 and de Walque et al. 2021.

Note: Solid markers indicate statistically significant estimates (*p* < .05); markers that are open indicate imprecise estimates. "Whiskers" around markers represent 95% confidence intervals. Components of the drugs index are in **bold** along the y axis. PBF = performance-based financing.

In addition, there is evidence from several LMICs that PBF can be an effective strategy in terms of its impacts on health service utilization. As shown by evidence from Burundi (Falisse et al. 2014), Nigeria (Khanna et al. 2021), Rwanda (Basinga et al. 2011), Zambia (Friedman et al. 2016), and Zimbabwe (Friedman, Das, and Mutasa 2017), PBF appears to be particularly successful at increasing the rate of institutional deliveries or deliveries attended by skilled birth attendants. Some studies, notably two in Argentina (Gertler, Giovagnoli, and Martinez 2014; Celhay et al. 2019), also find increases in ANC utilization, while a few others report impacts on immunization of the mother or child (Argentina, Cameroon, Nigeria, Rwanda, and Zambia). The impact evaluation of Plan Nacer in Argentina (box 5.1) demonstrates impacts on health outcomes such as low birth weight and neonatal mortality. Despite some heterogeneity in the results,

---

Box 5.1   In Focus: A middle-income country's experience with performance-based financing: The case of Argentina and Plan Nacer and Programa Sumar

The 2001 economic crisis plunged more than half of Argentina's population into poverty and resulted in high unemployment (Fiszbein, Giovagnoli, and Adúrez 2003). Many Argentines lost their health coverage and turned to the public health system for care. The increased demand strained the system's capacity to deliver services, and basic health indicators deteriorated. Between 2000 and 2002, Argentina's infant mortality rate increased from 16.6 to 16.8 per 1,000, and in the country's poorer northeastern and northwestern provinces, infant mortality was as high as 25 per 1,000 (Cortez and Romero 2013). As a result, the government of Argentina developed Plan Nacer to reduce infant mortality by increasing access to health care to uninsured pregnant women and children under age six, and to improve the efficiency and quality of the public health system by introducing changes in the incentive framework.

Plan Nacer's performance-based financing (PBF) mechanisms created two levels of incentives: one between the national and provincial governments, and the other between the provincial governments and health facilities. Provincial governments received capitation payments from the National Ministry of Health based on the number of beneficiaries enrolled in Plan Nacer, and on the achievement of specified health indicator targets. Health facilities received fee-for-service payments from the provincial government according to the number and quality of services they provided (Cortez 2009). The health facilities benefitted from substantial autonomy in deciding how to use the PBF incentives. Some paid bonuses to health workers, while others reinvested in the facility to make improvements in infrastructure and service delivery (Heard 2012).

The government launched phase I of Plan Nacer in nine of Argentina's poorest provinces in 2005 and brought the program to the 14 remaining provinces and the Autonomous City of Buenos Aires in phase II in 2007.

(Continued)

109

Box 5.1 *continued*

Impact evaluation

The impact evaluation of Plan Nacer used a unique data set based on birth and medical records combined with administrative data to estimate the causal impact of Plan Nacer on specific birth outcomes during 2004–08 in six of the program's nine initial provinces. The results show that the use and quality of prenatal services increased, resulting in reduced incidence of low birth weight (less than 2,500 grams) and lower in-hospital neonatal mortality (Gertler, Giovagnoli, and Martinez 2014). Specifically, the program beneficiaries were 19 percent less likely to be low birth weight compared with nonbeneficiaries. They also had a 74 percent lower chance of in-hospital neonatal mortality in larger facilities. Approximately half of the reduction in deaths is attributed to better prenatal care that prevented low birth weight, while the other half is the result of better postnatal care. The program also increased the use and quality of prenatal care services as measured by the number of prenatal care visits and the probability of pregnant women receiving a tetanus vaccine.

The results further show that the financial autonomy provided to facilities by Plan Nacer allowed a better allocation of scarce resources, which in turn had a positive impact on the health outcomes of the beneficiaries. The cost-effectiveness analysis finds Plan Nacer to be highly cost-effective compared with Argentina's gross domestic product per capita over this period. However, the study also finds small negative spillover effects on prenatal care utilization of nonbeneficiary populations in clinics covered by Plan Nacer, but no spillover was detected on birth outcomes.

Beyond Plan Nacer

Lessons from Plan Nacer's results were particularly valuable as the government of Argentina started to implement Programa Sumar (Ministerio de Salud Argentina 2013). This new program used Plan Nacer's PBF mechanisms. While extending health coverage to uninsured children and adolescents under age 19 and to uninsured women between ages 20 and 64, it also continued to provide coverage for uninsured pregnant women.

the evidence supports the conclusion that PBF pilots can lead to improvements in some aspects of maternal and child health, particularly institutional deliveries.

In two instances, however, impact evaluations failed to find evidence of significant changes in any of the targeted service utilization indicators: in Afghanistan and in a pilot in Haut-Katanga province in the Democratic Republic of Congo (Huillery and Seban 2021). In Afghanistan, two studies were conducted, but the periods covered overlapped with a significant increase in armed conflict across the country, which may have contributed to the lack of impact of the PBF pilot on service utilization. In the pilot in the Democratic Republic of Congo, the authors note that an implementation error led to health workers in treated facilities facing a 42 percent reduction in their remuneration. Unsurprisingly, this was accompanied by a large decrease in health worker motivation and satisfaction (further discussed in the following section) and may be tied to the lack of impact of the pilot.

Most of the impact evaluations were conducted 18 to 24 months after the intervention started, and few studies have looked at the sustained impacts of the pilots. One exception is Ngo and Bauhoff (2021), who use data from the Rwanda Demographic and Health Surveys to look at the short- and medium-term impacts of the Rwanda PBF pilot studied in Basinga et al. (2011). They find that in the short run, the program increased institutional deliveries and the completion of four ANC visits, and in the medium run there were further improvements in institutional deliveries. However, they also find that decentralized but unconditional financing was an effective alternative to PBF. Chapter 6 returns to the topic of direct facility financing as an alternative to PBF.

However, the impact evaluations present mixed evidence of effectiveness—perhaps except for institutional delivery—thereby highlighting the uneven impact of PBF programs in improving coverage, quality, and effective coverage (Diaconu et al. 2020). Such unevenness may not necessarily be surprising: broad-based health system reforms are typically complex and depend on both local context and the quality of implementation. PBF is no exception.

While effective coverage is the intermediate step, the end goal of health interventions is to improve population health outcomes. In maternal and child health, an example of such improvements to health outcomes would be reductions in maternal and neonatal mortality. Few studies examine such impacts. In secondary care settings, there is some evidence that PBF interventions can lead to reductions in mortality or closely related health outcomes. In Argentina, Celhay et al. (2019) find evidence of a large (74 percent) reduction in in-hospital mortality and a 19 percent reduction in the probability of low birth weight in larger health facilities but not in primary care settings. In the Kyrgyz Republic, Friedman and Kandpal (2021) find that a PBF intervention significantly reduced maternal blood loss and the incidence of severe postpartum hemorrhage, as well as improved a summary score of a newborn's condition at birth. However, both studies examine impacts on large, secondary hospitals. This experience is broadly consistent with high-income countries' experiences tying PBF to improved health outcomes in large hospitals (Mendelson et al. 2017).

However, most Health Results Innovation Trust Fund pilots typically intervened in the primary health setting. Here, evidence of health impacts is more limited. In the initial Rwanda pilot, there was evidence of a 69 percent reduction in wasting among children younger than age three, and in Zimbabwe, a 36 percent reduction in severe stunting.

Apart from these instances, in primary health care, evidence linking PBF to improved health outcomes is rare. For instance, Gage and Bauhoff (2020) assess the impact of PBF programs on neonatal health outcomes in Africa. They pool Demographic and Health Surveys and Multiple Indicator Cluster Surveys in Burundi, Lesotho, Senegal, Zambia, and Zimbabwe to estimate the effect of World Bank-supported PBF projects on early neonatal mortality and low birthweight. They do not find a statistically significant impact of PBF on neonatal mortality. In contrast, Kaila and Kandpal (2021) use nationally representative household surveys and administrative data from Nigeria and find that the PBF intervention reduced neonatal mortality relative to business-as-usual, although not to the policy counterfactual of direct facility financing (discussed in chapter 6).

Impact of PBF on health worker motivation and satisfaction in six countries

There have been long-standing concerns that PBF schemes can lead to reductions in health worker motivation (Paul et al. 2018). Scholars have argued, as discussed in further detail in box 5.2, that while PBF may improve extrinsic motivation driven by financial rewards, there can be an equal or more powerful crowding-out of intrinsic motivation, resulting in an ambiguous effect on overall health worker motivation. Intrinsic motivation, driven by factors such as autonomy, altruism, and purpose, is likely to be strong among health providers who perform cognitively complex tasks in suboptimal settings (Lohmann, Houlfort, and De Allegri 2016; Himmelstein, Ariely, and Woolhandler 2014). Given this, the idea of "intrinsic motivation crowding-out" is important in the context of LMIC health systems.

Although health worker motivation is recognized to be a key element in bringing about changes in health worker performance, the exact motivation mechanisms through which PBF affects health worker performance are poorly understood in the context of LMIC health systems

Box 5.2   In Focus: Theoretical underpinnings of health worker motivation and paying for performance

The idea that rewards—and, specifically, monetary rewards—may undermine and crowd out intrinsic motivation is usually traced back to Richard Morris Titmuss's seminal book, *The Gift Relationship*. In it, he argues, comparing blood donation systems in the United States and the United Kingdom, that paying for blood undermines the inherent social value of altruism and thereby reduces or totally eliminates the willingness to donate blood (Frey and Jegen 2001; Titmuss 1970). In his book, Titmuss argues that paying for blood leads to not only "worse blood," but also "less blood."

Another strand of literature where this idea has been identified and studied is cognitive social psychology, where under the theoretical umbrella of cognitive evaluation theory, intrinsically and extrinsically motivated behaviors are clearly identified and distinguished. Deci (1972, 217) summarizes intrinsic motivation as "perform[ing] an activity for no apparent reward except for the activity itself" and extrinsic motivation as the performance of an activity because it leads to external rewards. An expanded definition of intrinsic motivation includes motivation that stems from the opinion of one's peers (Leonard and Masatu 2017). Many studies discuss the link between prosocial motivation, which is derived from the opinion of peers or even the community, and interventions that track and share data on performance. Generally, these studies find that tracking performance and providing feedback on it, as done by performance-based financing (PBF) programs, can at least in theory improve performance for pro-socially motivated workers (Peabody et al. 2014; Malin et al. 2015).

Another theoretical approach, self-determination theory, explicitly recognizes the importance of a multidimensional approach to motivation (Deci and Ryan 1985; Lohmann, Houlfort, and De Allegri 2016; Borghi et al. 2018). It places motivation on a continuum where individuals engage in tasks because they find them interesting, enjoyable, or challenging (intrinsic motivation) on one extreme or for purely instrumental reasons, such as rewards or punishment, on the other (extrinsic motivation or external regulation). Between these two extremes, there are different types of extrinsic motivation that may be driven by a combination of internal and external factors. When motivation is driven by external factors (that is, driven by rewards, punishment, or performance), it is called controlled. When motivation is caused by internal factors (that is, driven by interest and enjoyment in the task itself), it is called autonomous (Lohmann, Houlfort, and De Allegri 2016).

In contrast, standard economic theory does not normally differentiate between different sources of motivation. Economic thinking typically assumes intrinsic motivation to be a constant and theorizes extrinsic motivation—which responds to monetary incentives. In standard principal-agent models, PBF rewards raise performance by imposing a higher marginal cost of shirking or increasing the marginal benefit of working, thereby increasing total motivation. Therefore, by treating motivation as a unidimensional measure, an overall measure, or simply additive, standard principal-agent models ignore intrinsic motivation (Lohmann, Houlfort, and De Allegri 2016; Himmelstein, Ariely, and Woolhandler 2014; Renmans et al. 2016). Given that the underlying logic of PBF schemes is based on economic theory, Himmelstein, Ariely, and Woolhandler (2014) point out that PBF schemes assume that financial incentives will increase total motivation by failing to distinguish between the different types

(Continued)

Box 5.2 *continued*

or sources of health care provider motivation. Further, simply assuming that rational individuals would respond to monetary rewards ignores the complexity of the health systems within which health care providers and managers work. Several studies provide evidence of health workers expressing intrinsic motivation, suggesting that ignoring it may provide an incomplete understanding of the effect of PBF on overall health worker motivation (Kalk, Paul, and Grabosch 2010; Olasfsdottir, Bakhtiari, and Barman 2014).

(Lohmann et al. 2018). Lohmann et al. (2018, table 3) find that the Malawian Results-Based Financing for Maternal and Newborn Health Initiative motivated health workers to improve their performance by "triggering a sense of accomplishment," "altering social dynamics by creating a sense of common goals," and "providing direction and goals to work toward," among other positive changes. In Burundi, health workers found that PBF reinforced feelings of professionalism (Bertone and Meessen 2013). In Rwanda, health workers reported greater appreciation of their work, greater attention to their work by managers, and increased feelings of responsibility (Kalk, Paul, and Grabosch 2010). In Mali, Zitti et al. (2019) find that PBF led health workers to feel more motivated to perform their tasks—this was not driven by financial rewards but by PBF allowing them to work more efficiently. All these studies point toward different sources of motivation beyond those driven by monetary rewards, which are often just one component of PBF interventions.

Frey and Jegen (2001) incorporate two main psychological processes through which external interventions may affect intrinsic motivation into economic thinking that enable unpacking "intrinsic motivation crowding-out" in the context of PBF interventions. These are (1) impaired self-determination and (2) impaired self-esteem. External interventions such as PBF may impair self-determination if individuals feel compelled to behave in a specific way by an external intervention. In this case, intrinsic motivation is substituted by extrinsic motivation. Additionally, external interventions may also impair self-esteem when an individual feels their involvement is not appreciated. Intrinsically motivated persons may reduce effort when a monetary reward is offered because they are deprived of the chance to display their interest and involvement. Given these two processes, Frey and Jegen (2001) theorize that external interventions such as PBF may *crowd out* intrinsic motivation if individuals perceive them to be *controlling* and may *crowd in* intrinsic motivation if individuals perceive them to be *supportive*.

While the phenomenon of "intrinsic motivation crowding-out" has been confirmed by studies in behavioral economics and social psychology, these are largely confined to high-income contexts or those involving the introduction of payments to hitherto non-incentivized tasks such as blood donation (Lohmann, Houlfort, and De Allegri 2016; Gneezy and Rustichini 2000; Ariely, Bracha, and Meier 2009; Deci, Koestner, and Ryan 1999). To date, beyond a few studies, there is little and inconclusive evidence on this issue in the context of health systems in LMICs (Binyaruka, Lohmann, and De Allegri 2020). One exception is the Malawian PBF pilot whose effect on intrinsic health worker motivation has been studied by Lohmann et al. (2018). The authors report that PBF did not affect health workers' intrinsic motivation levels. Shen et al. (2017) also find similar results in Zambia. There is a need for a larger number of field experiments that study this phenomenon in the context of payments to health workers (Renmans et al. 2016).

Beyond the study of "intrinsic motivation crowding-out," there is at best mixed evidence that paying health workers for performance improves health worker motivation in low-income settings. A systematic review of 35 peer-reviewed articles (Renmans et al. 2016) points toward contradictory findings from evaluations and calls for more research on the influence of the context and design of PBF schemes. Further, considering that PBF intervention packages often consist of many elements in addition to financial incentives, it has been difficult to disentangle the effects of pure incentives from increased autonomy (Ireland, Paul, and Dujardin 2011; Lohmann et al. 2018). Renmans et al. (2017) argue that viewing PBF exclusively as a payment-related incentive is inadequate and the different aspects and implications of the broad PBF package should be explained to unpack the effects on worker motivation. Binyaruka, Lohmann, and De Allegri (2020) emphasize the need to assess how PBF works across settings as well as within settings, by studying the heterogeneous effects of PBF on different cadres of health workers and health facilities.

Against this background, the rest of this section presents experimental evidence (from five randomized controlled trials and one nonrandomized controlled trial experiment) of the impact of PBF on health worker motivation, satisfaction, and well-being in four countries in Sub-Saharan Africa

(Cameroon, Nigeria, Zambia, and Zimbabwe) and two in Central Asia (the Kyrgyz Republic and Tajikistan), using data from health worker surveys. Aside from the contrast with PBF, these experimental settings also enable a comparison of pure control facilities with PBF, using difference-in-differences across multiple contexts. Box 5.3 presents the details on how worker motivation and satisfaction were measured and standardized across these six studies.

The section also examines whether there is any evidence of "intrinsic motivation crowding-out" in the context of PBF given the salience that this phenomenon has attained in the field. This is investigated by unpacking the overall measure of motivation into subconstructs of motivation for each of the six countries.

Box 5.3   In Focus: Measurement of worker motivation and satisfaction

The six-country study consistently measured health worker motivation and satisfaction using Likert scales and their well-being using the WHO-5 Well-Being Index. For the motivation scale, respondents were asked to what extent they agreed with statements such as "staff willingly share their expertise with other members" and could respond with (1) most of the time (=5), (2) more than half the time (=4), (3) less than half the time (=3), (4) only rarely (=2), and (5) never (=1).[a] Similarly, to assess job satisfaction, respondents were asked to what extent they were satisfied with different aspects of their life while working in a health facility.

To demonstrate, an example of a statement for the satisfaction scale is "working relationships with other facility staff," to which respondents could respond with (1) extremely dissatisfied (=1), (2) dissatisfied (=2), (3) indifferent (=3), (4) satisfied (=4), or (5) extremely satisfied (=5). Although many of the items overlap across countries, these scales were adapted to local contexts and languages for each country and therefore differ at the individual item level as well as the total number of items in

each scale. The motivation and satisfaction of health workers are treated as multidimensional constructs so that the effects of performance-based financing (PBF) schemes on different sources of motivation can be estimated.

Motivation subconstructs

The analysis takes a multidimensional approach, or a compositional approach, to motivation in order to unpack the sources of motivation and examine the phenomenon of "intrinsic motivation crowding-out" in the context of the six countries. The motivation scales in the six countries were not designed to capture the entire continuum of the types of motivation in self-determination theory—extracted constructs of motivation consist of elements that are autonomous (intrinsic) and controlled (extrinsic) and can at best be considered to be partly controlled and partly autonomous. Therefore, the motivation subconstructs are named based on the source of the motivation, such as empowerment or support from leadership, rather than the extent to which they are

(Continued)

Box 5.3 *continued*

autonomous or controlled or the degree to which they are self-determined.

Satisfaction subconstructs

Similar to the approach taken for motivation—although there is no theoretical framework underpinning satisfaction among health workers—the analysis breaks down the satisfaction results to understand the effect of PBF on satisfaction subconstructs, such as satisfaction with working conditions or relation with peers.

a. Statements in Likert scales that were framed negatively were recoded so that they are ordered in the same way as the rest of the statements. For instance, the statement "staff spend time complaining about work-related issues" was recoded so that 5 = *never* and 1 = *all the time.*

Results

The results indicate that compared with the control facilities, PBF did not have any systematic demotivating effects for each of the six study contexts. In Nigeria and Zimbabwe, health workers in PBF facilities experienced an approximately 5 percent statistically significant increase in motivation between baseline and endline compared with health workers in control facilities (figure 5.3). The analysis also found increases of 14 and 17 percent in health worker satisfaction between baseline and endline among health workers in PBF facilities compared with health workers in control facilities in Nigeria and Tajikistan (figure 5.4). In contrast, the analysis did not find any significant increase or decrease in health worker well-being between baseline and endline among health workers in PBF facilities compared with control facilities in five of the six countries. There is a small negative effect of PBF on health worker well-being in Zimbabwe (figure 5.5).

There is a positive effect of PBF on overall health worker motivation in Nigeria, driven by a positive impact of PBF on almost all the extracted subconstructs of (1) workplace relationships and job content, (2) self-concept, (3) procedures and performance, (4) risk taking among supervisors and peers, (5) changes, and (6) difficulties with supervisors and peers. Workplace relationships and job content consist of motivation from sources such as staff and supervisor relationships, sharing and treating each other as family, perceived complexity of the job, and perceived benefits of the job to the community. The results suggest that compared with health workers in control facilities, health workers in PBF facilities experienced a 3.8 percent increase in motivation, driven by workplace relationships and job content between baseline and endline. Self-concept consists of

Figure 5.3 Impact of PBF on health worker motivation: Treatment effect (%), PBF vs. control

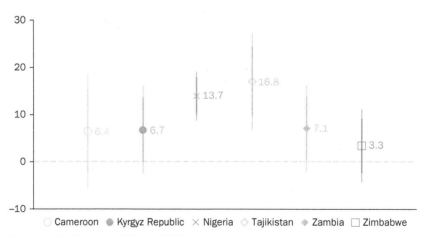

Source: Lamba, Friedman, and Kandpal 2022.

Note: The figure shows 99 and 95 percent confidence intervals. Coefficient rescaled to show percent. The individual-level controls are sex, marital status, education, cadre, and salary receipt. PBF = performance-based financing.

Figure 5.4 Impact of PBF on health worker satisfaction: Treatment effect (%), PBF vs. control

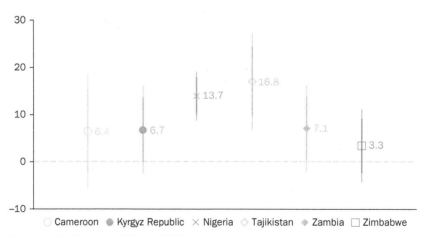

Source: Lamba, Friedman, and Kandpal 2022.

Note: The figure shows 99 and 95 percent confidence intervals. Coefficient rescaled to show percent. The individual-level controls are sex, marital status, education, cadre, and salary receipt. PBF = performance-based financing.

Figure 5.5 **Impact of PBF on health worker well-being: Treatment effect (%), PBF vs. control**

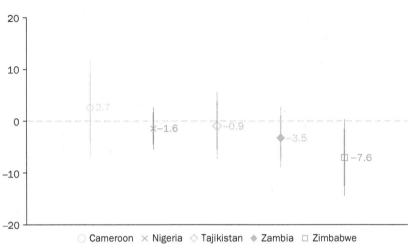

Source: Lamba, Friedman, and Kandpal 2022.

Note: The figure shows 99 and 95 percent confidence intervals. Coefficient rescaled to show percent. The individual-level controls are sex, marital status, education, cadre, and salary receipt. Data on well-being are unavailable for the Kyrgyz Republic. PBF = performance-based financing.

statements such as "I always wanted to be a health worker," "I am proud to tell others that I am a health worker," and "I am confident about my ability to do my job." The findings show that health workers in Nigerian health facilities that were part of the PBF intervention experienced a 5.3 percent increase in motivation, driven by self-concept between the baseline and endline surveys compared with health workers in control facilities. Hence, among Nigerian health workers, there is no evidence of "intrinsic motivation crowding-out." Instead, motivation driven by self-concept—a combination of intrinsic and extrinsic factors—increased. Similarly, health worker motivation driven by procedures and performance, risk taking among supervisors and peers, changes, and difficulties with supervisors and peers increased by 5, 8.1, and 8.7 percent, respectively. Box 5.4 examines the characteristics of the health workers who showed greater motivation between the baseline and endline in PBF facilities, to understand whether performance pay might be used to target certain types of workers effectively.

Box 5.4 In Focus: Heterogeneous effects of performance-based financing on motivation and satisfaction: An example from Nigeria

One way to understand how these performance-based financing (PBF) interventions affected health worker motivation, satisfaction, and well-being is through examining the heterogeneity of treatment effects among health workers in different cadres. This box presents the findings of heterogeneous effects for health workers in Nigeria. It uses difference-in-difference regression models with the addition of an interaction between broad cadres with the PBF treatment variable, to investigate the heterogeneity of effects by cadre of the health worker. This analysis helps to break down who among the health

workers exhibited an improvement in motivation between the baseline and endline in PBF facilities compared with control facilities. The following broad cadres are defined: (1) doctors/medical officers, (2) nurses/midwives, (3) community health workers, and (4) others (pharmacists, laboratory technicians, and other clinical officers).

Figure B5.4.1 shows the differences in treatment effects between doctors/medical officers (reference category) and other cadres of health workers. The findings show that overall motivation for community health workers working in

Figure B5.4.1 Impact of PBF on health worker motivation: Heterogeneity in treatment effects (%), by cadre, PBF vs. control

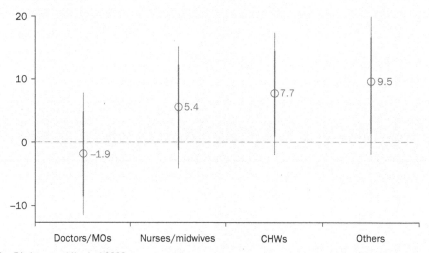

Source: Lamba, Friedman, and Kandpal 2022.

Note: The figure shows 99 and 95 percent confidence intervals. The individual-level controls are sex, marital status, education, cadre, and salary receipt. CHWs = community health workers; MOs = medical officers; PBF = performance-based financing.

(Continued)

Box 5.4 *continued*

PBF facilities increased by 5.8 percent (7.7 – 1.9) between baseline and endline compared with community health workers working in control facilities. Similarly, overall motivation for other health workers (pharmacists, laboratory technicians, and others) working in PBF facilities increased by 7.6 percent between baseline and endline compared with health workers in these cadres working in control facilities. The PBF intervention did not have a statistically significant effect on the motivation for doctors/medical officers or nurses/midwives.

In contrast, in Zimbabwe, the positive effect of PBF on overall health worker motivation is solely driven by recognition (6.9 percent increase) and inspiring work environment (8.5 percent increase). The results also show a positive effect of PBF on motivation driven by self-concept.[2] Although these constructs are not comparable, the results conclusively do not provide any evidence of "intrinsic motivation crowding-out" in Nigeria and Zimbabwe. In addition, there is no statistically significant effect of PBF on the subconstructs of motivation in the other four countries—Cameroon, the Kyrgyz Republic, Tajikistan, and Zambia—except for a reduction in motivation from negative peer attitudes in Tajikistan.

Among the countries where increases are observed in health worker satisfaction in PBF facilities between baseline and endline compared with the control facilities in figure 5.2, these appear to be driven by increases in health worker satisfaction with working conditions. There are very large increases in health worker satisfaction with working conditions of 32 percent in Nigeria and 20 percent in Zambia. Although there is no increase in overall health worker satisfaction in Cameroon, when the analysis unpacks satisfaction into subconstructs, the findings show that health workers in PBF facilities reported an increase in satisfaction with working conditions between baseline and endline compared with those in the control facilities. Finally, the analysis estimates a 10 percent increase in health worker satisfaction with rewards and benefits among health workers in PBF facilities compared with the control facilities in Nigeria.

PBF, quality of care, and idle capacity

Having established that PBF does not appear to reduce health worker motivation or satisfaction, this section turns to estimating the impact of PBF approaches on quality of care. In theory, PBF may increase quality of care by improving structural quality, increasing health worker knowledge, and eliciting greater effort. PBF programs explicitly provide funding for structural quality improvements, through enhanced financing to the facility and typically by including some measures of structural quality in the checklist. For instance, most PBF programs financially reward facilities for having correctly stored and available drugs and supplies, functioning essential equipment, and even essential infrastructure like running water and electricity. Concomitantly, the PBF pilots give facilities an infrastructure budget and autonomy over the budget so that they may respond to stockouts or equipment failure in a timely manner. Theoretically, PBF pilots could also improve health knowledge by increasing the salience of certain protocols or through supportive supervision or verification visits. In addition, most PBF pilots include at least some measures of process quality that are directly incentivized.

As reviewed above in the discussion of the impacts of PBF on the quantity of health service delivery, the literature shows that PBF significantly improves at least some measures of structural capacity across the board, highlighting the need for continued investments in facility infrastructure. However, the literature finds little evidence of impact on health worker knowledge. Finally, the evidence on the effectiveness of PBF on effective coverage or process quality is mixed. As such, although PBF may have alleviated some structural constraints, it has not lifted knowledge constraints.

This section uses the know-can-do gap framework to assess the impact of PBF on idle capacity. There are sufficient endline data—that is, surveys that included health facility assessments and direct clinical observations of patient-provider interactions—for Cameroon and Nigeria. The results are presented in figure 5.6. Idle capacity represents the scope for improvement, and a reduction in idle capacity is desirable from a quality of care standpoint. Thus, reductions in idle capacity would lie to the left of the zero vertical line in the figure, and increases in idle capacity, that is, a worsening of quality, would lie to the right. Further, a summary index of idle capacity is represented above the dotted line. Below the dotted line are the subcomponents that go into the summary index.

Figure 5.6 Impacts of performance-based financing on idle capacity—or the know-can-do gap—in Cameroon and Nigeria

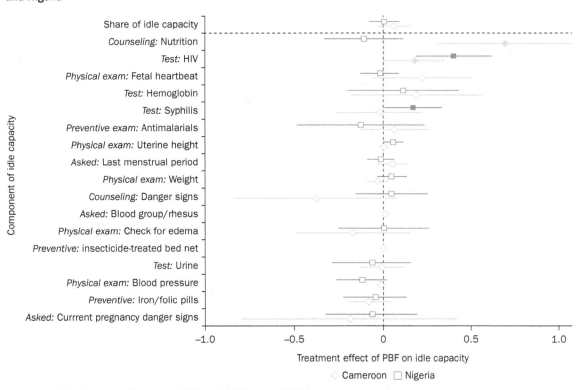

Sources: World Bank, based on Khanna et al. 2021 and de Walque et al. 2021.

Note: Markers above the dashed line indicate a summary effect. Solid markers indicate statistically significant estimates ($p < .05$); markers that are open indicate imprecise estimates. "Whiskers" around markers represent 95% confidence intervals. PBF = performance-based financing.

Overall, the findings do not show that PBF reduces idle capacity compared with business-as-usual. If anything, they show a small increase in idle capacity in Cameroon. Unpacking these overall estimates, significant and large increases are estimated for idle capacity in both Cameroon and Nigeria for some dimensions of clinical quality. For instance, in Cameroon, a large increase is estimated in idle capacity in nutrition counseling, although the analysis also estimates a sizable reduction in idle capacity for counseling for danger signs. In Nigeria, there are increases in idle capacity for essential testing, including for HIV and syphilis. While the increases in idle capacity may be cause for concern, they may at least partially be explained by the role played by out-of-pocket payments at baseline. For instance, in Nigeria, at baseline the average out-of-pocket payment was US$2.40 (Kandpal et al. 2019), although in Cameroon out-of-pocket payments are not typically made for ANC (de Walque et al. 2021). The PBF intervention in both countries included the removal of user fees, but this displaced a greater source of revenue in Nigeria. To some extent, health workers may have compensated by cutting back on some dimensions of the quality of care, including tests for which they may have received additional payments from the patients, as the health workers' income was less dependent on these payments.

Conclusions

This chapter considered the evidence available from impact evaluations of PBF pilots, as well as from the academic literature, to shed light on several questions about the use of PBF to improve effective coverage. It began with a stylized theoretical discussion of the various channels through which PBF interacts with the health system to possibly produce changes in population health. The channels discussed are consistent with an early hypothesis that PBF would improve health worker effort and thus the quality of care provided in primary health care settings (Fritsche, Soeters, and Meessen 2014). At the same time, these PBF programs have come under criticism on several counts, in particular their complexity of design and implementation, donor-driven backing, and potential to degrade health systems by crowding out intrinsic health worker motivation (Shroff, Bigdeli, and Meessen 2017; Ireland, Paul, and Dujardin 2011; Meessen, Soucat, and Sekabaraga 2011; Paul et al. 2018; Paul, Brown, and Ridde 2020). The chapter thus considered impacts on service utilization and quality of care as well as health worker motivation and satisfaction.

A review of the evidence and results from the primary analysis showed that PBF improves at least some measures of structural capacity, highlighting the need for continued investments in facility infrastructure. Then, the chapter delved further into the evidence on PBF schemes and their impacts on effective coverage. It found that in most contexts, PBF leads to some improvements in terms of coverage. However, the chapter found limited and mixed evidence that PBF has a significant impact on effective coverage or quality of care, although it did not find that PBF negatively impacts health worker motivation. Perhaps the most salient takeaway from this analysis is that heterogeneity in impact highlights the complexity of implementation. Chapter 6 further investigates the impact of PBF and compares it with policy alternatives such as demand-side incentives and direct facility financing.

Notes

1. As discussed in chapter 3, idle capacity is the proportion of all necessary components of antenatal care that are not provided by workers despite having all the equipment, supplies, and knowledge necessary to provide the care.
2. Recognition consists of the statements "it is important for me that the community recognizes my work as a professional" and "it is important for me that my peers recognize my work as a professional." Inspiring work environment consists of the statements "I am proud to be working for this health facility," "I am glad that I am working for this facility rather than in other facilities," and "this health facility inspires me to do my very best on the job." Self-concept in the Zimbabwean context is composed of the statements "I complete my tasks efficiently and effectively," "I am a hard worker," and "I am punctual about coming to work." Note the difference between the composition of the subconstruct self-concept across Nigeria and Zimbabwe.

References

African Union. 2014. *Universal Health Coverage in Africa—From Concept to Action*. Addis Ababa: World Health Organization.

Ariely, D., A. Bracha, and S. Meier. 2009. "Doing Good or Doing Well? Image Motivation and Monetary Incentives in Behaving Prosocially." *American Economic Review* 99 (1): 544–55.

Basinga, P., P. J. Gertler, A. Binagwaho, A. L. Soucat, J. Sturdy, and C. M. Vermeersch. 2011. "Effect on Maternal and Child Health Services in Rwanda of Payment to Primary Health-Care Providers for Performance: An Impact Evaluation." *The Lancet* 377 (9775): 1421–28.

Bauhoff, S., and E. Kandpal. 2021. "Information, Loss Framing, and Spillovers in Pay-for-Performance Contracts." Policy Research Working Paper 9687, World Bank, Washington, DC.

Bertone, M. P., and B. Meessen. 2013. "Studying the Link between Institutions and Health System Performance: A Framework and an Illustration with the Analysis of Two Performance-Based Financing Schemes in Burundi." *Health Policy and Planning* 28 (8): 847–57.

Binyaruka, P., J. Lohmann, and M. De Allegri. 2020. "Evaluating Performance-Based Financing in Low-Income and Middle-Income Countries: The Need to Look beyond Average Effect." *BMJ Global Health* 5 (8): e003136.

Borghi, J., J. Lohmann, E. Dale, F. Meheus, J. Goudge, K. Oboirien, and A. Kuwawenaruwa. 2018. "How to Do (or Not to Do) … Measuring Health Worker Motivation in Surveys in Low- and Middle-Income Countries." *Health Policy and Planning* 33 (2): 192–203.

Celhay, P., P. Gertler, P. Giovagnoli, and C. Vermeersch. 2019. "Long-Run Effects of Temporary Incentives on Medical Care Productivity." *American Economic Journal: Applied Economics*. 11 (3): 92–127.

Cortez, R. 2009. "Argentina: Provincial Maternal and Child Health Insurance—A Results-Based Financing Project at Work." En Breve No. 150, World Bank, Washington, DC.

Cortez, R., and D. Romero. 2013. *Increasing Utilization of Health Care Services among the Uninsured Population: The Plan Nacer Program.* Universal Health Coverage Study Series. Washington, DC: World Bank.

de Walque, D., P. J. Robyn, H. Saidou, G. Sorgho, and M. Steenland. 2021. "Looking into the Performance-Based Financing Black Box: Evidence from an Impact Evaluation in the Health Sector in Cameroon." *Health Policy and Planning* 36 (6): 835–47.

Deci, E. L. 1972. "The Effects of Contingent and Noncontingent Rewards and Controls on Intrinsic Motivation." *Organizational Behavior and Human Performance* 8 (2): 217–29.

Deci, E. L., R. Koestner, and R. M. Ryan. 1999. "A Meta-Analytic Review of Experiments Examining the Effects of Extrinsic Rewards on Intrinsic Motivation." *Psychological Bulletin* 125 (6): 627.

Deci, E. L., and R. M. Ryan. 1985. "The General Causality Orientations Scale: Self-Determination in Personality." *Journal of Research in Personality* 19 (2): 109–34.

Diaconu, K., J. Falconer, A. Verbel, A. Fretheim, and S. Witter. 2020. "Paying for Performance to Improve the Delivery of Health Interventions in Low- and Middle-Income Countries." *Cochrane Database of Systematic Reviews* 12: CD007899.

Diamond, J. 2013. "Good Practice Note on Sequencing PFM Reforms." PEFA Secretariat, World Bank, Washington, DC.

English, M., G. Irimus, A. Agweyu, D. Gathara, J. Oliwa, P. Ayieko, F. Were, et al. 2016. "Building Learning Health Systems to Accelerate Research and Improve Outcomes of Clinical Care in Low- and Middle-Income Countries." *PLoS Medicine* 13 (4): e1001991.

Falisse, J.-B., J. Ndayishimiye, V. Kamenyero, and M. Bossuyt. 2014. "Performance-Based Financing in the Context of Selective Free Health-Care: An Evaluation of Its Effects on the Use of Primary Health-Care Services in Burundi Using Routine Data." *Health Policy and Planning* 30: 1251–60.

Fiszbein, A., P. I. Giovagnoli, and I. Adúrez. 2003. "Argentina's Crisis and Its Impact on Household Welfare." *CEPAL Review* 2003 (79): 143–58.

Frey, B. S., and R. Jegen. 2001. "Motivation Crowding Theory." *Journal of Economic Surveys* 15 (5): 589–611.

Friedman, J., A. Das, and R. Mutasa. 2017. "Rewarding Provider Performance to Improve Quality and Coverage of Maternal and Child Health Outcomes." Zimbabwe Results-Based Financing Pilot Program: Evidence to Inform Policy and Management Decisions. World Bank, Washington, DC.

Friedman J., and E. Kandpal. 2021. "The Roles of Financial Incentives and Performance Monitoring in Improving the Quality of Health Care: Evidence from a National Pay-for-Performance Trial in the Kyrgyz Republic." World Bank, Washington, DC.

Friedman, J., J. Qamruddin, C. Chansa, and A. K. Das. 2016. "Impact Evaluation of Zambia's Health Results-Based Financing Pilot Project." World Bank, Washington, DC.

Friedman, J., and R. M. Scheffler. 2016. "Pay for Performance in Health Systems: Theory, Evidence and Case Studies." In *World Scientific Handbook of Global Health Economics and Public Policy, Volume 3: Health System Characteristics and Performance*, edited by R. M. Scheffler, 295–332. World Scientific.

Fritsche, G. B., R. Soeters, and B. Meessen. 2014. *Performance-Based Financing Toolkit*. Washington, DC: World Bank.

Gage, A., and S. Bauhoff. 2020. "Health Systems in Low-Income Countries Will Struggle to Protect Health Workers from COVID-19." Center for Global Development, Washington, DC.

Gertler, P., P. Giovagnoli, and S. Martinez. 2014. "Rewarding Provider Performance to Enable a Healthy Start to Life: Evidence from Argentina's Plan Nacer." Policy Research Working Paper 6884, World Bank, Washington, DC.

Gneezy, U., and A. Rustichini. 2000. "Pay Enough or Don't Pay at All." *Quarterly Journal of Economics* 115 (3): 791–810.

Heard, A. 2012. "Argentina Builds on Plan Nacer to Evolve into Plan Sumar." RBFHealth, World Bank, Washington, DC. www.RBFhealth.org.

Himmelstein, D. U., D. Ariely, and S. Woolhandler. 2014. "Pay-for-Performance: Toxic to Quality? Insights from Behavioral Economics." *International Journal of Health Services* 44 (2): 203–14.

Holmstrom, B., and P. Milgrom. 1991. "Multitask Principal-Agent Analyses: Incentive Contracts, Asset Ownership, and Job Design." *Journal of Law, Economics, and Organization* 7: 24–52.

Huillery, E., and J. Seban. 2021. "Financial Incentives, Efforts, and Performances in the Health Sector: Experimental Evidence from the Democratic Republic of Congo." *Economic Development and Cultural Change* 69 (3): 1115–64.

Ireland, M., E. Paul, and B. Dujardin. 2011. "Can Performance-Based Financing Be Used to Reform Health Systems in Developing Countries?" *Bulletin of the World Health Organization* 89: 695–98.

Kaila, H., and E. Kandpal. 2021. "A Pay-for-Performance Trial in Nigeria Saved Maternal and Neonatal Lives." World Bank, Washington, DC.

Kalk, A., F. A. Paul, and E. Grabosch. 2010. "'Paying for Performance' in Rwanda: Does It Pay Off?" *Tropical Medicine & International Health* 15 (2): 182–90.

Kandpal, E. 2016. "Completed Impact Evaluations and Emerging Lessons from the Health Results Innovation Trust Fund Learning Portfolio." RBFHealth, World Bank, Washington, DC.

Kandpal, E., B. P. Loevinsohn, C. M. Vermeersch, E. Pradhan, M. Khanna, M. K. Conlon, and W. Zeng. 2019. "Impact Evaluation of Nigeria State Health Investment Project." No. 135384, World Bank, Washington, DC.

Khanna, M., B. Loevinsohn, E. Pradhan, O. Fadeyibi, K. McGee, O. Odutolu, G. B. Fristche, et al. 2021. "Improving Maternal and Neonatal Health in Nigeria: Performance-Based Financing versus Decentralized Facility Financing." *BMC Medicine* 19: Article 224.

Lamba, S., J. Friedman, E. Kandpal 2022. "The Effect of Performance-Pay on Health Worker Motivation and Satisfaction: Experimental Evidence from Five Countries." World Bank, Washington, DC.

Lazear, E. P. 2000. "Performance Pay and Productivity." *American Economic Review* 90 (5): 1346–61.

Leonard, K. L., and M. C. Masatu. 2017. "Changing Health Care Provider Performance through Measurement." *Social Science & Medicine* 181: 54–65.

Lohmann, J., N. Houlfort, and M. De Allegri. 2016. "Crowding Out or No Crowding Out? A Self-Determination Theory Approach to Health Worker Motivation in Performance-Based Financing." *Social Science & Medicine* 169: 1–8.

Lohmann, J., D. Wilhelm, C. Kambala, S. Brenner, A. S. Muula, and M. De Allegri. 2018. "'The Money Can Be a Motivator, to Me a Little, but Mostly PBF Just Helps Me to Do Better in My Job': An Exploration of the Motivational Mechanisms of Performance-Based Financing for Health Workers in Malawi." *Health Policy and Planning* 33 (2): 183–91.

Maisey, S., N. Steel, R. Marsh, S. Gillam, R. Fleetcroft, and A. Howe. 2008. "Effects of Payment for Performance in Primary Care: Qualitative Interview Study." *Journal of Health Services Research & Policy* 13 (3): 133–39.

Malin, J., A. Nguyen, S. E. Ban, V. Willey, R. Quimbo, J. Barron, P. Inches, et al. 2015. "Impact of Enhanced Reimbursement on Provider Participation a Cancer Care Quality Program and Adherence to Cancer Treatment Pathways in a Commercial Health Plan." *Journal of Clinical Oncology* 33 (15, suppl): 6571.

Meessen, B., A. Soucat, and C. Sekabaraga. 2011. "Performance-Based Financing: Just a Donor Fad or a Catalyst towards Comprehensive Health-Care Reform?" *Bulletin of the World Health Organization* 89: 153–56. PMID:21346927. doi:10.2471/BLT.10.077339.

Mendelson, A., K. Kondo, C. Damberg, A. Low, M. Motúapuaka, M. Freeman, M. O'Neil, et al. 2017. "The Effects of Pay-for-Performance Programs on Health, Health Care Use, and Processes of Care: A Systematic Review." *Annals of Internal Medicine* 166 (5): 341–53.

Ministerio de Salud Argentina. 2013. "El programa SUMAR es más salud." Argentine Ministry of Health, Buenos Aires, Argentina. www.msal.gov.ar.

Ngo, D. K., and S. Bauhoff. 2021. "The Medium-Run and Scale-Up Effects of Performance-Based Financing: An Extension of Rwanda's 2006 Trial Using Secondary Data." *World Development* 139: 105264.

Ogbuoji, O., I. Bharali, N. Emery, and K. Kennedy McDade. 2019. "Closing Africa's Health Financing Gap." *Brookings Institution Blog*, March 1. https://www.brookings.edu/blog/future-development/2019/03/01/closing-africas-health-financing-gap/.

Olafsdottir, S., E. Bakhtiari, and E. Barman. 2014. "Public or Private? The Role of the State and Civil Society in Health and Health Inequalities across Nations." *Social Science & Medicine* 123: 174–81.

Paul, E., L. Albert, B. N'Sambuka Bisala, O. Bodson, E. Bonnet, P. Bossyns, S. Colombo, et al. 2018. "Performance-Based Financing in Low-Income and Middle-Income Countries: Isn't It Time for a Rethink?" *BMJ Global Health* 3 (1): e00064.

Paul, E., G. W. Brown, and V. Ridde. 2020. "Misunderstandings and Ambiguities in Strategic Purchasing in Low- and Middle-Income Countries." *International Journal of Health Planning and Management* 35 (5): 1001–08.

Peabody, J. W., R. Shimkhada, S. Quimbo, O. Solon, X. Javier, and C. McCulloch. 2014. "The Impact of Performance Incentives on Child Health Outcomes: Results from a Cluster Randomized Controlled Trial in the Philippines." *Health Policy and Planning* 29 (5): 615–21.

Rabin, M. 2000. "Diminishing Marginal Utility of Wealth Cannot Explain Risk Aversion." In *Choices, Values, and Frames*, edited by D. Kahneman and A. Tversky, 202–06. New York: Cambridge University Press.

Reich, M. R., J. Harris, N. Ikegami, A. Maeda, C. Cashin, E. C. Araujo, K. Takemi, and T. G. Evans. 2016. "Moving towards Universal Health Coverage: Lessons from 11 Country Studies." *The Lancet* 387 (10020): 811–16.

Renmans, D., N. Holvoet, B. Criel, and B. Meessen. 2017. "Performance-Based Financing: The Same Is Different." *Health Policy and Planning* 32 (6): 860–68.

Renmans, D., N. Holvoet, C. G. Orach, and B. Criel. 2016. "Opening the 'Black Box' of Performance-Based Financing in Low- and Lower Middle-Income Countries: A Review of the Literature." *Health Policy and Planning* 31 (9): 1297–1309.

Ridde, V., L. Gautier, A.-M. Turcotte-Tremblay, I. Sieleunou, and E. Paul. 2018. "Performance-Based Financing in Africa: Time to Test Measures for Equity." *International Journal of Health Services* 48 (3): 549–61.

Savedoff, W. D., and S. Partner. 2010. "Basic Economics of Results-Based Financing in Health." Social Insight, Bath, ME.

Shen, G. C., H. T. Nguyen, A. Das, N. Sachingongu, C. Chansa, J. Qamruddin, and J. Friedman. 2017. "Incentives to Change: Effects of Performance-Based Financing on Health Workers in Zambia." *Human Resources for Health* 15 (1): 20. https://doi.org/10.1186/s12960-017-0179-2.

Shroff, Z. C., M. Bigdeli, and B. Meessen. 2017. "From Scheme to System (Part 2): Findings from Ten Countries on the Policy Evolution of Results-Based Financing in Health Systems." *Health Systems & Reform* 3 (2): 137–47.

Titmuss, R. 1970. *The Gift Relationship: From Human Blood to Social Policy.* Bristol, UK: Policy Press.

Turcotte-Tremblay, A.-M., J. Spagnolo, M. De Allegri, and V. Ridde. 2016. "Does Performance-Based Financing Increase Value for Money in Low- and Middle-Income Countries? A Systematic Review." *Health Economics Review* 6 (1): 1–18.

World Health Organization. 1978. *Report of the International Conference on Primary Health Care.* Alma-Ata, USSR, September 6–12.

World Health Organization. 2010. *The World Health Report: Health Systems Financing: The Path to Universal Coverage.* Geneva: WHO.

World Health Organization. 2013. *State of Health Financing in the African Region.* Geneva: WHO.

World Health Organization. 2018. *Delivering Quality Health Services: A Global Imperative.* Geneva: WHO, Organisation for Economic Co-operation and Development, and World Bank.

Zitti, T., L. Gautier, A. Coulibaly, and V. Ridde. 2019. "Stakeholder Perceptions and Context of the Implementation of Performance-Based Financing in District Hospitals in Mali." *International Journal of Health Policy and Management* 8 (10): 583–92.

CHAPTER 6

Policy Alternatives to Performance-Based Financing

Introduction

The literature provides evidence of some gains in coverage and effective coverage from the introduction of performance-based financing (PBF), typically when compared with business-as-usual. However, these are not ordinarily the only two alternatives available to policy makers. When assessing the overall evidence on PBF interventions, a relevant question thus becomes, what are the policy alternatives or complements to PBF? As this chapter shows, many of the gains from PBF interventions become less salient when the impacts of other policy alternatives are considered. For instance, a growing body of high-quality evidence demonstrates the importance of approaches such as user-fee removal and engaging the local community in overseeing the local health facility, whether in combination with financial incentives on the supply side or alone (Falisse et al. 2014; Björkman and Svensson 2009). A demand-side alternative or complement to PBF may be cash transfers to patients or care seekers. Similarly, studies in Cameroon (de Walque et al. 2021) and the Kyrgyz Republic (Friedman and Kandpal 2021) examine the potential of supportive supervision. In Cameroon, additional financing, whether performance based or unconditional, drove program gains, but in the Kyrgyz Republic pilot (box 6.1), supervision, even without financial incentives, improved process quality, although health outcomes only improved in the PBF arm.

This chapter thus investigates the evidence on PBF's impact relative to other key interventions designed to increase effective coverage in health. It first presents results from a systematic review and meta-analysis of demand- and supply-side financial incentives to increase the use of reproductive, maternal, and child health services. Next, the chapter conducts a detailed

Box 6.1   In Focus: Kyrgyz Republic PBF pilot

In the Kyrgyz Republic performance-based financing (PBF) pilot—as well as in an additional study arm in Cameroon—a similar supervision approach was used in the PBF and enhanced supervision arms (Friedman and Kandpal 2021). It included a hospital-level PBF intervention that paid only for the quality of maternal and child health services. In both the Kyrgyz Republic and Cameroon, the enhanced supervision received no additional funding whatsoever. The hypothesis behind such a supportive supervision arm was that performance monitoring and supervision may affect health worker performance by increasing information about best practices and signaling to staff that their work is deserving of supervisor attention. Supportive supervision, if found effective at improving quality and outcomes, could thus represent an attractive nonpecuniary alternative to PBF, particularly in under-resourced settings.

The impact evaluation in the Kyrgyz Republic assessed the effectiveness of enhanced supervision against enhanced supervision plus PBF as well as business-as-usual in improving the quality of labor and delivery services in the country. It used rich, facility-level data on quality of care from two rounds of facility surveys with administrative data from the Kyrgyz National Birth Registry on the outcomes of all births in the study hospitals

(all 63 secondary hospitals in the country participated in the trial) during the study period. The facility-level data include direct observations of labor and delivery services, allowing the researchers to link provider practices to changes observed in birth outcomes.

The results suggest that while benchmarking performance and supportive feedback can improve clinical process quality, only by linking these efforts to financial incentives through PBF did population health outcomes significantly increase. These results contrast with the findings of many of the other studies discussed in this report. This may not be surprising—the Kyrgyz Republic context is different from the low-income settings that form the bulk of the evidence. It is a lower-middle-income country with the pilot being implemented in secondary hospitals rather than at the primary level. This setup makes it considerably closer to that found in high- and middle-income countries where performance pay has been shown to be more effective (Doran and Roland 2011; Gertler, Giovagnoli, and Martinez 2014). The fact that the Kyrgyz Republic PBF pilot led to significant gains suggests that as countries—and their health systems—develop, PBF approaches may become a more suitable policy option than direct financing of health facilities.

comparison of PBF with the direct financing of health facilities (DFF), a key policy counterfactual on the supply side in which additional funding is made available to frontline health facilities without conditionality, that is, without linking disbursements to increases in quantity and improvements in quality.

In addition, the chapter touches on why institutional deliveries may be the one indicator that is consistently improved by successful PBF interventions over and above DFF-type approaches. It also discusses potential complementarities of the PBF and DFF approaches and concludes with a consideration of PBF's impacts on health systems and how these impacts may be better understood. This discussion touches on why typical intervention evaluations may not successfully capture the entirety of a PBF program's impacts—particularly those at the system level—and how policy makers and researchers can begin to understand these impacts in the absence of standard evaluative evidence.

Systematic review and meta-analysis of demand- and supply-side financial incentives

The push toward performance-linked financing, such as through PBF, in the health sector is occurring in an environment where demand-side financial incentive mechanisms aimed at households, such as maternity care vouchers and conditional cash transfer (CCT) schemes, are also being introduced and scaled up. For example, faced with low screening rates for noncommunicable diseases despite the introduction of incentives on the supply side and mass communication campaigns, the Armenian government piloted and tested demand-side incentives and interventions to increase screening rates for hypertension and diabetes (box 6.2).

The different financing approaches have the common aim to lower the relative price of accessing or providing care relative to income. Supply- and demand-side financial incentives are to some degree complementary but not perfectly. They can be complements if they relieve different financial or behavioral constraints, but they may also serve as substitutes. For example, incentivizing patients might also reduce effort by providers to perform outreach activities, or it might reduce quality by increasing volumes at the facilities.

Thus, policy makers can legitimately ask whether it is wiser to use supply- or demand-side financial incentives. As illustrated in figure 6.1 and acknowledging that in practice some of the distinctions across programs can be less clear-cut, financial incentives can be described as varying by whether they operate on the supply or demand side and whether they reduce the patient's user fees, increase the household's income, or affect the provider's income (Neelsen et al. 2021). For example, performance pay approaches, including PBF programs, reward providers of primary or secondary care reproductive, maternal, and child health (RMCH) services. Vouchers give beneficiaries free or subsidized access to RMCH services for which providers are reimbursed on a fee-for-service basis, while CCTs

Box 6.2 In Focus: Demand-side interventions and incentives for increasing preventive screening for noncommunicable diseases in Armenia

More people around the world are dying from noncommunicable diseases than ever before. These diseases, which include cancer, chronic respiratory diseases, diabetes, and heart disease, prematurely kill more than 15 million people between ages 30 and 69 each year. The largest disease burden of noncommunicable diseases is in low- and middle-income countries, where 85 percent of related deaths now occur (WHO 2020), putting an extra strain on governments' health budgets—and families—due to medical expenditures, productivity losses, disability, and deaths. Although early screenings can lead to life-saving treatment, screening rates tend to be low, and discovery of these diseases thus often occurs too late for effective and efficient treatment.

Many countries, such as Armenia, have made efforts in recent years to tackle noncommunicable diseases by launching mass media campaigns and equipping medical providers to detect and treat these diseases. Despite these efforts, most people are still not getting tested. Policy makers are therefore looking for cost-effective approaches to motivate people to go to the doctor and get screened, and they are teaming up with behavioral scientists to answer key questions such as the following: Are people more compelled to get tested if they know how many of their peers have done so? Do they respond to a personal invitation? What about a small financial incentive?

In an individually randomized controlled trial designed to shed light on these questions, researchers tested the impact of four approaches: (1) a personal invitation for patients to come in for screening, (2) a personal invitation that also conveyed statistics on how many of the patient's peers have been screened, (3) a personal invitation with an unconditional pharmacy voucher labeled as an encouragement to get screened, and (4) a personal invitation and conditional pharmacy voucher that could only be used after the patient went for screening (de Walque, Chukwuma et al. 2022). The study participants were individuals ages 35–68 who had not been screened in the past 12 months.

After five months, people in the control group had very low screening rates: a mere 3.5 percent of people got screened for diabetes and hypertension. The personal invitation increased this rate to about 18.5 percent, with no additional impact from the unconditional voucher or the statistics about peers' screening. The pharmacy voucher that was conditional on screening, however, was the most effective, nearly doubling the percentage of people who got screened, to 34.7 percent. Since it was more expensive to implement, however, the conditional voucher and the personal invitation alone were equally cost-effective. Overall, the findings suggest that very simple personalized invitations and conditional financial incentives can lead to more life-saving health screenings in Armenia.

This research finds that conditional incentives and personalized invitations can substantially increase screening for diabetes and hypertension for those who have not been screened recently. Adding a conditional incentive to the personal invitation doubled its effectiveness. The two approaches were equally cost-effective. It is likely that these interventions would also be effective in other settings where screening rates are low and people have not responded to the usual mass communication campaigns encouraging them to go for preventive health screenings.

Figure 6.1 Typology and theory of change of included financial incentive interventions

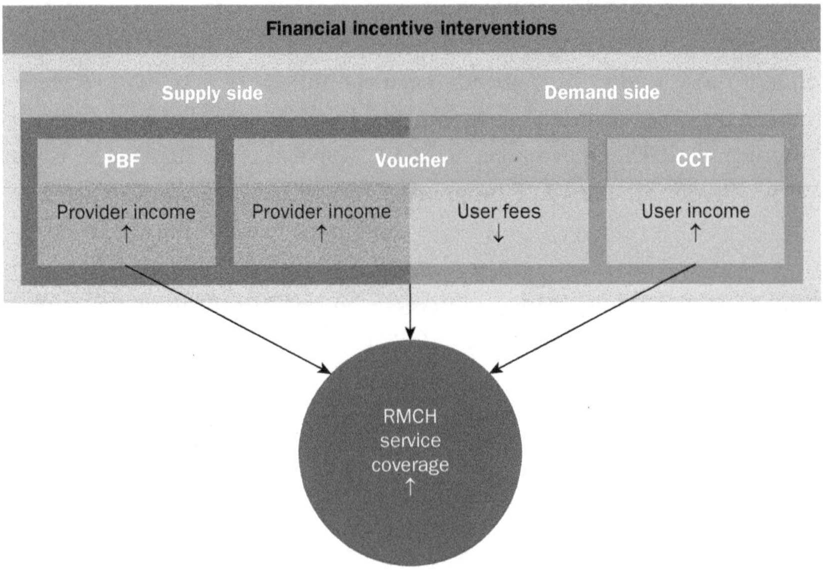

Source: Reproduced from Neelsen et al. 2021.

Note: CCT = conditional cash transfer; PBF = performance-based financing; RMCH = reproductive, maternal, and child health.

financially reward enrollees for complying with maternal and child health (MCH) service use conditions.

Performance pay, included in PBF programs, is thus essentially a supply-side intervention that increases health providers' income when more and higher quality–targeted services are provided to patients, but it does not directly affect the user fees paid by households or their income. CCTs act on the demand side by increasing the household's income when they use targeted services, but they do not directly increase providers' incomes. Vouchers play a role on both the supply and demand sides: when a voucher is redeemed for specific services, the fee paid by patients is reduced and the income received by providers increases.

A growing evaluative literature has explored the effectiveness of financial incentive interventions on health service coverage in low- and middle-income countries (LMICs), and an increasing number of reviews are available that synthesize this growing evidence base. For the emerging literature on PBF, the most recent comprehensive review (Diaconu et al. 2020), for which literature searches were conducted in 2018, finds the evidence on RMCH service coverage to be inconsistent and of low overall certainty. The literature on demand-side financial incentive schemes, including CCT programs and maternal voucher schemes, is older and more extensive, and some of those studies have already been the subject of systematic reviews (see, for example, Gaarder, Glassman, and Todd 2010; Bellows et al. 2016; Bassani et al. 2013; Glassman et al. 2013; Gopalan et al. 2014). The latest reviews of voucher and CCT programs—for which literature searches date back five years or longer—find more consistent positive impacts, particularly on family planning (vouchers) and maternity care, whereas effects on childhood vaccination are inconclusive (de Souza Cruz, Azevedo de Moura, and Soares Neto 2017; Hunter et al. 2017; Taaffe, Longosz, and Wilson 2017).

Except for a small number of CCT program reviews (Gaarder, Glassman, and Todd 2010; Bassani et al. 2013; Glassman et al. 2013; Oyo-Ita et al. 2016) and one review of voucher impacts on family planning (Belaid et al. 2016), the available reviews are narrative in nature. Due to this absence of quantitative syntheses, the average magnitude and heterogeneity of effect sizes of financial incentive interventions, which form important parameters for policy decisions, remain unknown to date. This section summarizes the findings of a recent systematic review and meta-analysis that attempts to close this knowledge gap as follows (Neelsen et al. 2021). First, conducting a meta-analysis across PBF, voucher, and CCT schemes can determine whether financial incentives, on average, improve access to RMCH service utilization. Next, the meta-analysis allows estimation of the mean effects of PBF, voucher, and CCT interventions for increasing RMCH service utilization. Finally, the analysis investigates selected contextual and program features of financial incentive programs for RMCH service utilization impacts.

Previous systematic reviews of financial incentives for RMCH have typically cited dissimilarities across interventions as a reason not to conduct quantitative syntheses of program impacts. However, if outcomes and interventions are similar enough, meta-analysis is indicated as soon as two studies are available (Valentine, Pigott, and Rothstein 2010; Higgins and Green 2011; Ryan and Cochrane Consumers and Communication Review Group 2016). As discussed in this chapter, although the outcome variable definitions are very similar across the studies in this review, differences in intervention designs and contexts can be substantial even within the three intervention types.

While cognizant of this limitation, a quantitative synthesis of individual studies is still useful and timely, as financial incentive interventions as a whole, and each of the three intervention groups individually, have well-defined common characteristics (figure 6.1). Because of these common features, policy discussions typically aggregate "financial incentives in health" into three general groups: PBF, vouchers, and CCT programs. Obtaining mean effect sizes through meta-analysis of all available evidence is therefore preferable over the ad-hoc, implicit aggregation of often selective study results, which is frequently undertaken.

Methodology

This chapter's results were obtained using systematic reviews and meta-analysis methodology (see, for example, Higgins and Green 2011; Waddington et al. 2012; Card 2015). Table 6.1 summarizes the main inclusion criteria that were used to identify relevant studies.

Table 6.1 Inclusion criteria for the systematic review and meta-analysis

Type of inclusion criteria	Criteria used in this study
Publication format	Studies in English that were published in peer-reviewed scientific journals, as part of a working paper series, in books (with ISBN numbers), as doctoral dissertations, or official research or project reports
Interventions	Performance-based financing, voucher, and conditional cash transfer schemes[a] occurring in countries classified as low or middle income by the World Bank
Outcomes	Six indicators that represent the official and supplemental reproductive, maternal, and child health indicators of the Millennium Development Goals (Wagstaff and Claeson 2004) or are intermediate indicators critical to their achievement, namely, the shares of (1) women of fertile age who use modern contraceptives, (2) pregnancies with four or more antenatal care checks, (3) pregnant women receiving tetanus vaccinations, (4) births occurring in health facilities, (5) births with postnatal care, and (6) children receiving the full course of vaccinations recommended for the first year of life
Data source	Only evidence from household survey data due to sample selectivity and reporting bias concerns in health facility and administrative data sets from low- and middle-income countries (Chiba, Oguttu, and Nakayama 2012; Hahn, Wanjala, and Marx 2013; Sharma et al. 2016)
Study design	Randomized controlled trials as well as evaluations of nonrandomized interventions that identify impacts using regression discontinuity design, instrumental variables, or double difference and triple difference models

Source: World Bank.

a. Because they are based on a different theory of change, the review does not consider interventions that affect the monetary price of providing or using MCH services only indirectly or implicitly. On the supply side, omitted interventions include health worker training, provider performance tournaments, and the introduction of mobile health units or health worker home visits. On the demand side, excluded interventions include information campaigns, unconditional cash transfers, and conditional cash transfer schemes that do not condition on MCH service use or employ soft conditions or co-responsibilities. MCH = maternal and child health.

The outcomes included are mainly service indicators because they are the ones most often and most uniformly reported by the studies included in the analysis. However, some of the indicators considered, such as tetanus vaccination during antenatal care (ANC), at least four ANC visits, and full vaccination, also have a quality component. Importantly, the analysis only includes impact estimates of outcomes whose provision is financially incentivized by the interventions under study. This incentivization may be direct (for example, a fee a health facility receives for each birth taking place in it) or indirect (for example, a maternal tetanus vaccination being incentivized in a CCT that rewards pregnant women for ANC visits during which maternal tetanus vaccinations are carried out). By contrast, the analysis excludes impact estimates of outcomes without financial incentivization, for example, those measuring an intervention's unintended consequences.

Further, the parameter of interest in this review is a program's intention-to-treat effect—the impact on its full target population that consists of both compliers and noncompliers. Thus, the excluded effects are estimated only for compliers, for example, only for enrollees in a CCT scheme as opposed to its entire target group. As a requirement for the meta-analysis, impact estimates are only included if they are presented with a measure of statistical uncertainty.

Intervention characteristics

The results of the search are described in greater detail in box 6.3. Table 6A.1, in annex 6A, provides an overview of the 52 programs in the review and their underlying reports. The study design, program characteristics, and implementation contexts vary both across and within the three intervention groups. About 55 percent of the studies in the review have randomized designs, which are most common for CCT programs, and only three studies rely on instrumental variable and regression discontinuity design models to identify program impacts. Due to the review's strict methodological inclusion criteria, the share of studies with high bias risk is only 29 percent, 45 percent of studies are classified as having medium bias risk, and 26 percent as having low bias risk.

In terms of implementation context, the geographic coverage of the review is illustrated in map 6.1. Among the PBF programs in the review, 82 percent are in Sub-Saharan Africa, compared with 40 percent of the voucher programs and 35 percent of the CCT programs. The distribution is more balanced across country income groups, where 55 percent of PBF,

Box 6.3   In Focus: Systematic review search results

Several comprehensive literature searches were conducted between September 2016 and March 2021. The repeated searches produced a total of 58 included references, with 24 reporting on PBF programs, one on vouchers and performance-based financing (PBF), eight on vouchers alone, and 25 on conditional cash transfer (CCT) programs alone. From the 58 references, 212 impact estimates were extracted across the six outcomes of interest: (1) women of fertile age who use modern contraceptives, (2) pregnancies with four or more antenatal care checks, (3) pregnant women receiving tetanus vaccinations, (4) births occurring in health facilities, (5) births with postnatal care, and (6) children receiving the full course of vaccinations recommended for the first year of life. Aggregating these

estimates to the program level yields 130 program-specific effect sizes, of which 75 come from 22 PBF programs, 31 from 10 voucher programs, and 34 from 20 CCT programs (for interventions with multiple treatment arms, the review considers as separate the treatment arms those that differ in terms of having status quo as opposed to income equalized control groups, and in terms of introducing complementary demand- or supply-side financial incentives).

Figure B6.3.1 provides a breakdown of the references, impact estimates, and program-specific effect sizes per maternal and child health outcome. Figure B6.3.2 displays the number of programs included per outcome and by financial incentive intervention type.

Figure B6.3.1   Search and data extraction results across all financial incentive intervention types

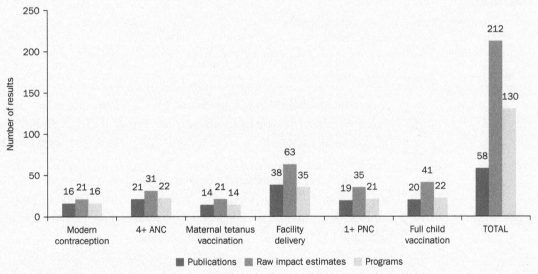

Source: World Bank.

Note: ANC = antenatal care; PNC = postnatal care.

(Continued)

Box 6.3 *continued*

Figure B6.3.2   Programs per outcome, by financial incentive intervention type

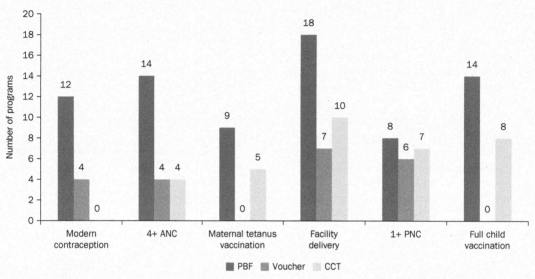

Source: World Bank.

Note: ANC = antenatal care; CCT = conditional cash transfer; PBF = performance-based financing; PNC = postnatal care.

70 percent of voucher, and 50 percent of CCT programs are in low-income countries. With a median first implementation year of 2011, PBF programs are somewhat younger than vouchers and CCT schemes, where the median year is 2009.

Key program characteristics are summarized in Neelsen et al. (2021, table 2).[1] Three PBF, five CCT, and, by definition, all 10 voucher programs combine demand- and supply-side financial incentives instead of incentivizing either the supply or demand side alone.[2]

Overall effects of financial incentives

Details on the statistical methods used to compute overall effect sizes and for the subgroup analyses are included in box 6.4. Figure 6.2 shows the overall mean effects of all the financial incentive interventions on the demand and supply sides, aggregating the results for PBF, voucher, and CCT schemes.

Map 6.1   Geographic coverage of studies included in the meta-analysis

IBRD 46457 | MARCH 2022

Source: World Bank.

Note: CCT = conditional cash transfers; PBF = performance-based financing.

For the six main outcomes, the analysis estimates a statistically significant mean effect size: 3.7 percentage points for modern family planning, 1.4 percentage points for pregnant women completing four or more ANC checks, 2.7 percentage points for maternal tetanus vaccination, 5.3 percentage points for facility delivery, 2.7 percentage points for postnatal care checks, and 4.4 percentage points for full childhood vaccination.

Effects by intervention type: PBF, vouchers, and CCTs

Figure 6.3 compares the mean effects of PBF, voucher, and CCT schemes on the same six outcomes. For modern family planning, the PBF mean effect size amounts to a statistically significant 2.4 percentage points. For the four voucher programs, the mean effect size is 6.2 percentage points, but it is statistically indistinguishable from zero.

Breaking programs down by intervention type for four or more ANC checks, the mean effect size for PBF is close to zero. For vouchers, the mean effect size amounts to a nonsignificant 2.7 percentage points, and the CCT effect size is a significant 4.4 percentage points.

Box 6.4 In Focus: Mean effect size computation and subgroup analysis

For the quantitative synthesis of intervention impacts, overall financial incentive and performance-based financing (PBF), voucher, and conditional cash transfer (CCT) mean effect sizes and confidence intervals were obtained using random effects models that take into account that differences between impact estimates across incentive intervention types may result from not only sampling error, but also genuine differences in program effectiveness (Borenstein, Hedges, and Higgins 2009). Because the review shows effect sizes in percentage points, impact estimates reported in other units—such as log odds ratios, odds ratios, or risk ratios—were converted to percentage points.

The analysis further estimates differences between mean effect sizes of different types of financial incentive interventions, namely, between the PBF, voucher, and CCT intervention groups. The intervention group–specific mean effect size

estimates give the relative effectiveness of PBF, voucher, and CCT programs. Comparisons of the statistical significance of mean effect sizes across groups should be avoided, however, as variation in the number of underlying program-specific effect sizes (and, in turn, the number of observations underlying them) can make such comparisons highly misleading. Instead, the chapter reports the statistical significance of mean effect size differences between subgroups from bivariate, random effects meta-regressions, assuming similar between-study variances across subgroups (Higgins and Green 2011). Because a relatively large number of meta-regression subgroup analyses are carried out, there is a risk of type I error (false positives) from multiple hypothesis testing. Following Borenstein, Hedges, and Higgins (2009), this risk is addressed by using the 99 percent instead of the 95 percent threshold to determine statistical significance.

Figure 6.2   Mean effect sizes for all incentive interventions combined

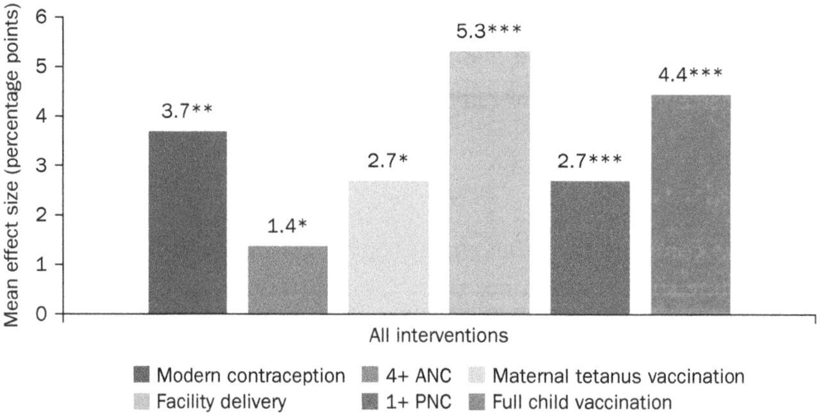

Source: World Bank.

Note: Mean effect sizes were obtained with random effects meta-analysis. ANC = antenatal care; PNC = postnatal care.

***$p < .01$, **$p < .05$, *$p < 0.1$.

Figure 6.3 Mean effect sizes, by intervention type

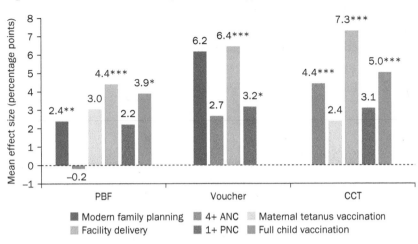

Source: World Bank.

Note: Mean effect sizes were obtained with random effects meta-analysis. ANC = antenatal care; CCT = conditional cash transfers; PBF = performance-based financing; PNC = postnatal care.

***p < .01, **p < .05, *p < 0.1.

For maternal tetanus vaccination, for PBF programs, the mean effect size is 3 percentage points, with a p-value just above the 5 percent level. For CCTs, the mean effect size is similar, at 2.4 percentage points, but there is substantial heterogeneity, driven by the significant negative impact of Indonesia's Program Keluarga Harapan, which contrasts with the positive effect sizes of the four other CCT programs.

For facility delivery, all the intervention group–specific mean effect sizes are statistically significant, with the PBF mean effect size being the smallest, at 4.4 percentage points, followed by the voucher mean effect of 6.4 percentage points and the CCT mean effect of 7.3 percentage points.

The mean effect size across all the financial incentive interventions for postnatal care checks is a modest but statistically significant 2.7 percentage points. A low degree of effect size heterogeneity across programs is mirrored in intervention type–specific mean effect sizes of similar magnitude: a nonsignificant 2.2 percentage points for PBF, 3.2 percentage points—and significant—for vouchers, and 3.1 percentage points and not significant for CCTs.

For PBF schemes, the mean effect size for full childhood vaccination is a significant 3.9 percentage points, and for CCTs, it is a significant 5 percentage points. Random effects meta-regressions were conducted to establish whether the differences between the mean effect sizes of the intervention groups were significant using a 1 percent threshold to account for multiple hypothesis testing. No significant differences were found except for ANC, for which the difference between the relatively large CCT and near-zero PBF mean effect sizes is statistically significant.

Box 6.5 provides more details on the heterogeneity of effect sizes, and box 6.6 reports the results from a heterogeneity analysis examining

Box 6.5 In Focus: Effect size heterogeneity

The dispersion of program-specific impact estimates around their estimated mean effect is an important policy parameter as it conveys a sense of how certain policy makers can be about the expected effects of a new program. To assess the degree of effect size heterogeneity across financial incentive intervention types and within intervention groups, I^2 statistics and their p values were calculated. The I^2 statistic represents the share of the variation around the mean effect size that is explained by genuine differences in program-specific effect sizes ("between-study variance") as opposed to mere sampling error ("within-study variance") (Borenstein, Hedges, and Higgins

2009). Following Cochrane collaboration guidelines, this study considers I^2 statistics of 0–40 percent, 40–60 percent, and 60+ percent to indicate low, moderate, and substantial heterogeneity, respectively (Borenstein, Hedges, and Higgins 2009). Table B6.5.1 displays the level of effect size heterogeneity for each outcome and each intervention. Except for maternal tetanus vaccination (overall and for CCT) and modern family planning for vouchers, heterogeneity is low to moderate for all the outcomes and intervention types. This indicates that despite the variation in contexts and intervention designs, the impact estimates tend to be similar across the financial incentive interventions.

Table B6.5.1 Level of effect size heterogeneity, measured by I^2 statistics

Maternal and child health outcome	Type of incentive intervention			
	PBF	Vouchers	CCT	All interventions
Modern family planning	Low	Substantial	n.a.	Moderate
4+ ANC checks	Low	Low	Low	Low
Maternal tetanus vaccination	Moderate	n.a.	Substantial	Substantial
Facility delivery	Moderate	Low	Moderate	Moderate
1+ PNC checks	Low	Low	Moderate	Low
Full child vaccination	Low	n.a.	Low	Low

Source: World Bank.

Note: Low = 0% ≤ I^2 < 40%; Moderate = 40% ≤ I^2 < 60%; Substantial = I^2 ≥ 60%. ANC = antenatal care; CCT = conditional cash transfer; n.a. = not applicable; PBF = performance-based financing; PNC = postnatal care.

Box 6.6   In Focus: Combining supply- and demand-side incentives

A reasonable hypothesis is that there exist complementarities between demand- and supply-side interventions. To test this hypothesis, this box examines whether the effect sizes of schemes that combine supply- and demand-side financial incentives are larger than those of schemes that only incentivize either the demand or supply side. While acknowledging the limited power in this subgroup analysis, the meta-regression results displayed in figure B6.6.1 provide little evidence for such complementarities. In no case is there a statistically significant difference between combined and single interventions, and for the three outcomes—maternal tetanus vaccination, facility delivery, and postnatal care—for which meaningful differences in effect size magnitudes are estimated, they indicate smaller effect sizes for programs combining supply- and demand-side interventions.

Figure B6.6.1   Difference in mean effect size between schemes combining supply- and demand-side interventions and schemes intervening only on the supply or demand side

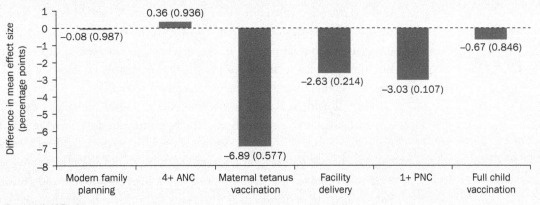

Source: World Bank.

Note: The labels on the bars indicate the magnitude and p-value (in parentheses) of the difference in mean effect size between schemes combining supply- and demand-side interventions and schemes intervening only on the supply or demand side from meta-regressions of the respective service utilization variable on an indicator variable that equals one if a program combines supply- and demand-side interventions and zero if a scheme affects only the supply or demand side, as well as on a categorical variable for intervention type (performance-based financing, voucher, and conditional cash transfer) and a constant. ANC = antenatal care; PNC = postnatal care.

whether programs combining supply- and demand-side incentives have larger impacts.

Comparing the PBF and DFF approaches

A key policy counterfactual to PBF is the direct financing of health facilities, also known as direct facility financing (DFF). Indeed, several evaluations of PBF programs have found that resource neutrality with decentralization can lead to equivalent gains in coverage albeit with differential impacts on quality of care (de Walque et al. 2021; Kandpal et al. 2019; Friedman et al. 2016; Friedman, Das, and Mutasa 2017). While PBF interventions provide an unconditional core budget and additional financial incentives conditional on performance, DFF interventions only provide additional unconditional financing. Often the financing—whether conditional or unconditional—is accompanied by autonomy, community engagement, and supportive supervision. In addition, PBF and DFF are perhaps best viewed as mechanisms that leverage input financing and user fees (Fritsche, Soeters, and Meessen 2014). In PBF facilities, providers were actively encouraged to lower user fees as a strategy to boost demand and in some cases to waive out-of-pocket fees. In addition to the strategic purchasing, a key difference between these two types of interventions, of course, is in the verification of facility performance reports. In the PBF arm, typically the quantity of services reported by the health facility was verified at fixed intervals, often quarterly, by an external verification agency. In DFF facilities, there was no such verification because there was no strategic purchasing (there were no prices attached to certain services).

The following is an example of how these two interventions work. Both sets of facilities can typically use the operating budget provided by the intervention, which is not conditional on performance, for health facility operating costs (at least 50 percent). Such costs include maintaining and repairing essential equipment; purchasing drugs, supplies, and consumables; engaging in outreach; and carrying out other related aspects of quality enhancement. In DFF facilities, none of the budget could be used for staff incentives. However, in PBF facilities, performance bonuses added about 10–20 percent to health worker salaries.

Whether comparing PBF with DFF that disbursed as much as PBF but had lower administrative costs, such as in Cameroon, or with DFF that had significantly lower disbursements to facilities, as in Nigeria and Zambia, the evidence suggests that different models of DFF may be as effective as PBF in increasing health service coverage. Further, DFF may be a cost-effective alternative to PBF because it does not entail directly measuring and verifying outputs. As such verification takes the form of routine third-party verification visits to all the treated facilities, by avoiding these visits, DFF can have significantly lower administrative costs (Zeng et al. 2021). DFF also has the benefit of causing fewer unintended effects, for instance, by not incentivizing gaming of the system (Petersen et al. 2006) or by not rewarding relatively easy but measurable tasks, like dispensing pills, while leaving aside tasks that are more difficult to measure (Bridges and Woolcock 2019). Further, in the PBF arm, the additional payments for salary "top-ups" or performance-based bonuses often do not have clear rules for allocation between facility staff. Different countries use different rules to divide these bonuses between staff, which in turn creates the potential for free riding, particularly as health workers operate in teams and individual performance can be difficult to observe (Leonard and Masatu 2010).

Another appealing aspect of DFF is that it is deemed to be easier to implement than PBF—not only cheaper—because it does not require selecting indicators for payment or routinely verifying facility performance, and there is almost mechanically less heterogeneity in payment schemes and program design. Finally, because DFF does not link payments to performance on specific tasks, some critics of PBF argue that DFF has fewer sustained impacts on worker motivation, in turn limiting any potential detriments caused by such effects (Paul et al. 2018; Ireland, Paul, and Dujardin 2011). As DFF is seen as a less radical approach at the facility level, it is argued to have fewer systemwide and long-term impacts than PBF programs (Paul et al. 2018; Ridde et al. 2018). Of course, often such health system impacts are typically a desired, or even an intended, part of the PBF intervention (Meessen, Soucat, and Sekabaraga 2011).

In the Health Results Innovation Trust Fund (HRITF) portfolio, five countries successfully piloted a DFF approach in addition to PBF: Cameroon, Nigeria, Zambia, Zimbabwe, and the initial Rwanda pilot (de Walque et al. 2021; Kandpal et al. 2019; Friedman, Das, and Mutasa 2017; Friedman et al. 2016; Basinga et al. 2011). The rest of this section pools the data from these five countries to assess the relative effectiveness of the PBF and DFF approaches when implemented side by side.

Table 6A.2, in annex 6A, summarizes the two interventions in each of these countries. In general, as implemented in the five countries, the DFF approaches were similar or even identical to PBF except that the payments to the health facilities were explicitly decoupled from the quantity or quality of services that were delivered, and no performance bonuses were paid to the health workers. In Cameroon, Zimbabwe, and Rwanda, the DFF and PBF arms received, on average, the same amounts. However, in Nigeria and Zambia, the amount of funds transferred to the DFF facilities was set, by design, to be exactly half the average of what PBF facilities in the same state earned. Broadly speaking, the budget equalization was implemented retrospectively. In other words, DFF income depended on the actual disbursements to PBF facilities for the past quarter.

In all these countries, DFF facilities were subject to the same reporting requirements as PBF facilities without the additional monthly third-party verification of quantity or quality. In addition, DFF facilities typically received the same level of autonomy in using their funds as the PBF facilities. In Nigeria, where community engagement was a part of the PBF intervention, the DFF facilities were also exposed to the same level of participation from the local ward development committees. In all the countries, the supervision and disbursement of funds were also comparable between PBF and DFF and distinct from business-as-usual. For instance, in Nigeria, in both the PBF and DFF arms, all income sources—including user fees and PBF or DFF disbursements—were managed collectively and even stored in the same bank account.

PBF and DFF interventions can often also serve as conduits for additional staff training. For example, in Cameroon and Nigeria, the quality of care provided was an additional target for the program, so a quality checklist that aimed to measure facility quality was implemented in both PBF and DFF facilities on a quarterly basis. The visit to implement this quality checklist was at the center of the enhanced supervision provided in these two countries. Both PBF and DFF facilities thus received a quarterly training visit for MCH staff. During this visit, district health supervisors implemented the quality checklist at the facility, calculating and communicating the scores to the facility. They then worked with the facility to identify areas for improvement and provided hands-on training on issues identified through this process. Thus, in some ways, this process resembled a continuous quality improvement approach whereby supervisors worked with facility staff to identify key challenges to the quality of care, aided facility staff in problem solving, and provided hands-on training in areas of need. In the PBF arm, the score was tied to an additional quality bonus; in the DFF arm, no additional funds were provided.

The Nigerian experience illustrates why PBF verification costs can be substantial: in addition to the verification of the quantities of services, the quality score was independently verified by an external verification agency. Since the quality visit and the verification were not on the same day, an algorithm to detect and address misreporting was needed. If the verification reports were more than 10 percent off the scores reported in the quality visit, the facility received a financial penalty. If a discrepancy of more than 10 percent happened more than three months in a row, the facility faced a punitive audit by the Federal Ministry of Health. DFF interventions, by design, provide unconditional funding, thereby avoiding all such administrative costs.

There were also important transparency and accountability interventions in all the PBF and DFF arms studied here. For instance, in all five countries, in both the PBF and DFF arms, the amount earned by the facility was transferred electronically to the facility's bank account. In cases like Nigeria, where community engagement was a central pillar of the intervention, the chair of the local area development committee was a co-signatory of the bank account.[3]

Table 6.2, reproduced from Khanna et al. (2021), summarizes the differences and similarities in the PBF, DFF, and business-as-usual arms in Nigeria, which is representative of the two approaches as implemented in the five countries studied. As the table illustrates, the DFF intervention was identical to the PBF intervention except for the strategic purchasing element. PBF facilities received a quarterly payment based on the quantity of targeted MCH services they reported providing over the previous quarter. Each of these targeted indicators had a predetermined price assigned to it, and the indicators and prices were provided to the facility ahead of time through a checklist. At the end of each quarter, the total payment for each participating health facility in the PBF arm was calculated by multiplying the number of people to whom each targeted service was provided by the price of that service plus the quality bonus calculated using a quality scorecard (see Khanna et al. (2021) for further details).

Table 6.2 Description of the PBF and DFF arms in Nigeria

Characteristic	Program arm		
	PBF	DFF	Control
Funds electronically transferred to health facility account	Yes	Yes	No
Autonomy of facility to allocate funds	Yes	Yes	No
Community engagement in facility management	Yes	Yes	No
Enhanced supervision using quantitative supervisory checklist	Yes	Yes	No
Facility payment linked to quantity and quality of services	Yes	No	No
Remoteness bonus	Yes	No	No
Salary bonuses to health workers based on performance	Yes	No	No
Level of overall incremental funding (US$ per capita per year)	$3.49	$1.74	$0.00

Source: Kandpal et al. 2019.

Note: DFF = direct facility financing; PBF = performance-based financing.

To provide an overall comparison of PBF and DFF as well as gain statistical power in comparing the impacts, a pooled analysis of the data from the five HRITF funded impact evaluations that allowed such a comparison is conducted. The results presented in figure 6.4 show that apart from institutional deliveries in public facilities, PBF does not lead to incremental gains over DFF—indeed, in aggregate, not even compared with business-as-usual. Even when the DFF arm disbursed significantly less than the PBF arm, with the additional resources in the PBF arm being used solely for performance pay, there is limited evidence of additional impact of PBF.

The fact that little evidence is found of a differential impact of PBF over DFF is indicative that in these LIC contexts, performance pay to health workers may not lead to greater impact than DFF. Further, although the analysis finds that PBF increases deliveries at public institutions, given that

Figure 6.4 Comparison of the pooled impact of performance-based and unconditional facility financing in five Sub-Saharan African countries (Cameroon, Nigeria, Rwanda, Zambia, and Zimbabwe)

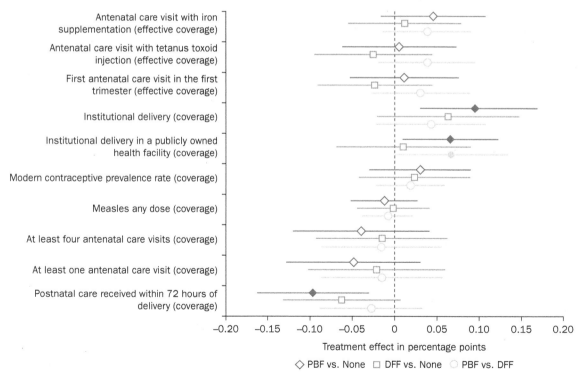

Sources: World Bank, based on de Walque, Friedman, et al. 2022.

Note: Solid markers indicate statistically significant estimates ($p < .05$); markers that are open indicate imprecise estimates. "Whiskers" around markers represent 95% confidence intervals. DFF = direct facility financing; PBF = performance-based financing.

facility quality is not observed, the welfare implications of this effect are unclear. If public institutions are of lower quality than private institutions, then, if anything, patients may be worse off due to this shift. It is also noteworthy that the analysis of pooled data from these five countries leads to a different finding than what might be suggested by individual impact evaluations. For example, in Nigeria, Rwanda, Zambia, and Zimbabwe, the findings show that PBF outperformed DFF for institutional delivery, while the pooled analysis does not find an aggregate effect of PBF on institutional deliveries. This difference between the individual impact evaluations and the pooled analysis highlights the salience of context as a mediator of PBF's impact.

Figure 6.5 compares the impacts of PBF and DFF on idle capacity. As discussed in chapter 3, idle capacity measures the potential for

Figure 6.5 Impacts of PBF relative to DFF on idle capacity in antenatal care consultations in Cameroon and Nigeria

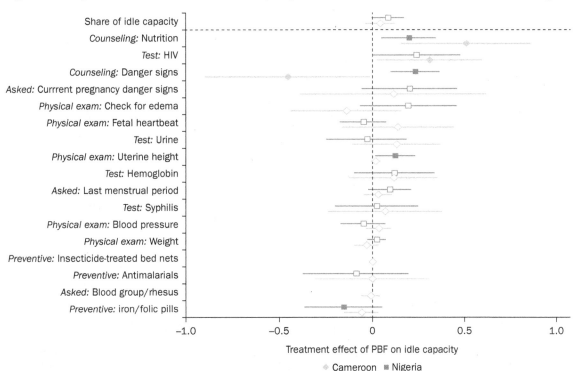

Source: World Bank, based on Khanna et al. 2021 and de Walque et al. 2021.

Note: Markers above the dashed line indicate a summary effect. Solid markers indicate statistically significant estimates ($p < .05$); markers that are open indicate imprecise estimates. "Whiskers" around markers represent 95% confidence intervals. DFF = direct facility financing; PBF = performance-based financing.

improvement in clinical quality that is truly in the health worker's locus of control. Because idle capacity should be zero in a normative sense, positive impacts, that is, where PBF reduced idle capacity compared with DFF, would be to the left of the zero line in the figure, and increases in idle capacity would be to the right. An overall index of idle capacity is presented above the dotted line, and the various subcomponents of the overall index of idle capacity are below the dotted line. In both countries, most of the impacts are on the right, suggesting that PBF increased idle capacity over DFF— although not all of the impacts are precisely estimated. Indeed, with the exception of counseling for danger signs, there are no significant reductions in idle capacity from PBF compared with DFF. Returning to the theme of equity in access to care, Box 6.7 explores whether these impacts on idle capacity vary by the socioeconomic status of the patient accessing care.

Box 6.7 In Focus: PBF and equity

As discussed in chapter 4, evidence suggests the presence of a wealth-quality gradient in antenatal care, including in many of the settings studied in this report. Figures B6.7.1 and B6.7.2 present baseline and endline concentration curves of the idle capacity (or know-can-do gaps) for Nigeria and Cameroon, respectively. In Nigeria, care at baseline is close to the line of equality, suggesting an equitable distribution. At endline, if anything, the intervention arms held constant while the business-as-usual arm became less equitable, with the poor facing greater idle capacity. In Cameroon, the performance-based financing (PBF) and business-as-usual arms became less pro-poor over the study period. Notably, however, the greatest detriments from PBF to the know-can-do gap often come from the middle of the wealth distribution rather than from the poorest of the poor.

In contrast, there were few changes in idle capacity in direct facility financing (DFF), and it ended the study period as the most pro-poor of the study arms. In particular, the DFF gains in quality came from the poorest wealth quintiles relative to PBF. This may be because the wealthy are (can be) more quality sensitive—which may take the form of being able to pay for additional tests, demand better care, travel further to better facilities, and live in wealthier areas. As a result, PBF facilities may have faced greater volume from relatively well-off patients. Indeed, the Nigeria impact evaluation documents that 40 percent of PBF's impact on institutional deliveries was actually a displacement from private to public facilities—by relatively wealthy women returning to the public sector in response to perceived improvements in public facilities (Kandpal et al. 2019).

(Continued)

Box 6.7 *continued*

Figure B6.7.1 Patient socioeconomic status, PBF, DFF, and know-can-do gaps in Nigeria

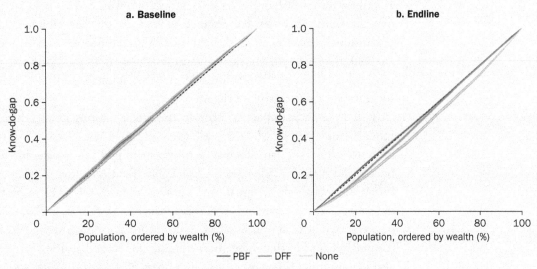

Source: World Bank, based on Kandpal et al. 2019 and de Walque et al. 2021.

Note: DFF = direct facility financing; PBF = performance-based financing.

Figure B6.7.2 Patient socioeconomic status, PBF, DFF, and know-can-do gaps in Cameroon

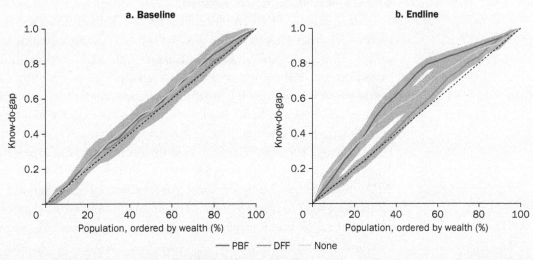

Source: World Bank, based on Kandpal et al. 2019 and de Walque et al. 2021.

Note: Shaded areas represent 95% confidence intervals. DFF = direct facility financing; PBF = performance-based financing.

PBF, DFF, and institutional deliveries

In many of the PBF pilots discussed in this chapter, including some where the PBF arm had little other impact on service utilization or quality of care, an indicator that PBF improves with respect to business-as-usual is the rate of institutional deliveries. For instance, in Rwanda, the PBF pilot increased institutional deliveries by 23 percent; in Nigeria, compared with business-as-usual, the PBF arm increased institutional deliveries by 7 percent; and in Zambia, where the PBF pilot had no other impacts, it also increased institutional deliveries by 7 percent.

This systematic impact of PBF on the rate of institutional deliveries raises the question of why these pilots are effective at increasing this one indicator even if the overall impact is otherwise muted. An explanation may be that the price for deliveries is often higher than for other services. For instance, in Nigeria, a vaginal birth earned the facility US$12 in performance pay, while a standard ANC visit earned it US$1.20. In Rwanda, a delivery earned US$4.60, while a standard ANC visit earned US$0.09. Although it appears that these prices substantially favor deliveries, deliveries also require more time and effort on the part of the health worker than a standard ANC visit. In addition, ANC visits are predictable, and facilities often offer ANC services on a given day of the week. In contrast, deliveries have unknown durations and uncertain outcomes. Therefore, even at these relatively nominal prices, the price per unit of effort may not necessarily be different for ANC visits and deliveries.

Further, often DFF interventions can lead to significant gains to institutional deliveries without paying specifically for the outcome (for instance, see the Nigerian example reported in Khanna et al. 2021). If the indicator price truly led to the disproportionate success of PBF programs, then it would not be the case that DFF performs almost as well as PBF in Nigeria. Further, assuming that health workers adjust effort in response to the price implies that they understand the incentive structure. In contrast, in Nigeria, where the PBF pilot increased the institutional delivery rate by 7 percent over business-as-usual and 10 percent over DFF (Khanna et al. 2021), it was found that approximately 60 percent of the workers did not understand how to increase their payment, and a quarter of those who worked in a PBF health facility were not even aware of the PBF program (Kandpal et al. 2019).

Bauhoff and Kandpal (2021) study the same set of health workers sampled in the impact evaluation of the Nigeria pilot. They show that even in a simple lab-in-the-field setup, health workers do not respond linearly to price. In their experiment, health workers received the incentives directly and in response to a simple payout structure. Despite this, as demonstrated in figure 6.6, most of the gains from incentives accrue from going from zero to a small positive price, and the authors estimate few additional gains from going from low to high prices. Although their estimated effort response is different from one canonical estimate of wage elasticity (Fehr and Goette 2007), it is broadly consistent with others (Oettinger 1999; Goldberg 2016). This result of the price acting as a signal is also in line with some of the literature on CCTs (Filmer and Schady 2011) and transfers acting as nudges (Baird, McIntosh, and Özler 2011; Benhassine et al. 2015). In turn, this lack of response by providers to the price highlights the potential slack in PBF payment schedules and suggests that PBF payments largely work to increase the salience of the information provided by the checklist. PBF may thus be made more cost-effective by reducing the prices of salient indicators like institutional deliveries.

Figure 6.6   Lab-in-the-field evidence on prices and provider effort

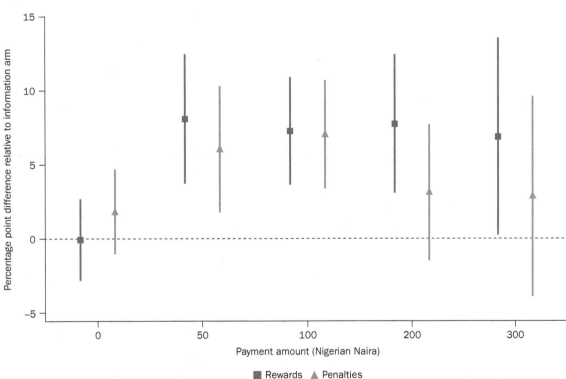

Source: Bauhoff and Kandpal 2021.

Note: "Whiskers" around point estimates represent 95% confidence intervals.

In addition, institutional delivery may be a particularly salient task, especially in primary care settings. It is also a task that may be intrinsically important and well aligned with the overall mission of providing care. Midwifing a new life may be seen as the culmination of the chain of care in maternity services (Cullen et al. 2016). As a result, nonpecuniary signals or incentives for deliveries may have a disproportionate impact on deliveries relative to their impact on other services because deliveries are a task of unusual salience to health workers. There are also important potential complementarities in the production of institutional deliveries with ANC but not vice versa. To be specific, whether a woman visits a facility for the first ANC visit is not within a health worker's control. Demand-side factors may keep women from seeking ANC, thus limiting the impact of the strategic purchasing of ANC services. However, once a woman decides to seek ANC in a health facility, the health worker may be able to convince her to come back to the facility for delivery. Indeed, such a pattern has been studied and established in several previous studies, including Basinga et al. (2011) in Rwanda and Van de Poel et al. (2016) in Cambodia. This discussion thus highlights the importance of considering the variety of factors to which health workers are required to respond in addition to the performance pay provided by the PBF pilot. Simply finding that PBF programs increase the utilization of a certain service does not necessarily imply that the impact is driven by the performance pay.

The literature presents evidence of other interventions, such as transportation vouchers and CCTs, increasing institutional deliveries, perhaps at a much lower cost and with less uncertainty in implementation. For indicators where baseline coverage is particularly low, demand-side barriers may be salient and at least partially addressed using low-cost cash transfers to patients/households. Many of the constraints to effective coverage are not in the health worker's locus of control and thus do not necessarily respond well to PBF incentives. As a result, perhaps unsurprisingly, the findings indicate that DFF, typically paired with facility-level autonomy and supervision reforms, can improve coverage and effective coverage to a similar degree as PBF—often at a lower cost since DFF does not require a verification mechanism.

PBF, DFF, and baseline effort

With the objective of increasing coverage or effective coverage of targeted health services, PBF programs are designed under the assumption that financial incentives will increase providers' effort toward delivering the incentivized services. If there is idle capacity in effort, providers may work more once the return to effort is higher. To prevent providers from increasing the provision of lower quality services, the PBF transfers typically also depend on indicators of quality of care, although the evidence provided in the previous chapter suggests that at least in Cameroon and Nigeria, PBF may have increased idle capacity anyway. Evaluations of PBF programs in low- and middle-income countries overall have found positive impacts on quality of care.

While performance pay for a single task provides a signal of the salience of the task and increases the marginal return to effort on that purchased task, PBF programs typically incentivize the provision of a set of services, each at a different rate, meaning the relative marginal return to effort on different actions is changed. The marginal return to effort on a specific service depends on whether the service is incentivized, the incentive size, and the amount of effort required to provide an additional service. The marginal return to effort exerted on one service might also depend on the number of other services provided if the services have common effort inputs, in other words, if they are complements in production (Mullen, Frank, and Rosenthal 2010; Bauhoff and Kandpal 2021). Consider, for example, the link between ANC and delivery services. Facilities establish contact with pregnant women during consultations, and preparation for delivery is one of the counseling topics that should be covered. Therefore, the effort exerted on outreach for ANC can reduce the effort required to bring women in for deliveries.

The effort required to provide an additional unit of service might also depend on other factors. For example, the marginal return to effort might not be constant but increasing. Consider a facility serving a large catchment area. The effort required to bring in individuals from nearby residences could be lower than that required to attract individuals from further villages. The characteristics of the catchment area a facility serves might also affect the marginal return to effort. For example, population density and poverty rates might affect the amount of effort required to bring in more individuals to receive services. Simply put, at high levels of coverage, the marginal effort required to increase service delivery may be higher than the performance pay offered for that service. It may also be the case that demand-side factors, not supply-side ones, keep some women from seeking care. In response, providers may reallocate effort to a lower effort task, that is, one for which existing coverage levels are low, even if that task has lower performance pay associated with it.

Figure 6.7 presents a preliminary analysis of data from the Nigeria PBF project's impact evaluation. Using triple differences to account for

Figure 6.7   PBF and DFF impact by baseline coverage of institutional deliveries and ANC in Nigeria

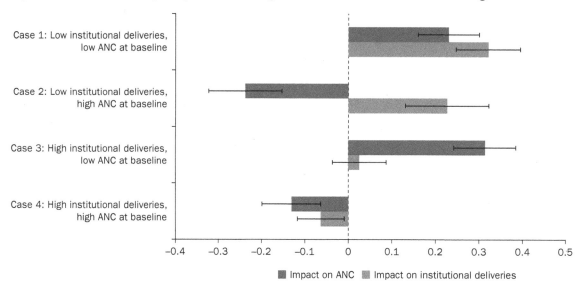

Case 1: Low institutional deliveries, low ANC at baseline

Case 2: Low institutional deliveries, high ANC at baseline

Case 3: High institutional deliveries, low ANC at baseline

Case 4: High institutional deliveries, high ANC at baseline

■ Impact on ANC   ■ Impact on institutional deliveries

Source: World Bank.

Note: "Whiskers" represent 95% confidence intervals. ANC = antenatal care; DFF = direct facility financing; PBF = performance-based financing.

differences in time trends, the figure compares the impacts of the PBF intervention on the coverage rates of timely uptake of ANC and institutional delivery, by baseline levels of coverage of the two services. This analysis allows teasing out the effects of the levels of performance pay for the two services, as otherwise the two impacts arose from the same PBF package—the only difference was in the levels of performance pay. The figure plots the coefficient on the interaction of the indicators for (1) PBF (versus DFF), (2) endline (versus baseline), and (3) above (or below) median baseline coverage of that indicator. The PBF program had an overall significant impact on in-facility deliveries but not on ANC coverage. When the coverage rates of both services were below median before the project was launched, as in case 1, there is a positive and statistically significant impact on both services, with a marginally greater impact on the service with a higher price, that is, institutional deliveries. When the rate of institutional deliveries was below median, but the ANC rate was above median, as in case 2, the estimates show a positive impact on deliveries and a negative one on ANC, perhaps suggesting a reallocation of resources to deliveries. When the baseline rate was high for deliveries but low for ANC, as in case 3, there is a significant impact only on ANC. However, when the coverage rates of the services were above median at baseline, as in case 4, the estimates reveal similarly negative impacts on both services, again perhaps indicating a reallocation of resources to other services.

These findings are consistent with an increasing marginal cost of providing additional services. When the rates of both services were below median, the performance pay amounts were higher than the marginal cost and the providers increased their effort on both services. When the provision of both services was already high at baseline, the providers might have shifted effort to other services. The facilities with low delivery coverage and high ANC coverage at baseline responded to the PBF intervention by increasing effort on deliveries and reducing effort on ANC. The overall similarity in results across PBF and DFF in Nigeria hides this heterogeneity in response to performance pay. This finding suggests that providers reallocate effort across tasks in response to the performance pay; similar but only indicative evidence is found from the data used in the meta-analysis presented in box 6.8.

Box 6.8 In Focus: How do impacts depend on the baseline outcome values? Results from the meta-analysis

Figure B6.8.1 uses the meta-analysis framework and data and shows the association of effect sizes with the targeted outcome values at baseline. The baseline value serves as a measure of pre-intervention health system effectiveness in reaching mothers and children with health services—a possible proxy for country income level and overall implementation context. In theory, a possible association can go in either direction. A negative relationship would result if, for instance, low baseline outcome levels indicated low capacity to implement financial incentives successfully. By contrast, a positive relationship would arise if, for example, a low baseline outcome level indicated larger populations within reach of marginal changes in effort induced by financial incentives. The results displayed in figure B6.8.1, using a binary variable indicating if the baseline value is below or above the sample median, show a mixed picture: for modern family planning, facility delivery, and childhood vaccinations, the point estimates indicate that baseline values below the median are associated with better outcomes, whereas for maternal tetanus vaccination and postnatal care, the reverse applies.

This pattern highlights that service provision may depend not only on the price, but also on the marginal effort required—and that performance-based financing (PBF) may be fruitfully deployed for indicators where coverage levels are relatively low and there is room for improvement. Further, this finding suggests a way to think about the potential complementarities between cash transfers, PBF, and direct facility financing. Policy makers may wish to view household cash transfers conditioned on service utilization and PBF as lying on a continuum. For instance, a low-cost option may be to identify areas where baseline demand is particularly weak for certain types of services, implement household-level conditional cash transfers (CCTs) to see how much they increase a given indicator, and only then consider PBF payments. Although PBF may be most effective at low levels of coverage, CCTs may be cheaper for increasing coverage when levels are especially low.

(Continued)

Box 6.8 *continued*

Figure B6.8.1   Effect size of the baseline health service utilization rate being below the sample median

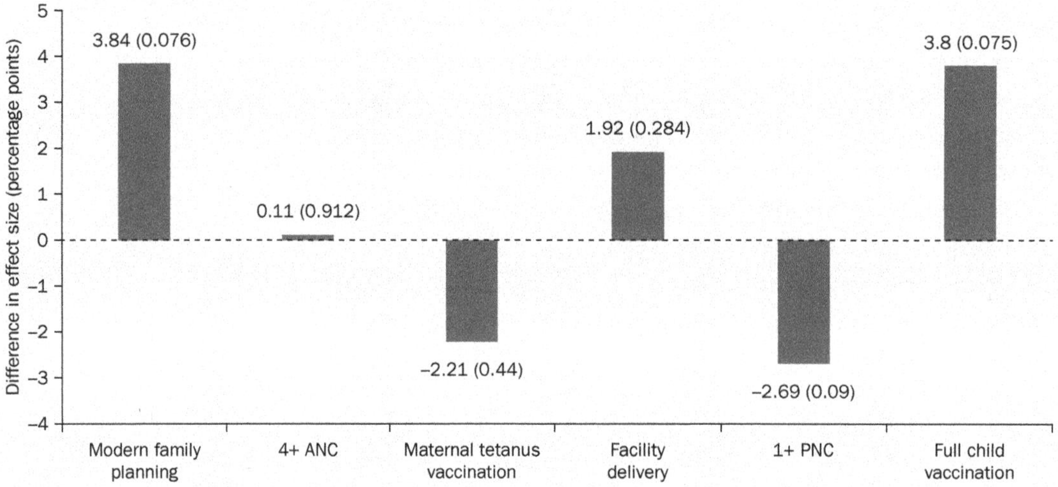

Source: World Bank.

Note: The labels on the bars indicate the magnitude and p-value (in parentheses) of the difference in mean effect size of the baseline health service utilization rate being below the sample median from meta-regressions of the respective service utilization variable on an indicator variable that equals one if the baseline health service utilization rate is below the sample median and zero if it is above the sample median, as well as on a categorical variable for intervention type (performance-based financing, voucher, and conditional cash transfer) and a constant. ANC = antenatal care; PNC = postnatal care.

Complementarities in the PBF and DFF approaches

The evidence presented above, linking the impact of performance pay to baseline coverage levels and the salience of the task, raises a broader point about the relationship between the PBF and DFF approaches. While thus far the chapter has explored the differences in the design, implementation, and impact of PBF and DFF, there may be important complementarities between the two approaches. For example, a crucial similarity is that both PBF and DFF disburse money directly to the frontlines, which can be an important difference in health system financing from the status quo. Indeed, without such approaches as DFF, primary health facilities in much of Sub-Saharan Africa (but also South Asia and parts of East Asia and the Pacific) often do not have a budget over which they have autonomous control. As discussed in chapter 1, health facilities in centralized systems have a staff roster, and typically the salary rolls are paid centrally, leaving facilities with limited ability to hire contract workers in response to demand increases or quality of care requirements. In addition, based on the size of the catchment area they serve, which is often documented through old and incomplete data, facilities receive a certain set of drugs and supplies at preset intervals. Beyond this, if something breaks or there is a stockout, procurement must proceed through centralized processes and can lead to sustained gaps in equipment and drug availability (Fritsche, Soeters, and Meessen 2014).

In contrast, both PBF and DFF approaches give health facilities a budget over which they have some autonomous control, which provides them a core fund for infrastructure. In addition, the DFF interventions studied here do not just send money to facilities without accountability—indeed, most incorporated the same accountability measures, such as business plans and dashboards, as the PBF arms in the same trial. Plus, like in the PBF arms, many of the DFF arms received additional supervision in the form of training visits. Finally, most of these interventions led to sustained effects on the Public Expenditure Tracking System (PETS), leading to downstream improvements in the regularity of disbursements (see Kandpal et al. (2019) for a discussion of the effects of the Nigerian PBF pilot on the local PETS; chapters 7 and 8 return to this topic).

All the DFF arms studied were nested within well-known PBF trials. As such, there may have been some anticipation effects among the DFF facilities that if they performed well, they too would receive the performance pay, which was almost always additional to the base salary. Of course, the exact contribution of such anticipation effects to the success of DFF interventions cannot be quantified, and it should not necessarily be expected that most or even all of the relative success of the DFF programs came from these effects rather than from the additional financing, autonomy, accountability, and PETS-level changes. However, even for DFF, a central point remains that it is unknown how much of the observed impact comes from the additional budget versus autonomy or the related changes. Indeed, the supervision-only intervention in the Kyrgyz Republic suggests that financing reform may not always be necessary to improve health service delivery. A fruitful channel for further inquiry may be to understand the role of these aspects of the DFF intervention.

Thus, the evidence presented here suggests that PBF and DFF have important complementarities. Ultimately, the question is what is feasible within the government system. PBF budgets are unpredictable because the payments vary by facility performance, making them difficult to reconcile with government systems that lack a dedicated purchasing agency. In many ways, this mirrors the discussion in the debate around CCTs and unconditional cash transfers (UCTs). On the one hand, the link to results might make PBF more politically palatable in some settings and may have attracted additional donor funding, which is the same reason offered for government preferences for CCTs relative to UCTs. On the other hand, with DFF and UCTs, governments know exactly how much to disburse to recipient facilities, and there is no need for verification, making implementation easier and less expensive.

One way of reducing the budget unpredictability imposed by PBF may be to use PBF and DFF together, with DFF as a core level of decentralized funding and PBF in selected areas for targeted indicators. This approach was scaled up in Nigeria because of the PBF impact evaluation finding that PBF only had an incremental impact on institutional deliveries relative to DFF. As a result, the project's national scale-up provides facilities a core budget and DFF as baseline, and it uses PBF for a small number of indicators, including institutional deliveries. Paying for a small number of indicators limits the uncertainty for government budgets.

A large source of the administrative expenses from PBF interventions comes from third-party verification, which is conducted in person at each participating facility at regular intervals, often quarterly or more frequently. Such costs can be substantial: in Nigeria, for instance, PBF administrative costs were 24 percent of all program expenditures (Zeng et al. 2021). The DFF arm did not entail these costs. Even with the hybrid PBF-DFF approach, verification may incur substantial costs, especially if it is conducted in person at all facilities with any regularity. However, recent work suggests that a risk-based algorithm may substantially reduce the need for in-person verification, in turn reducing verification costs by up to two-thirds (Grover, Bauhoff, and Friedman 2019).

On the issue of performance pay amounts, two sources of evidence suggest that the service-specific amount might not be central to any observed impacts on service delivery. First, a study on the Misiones province in Argentina estimates the effect of a threefold *temporary* increase in the level of performance pay for health care providers on the initiation of prenatal care in the first trimester of pregnancy. The increased pay led to a 34 percent increase in early initiation of prenatal care in the treatment group relative to business-as-usual during the treatment period. Notably, however, this effect persisted 12 months after the increase in performance pay ended, suggesting that providers respond to more than just the price. However, the study also finds that the quality of care may have remained a constraint to improving health outcomes as the increase in the early initiation of prenatal care did not have any effect on birth outcomes. Second, lab-in-the-field experimental price elasticity estimates from Nigeria (Bauhoff and Kandpal 2021) cast some doubt on the degree to which providers respond to increases in performance pay. This result suggests that the primary role of the price may be to increase the salience of the information conveyed by the checklist. This in turn suggests another way—instead of risk-based verification—in which PBF programs can be made more cost-effective, which is by simply providing token prices. Finally, it is also important to recognize that PBF can be difficult to implement (Paul et al. 2018), making it an expensive and perhaps risky way of getting money to the frontlines.

Discussion and conclusions

Several insights emerge from the analysis presented in this chapter. The results from the meta-analysis indicate that while on average financial incentives increase the coverage of all included RMCH service indicators, the effect sizes are relatively modest, ranging between 2 and 6 percentage points, with the largest effects being for facility delivery and full childhood vaccination (about 5 percentage points). Effect size heterogeneity across financial incentive programs is estimated to be low to moderate for all the indicators except maternal tetanus vaccination.

The low to moderate levels of effect size heterogeneity across financial incentive interventions is reflected in generally small differences in mean effect sizes across the PBF, voucher, and CCT interventions. The analysis is not sufficiently powered to determine precisely the magnitudes of these differences, but, overall, the results indicate that PBF might be slightly less effective in improving RMCH coverage than voucher and CCT schemes.

When testing for other possible drivers of effect size heterogeneity across financial incentive programs, the analysis finds neither systematic evidence of complementarities between supply- and demand-side incentives nor systematic evidence of an influence of baseline indicator levels. The results of the systematic review and meta-analysis are subject to limitations. The methodological inclusion criteria are demanding, which can be considered a strength of the analysis. The exclusion of studies with less rigorous empirical methods and study designs, however, further limits the statistical power, which, despite a growing evidence base, remains insufficient for conducting a more detailed analysis of the roles of intervention design features and implementation contexts. This limitation applies to comparisons of PBF, voucher, and CCT effect sizes—the differences reported should be given a strictly associational interpretation as the analysis cannot control for confounding factors. To allow more fine-grained subgroup comparisons going forward, future studies of financial incentive interventions should rely on rigorous impact evaluation methods, reduce avoidable heterogeneity by using standard outcome variable definitions, and include detailed information about program design features.

Another limitation is that the scope of indicators targeted by financial incentive interventions is usually larger than the narrow set of outcomes in this review. Many programs incentivize other health coverage indicators in and outside the RMCH domain (for a review and summary of the evidence on the demand side, see, for example, Neelsen et al. (2021)). CCT programs often also include education and job training conditionalities and, like vouchers, can have additional effects on household consumption and welfare. Similarly, incentives to improve the quality of facility equipment and cleanliness and to streamline administrative processes are almost always included in PBF programs, whose impacts on transparency, provider accountability, and data usage are often hoped to have a transformational effect on overall health systems (Friedman and Scheffler 2016; Ma-Nitu et al. 2018). For these reasons, it is important to stress that the results of the meta-analysis only support conclusions about the effects of financial incentives on the six included indicators but not about the overall (cost-) effectiveness of specific programs or entire intervention types.

Beyond the meta-analysis, evidence from the Nigeria impact evaluation suggests that performance pay may be most effective at improving coverage where the baseline levels of the indicator are low, suggesting that paying for indicators where baseline coverage is high may not be effective since the effort required to increase coverage is not commensurate with the price paid. For indicators where baseline coverage is particularly low, demand-side barriers may be salient and at least partially addressed using low-cost cash transfers to patients/households.

Many of the constraints to effective coverage are not in the health worker's locus of control and thus do not respond well to pay-for-performance incentives. As a result, perhaps unsurprisingly, the analysis finds that

DFF, typically paired with facility-level autonomy and supervision reforms, can improve coverage and effective coverage to a similar degree as PBF—often at lower cost, since DFF does not require a verification mechanism. This mixed evidence of effectiveness is a reminder that PBF, as probably any complex intervention, may fail to improve effective coverage, and this failure can be driven by a variety of reasons.

The mixed results on the effectiveness of PBF interventions presented in this chapter highlight the complexities of a PBF intervention and suggest that thinking of DFF, PBF, and demand-side cash transfers as a menu of potentially reinforcing policy options may be a fruitful means for increasing effective coverage. The evidence also raises questions about the appeal of PBF as the primary attempt at health financing in most of the developing world. It also begs the question as to whether the substantial donor finances channeled into PBF could be used more fruitfully—at least partially—in other types of health financing approaches. DFF or direct transfers to households may attain much of the progress achieved through PBF at a lower administrative cost and with less heterogeneity in impact. Even when PBF is used, it may make sense to purchase only a small number of targeted indicators. These may be selected for such strategic purchasing if they are within the health worker's locus of control. For instance, health workers may not be in a position to respond to incentives for ANC visits because of demand-side constraints, but once a woman uses ANC services, health workers may be able to use quality of care during those visits to convince her to come back for delivery (Basinga et al. 2011; Bonfrer, Van de Poel, and Doorslaer 2014). The chapter also provided several reasons that suggest caution in attributing the observed impact of PBF on institutional deliveries entirely to the price set in the PBF system. It further discussed suggestive evidence that a token price might capture much of the benefit of performance pay, suggesting that even effective PBF programs might be made more cost-effective.

The evidence brought to bear in this report comes, in large part, from a unique effort at systematically learning about the impact of PBF approaches. In 2008, at the onset of the first trust fund, HRITF, that funded these PBF trials and impact evaluations, there were many unanswered questions about the use of PBF to improve effective coverage in LMICs. As this chapter has demonstrated, the large number of pilot projects and impact evaluations funded by the HRITF has led to substantial learning about where, when, and why PBF approaches might work and how they can be strengthened.

Nonetheless, this body of evidence also highlights that PBF is far from the only, or even the most uniformly appealing, option on the path to sustainable health facility financing and universal health coverage. By shedding light on a menu of viable policy options available for health system financing and strengthening, this report aims to provide options for policy makers. Both PBF and DFF represent notable improvements over business-as-usual in moving forward with the desired transformation of health systems. Compared with PBF, the ease of implementation and low administrative costs of DFF may make it particularly appealing to country governments in responding to the health system challenges imposed by COVID-19, but the link to results in PBF approaches may make it more appealing to donors. Even with the gains from PBF or DFF, the end levels of effective coverage remain poor and much work remains to be done to meet the Sustainable Development Goal of good health and well-being for all. PBF or DFF alone is unlikely to close the entirety of the gap that remains. Thus, the report closes with two chapters that look ahead by building on the findings presented here. Chapter 7 presents a research agenda and cautionary evidence on the risks of overutilization of care on using PBF to develop health systems; chapter 8 closes with a discussion of the operational implications of the research reviewed here.

Annex 6A: Additional tables

Table 6A.1   Characteristics of included reports

Country	Intervention name	Start year	Reference	Years post-treatment data collected	Indicators with impact estimates						Randomized	Statistical model	Risk of bias
					Modern family planning	4+ ANC checks	Maternal tetanus vaccination	Facility delivery	1+ PNC checks	Full child vaccination			
Performance-Based Financing													
Afghanistan	System Enhancement for Health Action in Transition	2010	Engineer et al. (2016)	2010–2012	X				X		Yes	SD	Medium
Burkina Faso	Reproductive Health Project I	2013	De Allegri, Lohmann, and Hillebrecht (2018)	2015–2017	X	X	X	X	X	X	No	DID	Medium
Burkina Faso	Reproductive Health Project II	2013	De Allegri, Lohmann, and Hillebrecht (2018)	2015–2017	X	X	X	X	X	X	No	DID	Medium
Burundi	PBF Scheme	2006	Bonfrer et al. (2014)	2007–2010	X		X	X			No	DID	High
			Bonfrer et al. (2014)	2006–2011			X	X		X	No	DID	Medium
			Gage and Bauhoff (2021)	2006–2017		X		X			No	DID	Medium
			Rudasingwa, Soeters, and Basenya (2017)	2007–2008			X	X			No	DID	Medium
Cambodia	Contracting-in	2004	Van de Poel et al. (2014)	2004–2010				X		X	No	DID	Medium

(Continued)

Table 6A.1 *continued*

Country	Intervention name	Start year	Reference	Years post-treatment data collected	Modern family planning	4+ ANC checks	Maternal tetanus vaccination	Facility delivery	1+ PNC checks	Full child vaccination	Randomized	Statistical model	Risk of bias
					|—— Indicators with impact estimates ——|								
Cambodia	Government Scheme	2004	Van de Poel et al. (2014)	2004–2010				X		X	No	DID	Medium
Cameroon	Health Sector Support Investment Project I	2012	de Walque et al. (2021)	2013–2015	X		X			X	Yes	DID	Low
Cameroon	Health Sector Support Investment Project II	2012	de Walque et al. (2021)	2013–2015	X		X			X	Yes	DID	Low
Congo, Dem. Rep.	Health Sector Rehabilitation and Support Project	2010	Huillery and Seban (forthcoming)	2011–2012				X		X	Yes	SD	Medium
Congo, Rep.	Health Sector Services Development Project	2012	Zeng, Shepard, de Dieu Rusatira, et al. (2018); Zeng, Shepard, Nguyen, et al. (2018)	2012–2014	X	.		X	X		No	DID	Medium
Gambia, The	Maternal and Child Nutrition and Health Results Project	2014	Ferguson et al. (2020)	2014–2016				X		X	Yes	DID	Medium
Lesotho	Health System Performance Enhancement Project	2016	Gage and Bauhoff (2021)	2016–2018		X		X			No	DID	Medium
Nigeria	State Health Investment Project I	2014	Kandpal et al. (2016)	2015–2017	X	X		X		X	No	DID	Medium

(Continued)

Table 6A.1 *continued*

Country	Intervention name	Start year	Reference	Years post-treatment data collected	Indicators with impact estimates						Randomized	Statistical model	Risk of bias
					Modern family planning	4+ ANC checks	Maternal tetanus vaccination	Facility delivery	1+ PNC checks	Full child vaccination			
Nigeria	State Health Investment Project II	2014	Kandpal et al. (2016)	2015–2017	X	X		X		X	No	DID	Medium
Rwanda	PBF scheme	2006	Basinga et al. (2011)	2006–2008	X	X		X		X	No	DID	High
			Gertler and Vermeersch (2013)	2006–2008	X	X					No	DID	Medium
			Lannes et al. (2016)	2006–2008	X	X		X			No	DID	High
			Okeke and Chari (2015)	2006–2008		X	X				No	DID	Medium
			Priedeman Skiles et al. (2013)	2006–2008	X	X		X		X	No	DID	High
			Sherry, Bauhoff, and Mohanan (2017)	2006–2008	X	X	X	X		X	No	DID	Medium
Rwanda	Community Living Standards Grant	2009	Shapira et al. (2018)	2010–2014	X	X		X			Yes	SD	Low
Senegal	Health and Nutrition Financing Project	2012	Gage and Bauhoff (2021)	2012–2017		X		.X			No	DID	Medium
Tajikistan	Health Services Improvement Project	2015	Ahmed et al. (2006); Ahmed et al. (2022)	2015–2018	X	X				X	Yes	DID	Medium

(Continued)

169

Table 6A.1 continued

Country	Intervention name	Start year	Reference	Years post-treatment data collected	Modern family planning	4+ ANC checks	Maternal tetanus vaccination	Facility delivery	1+ PNC checks	Full child vaccination	Randomized	Statistical model	Risk of bias
					Indicators with impact estimates								
Tanzania	Pwani Pilot	2011	Binyaruka et al. (2015)	2012–2013		X	X	X	X		No	DID	Medium
Zambia	Zambia Health Services Improvement Project I	2012	Gage and Bauhoff (2021)	2012–2018		X		X			Yes	DID	Low
			World Bank (2016a, 2016b)	2012–2015		X	X	X	X	X	Yes	DID	Low
			Zeng, Shepard, de Dieu Rusatira, et al. (2018); Zeng, Shepard, Nguyen, et al. (2018)	2012–2015				X	X		Yes	DID	Low
Zambia	Zambia Health Services Improvement Project II	2012	World Bank (2016a, 2016b)	2012–2015		X	X	X	X	X	Yes	DID	Low
			Zeng, Shepard, de Dieu Rusatira, et al. (2018); Zeng, Shepard, Nguyen, et al. (2018)	2012–2015				X	X		Yes	DID	Low
Zimbabwe	Health Sector Development Support Project	2011	Gage and Bauhoff (2021)	2012–2015		X		X			No	DID	Medium
			World Bank (2016a, 2016b)	2012–2014	X		X	X	X	X	No	DID	Medium

(Continued)

Table 6A.1 *continued*

Country	Intervention name	Start year	Reference	Years post-treatment data collected	Modern family planning	4+ ANC checks	Maternal tetanus vaccination	Facility delivery	1+ PNC checks	Full child vaccination	Randomized	Statistical model	Risk of bias
Vouchers													
Cambodia	Reproductive Health Voucher	2010	Bajracharya et al. (2016)	2012–2013	X						No	DID	Medium
Cambodia	Targeted Maternal and Child Health Voucher	2007	Van de Poel et al. (2014)	2007–2010				X	X		No	DID	Medium
Cambodia	Universal Maternal and Child Health Voucher	2008	Van de Poel et al. (2014)	2008–2010		X		X	X		No	DID	Medium
Kenya	Reproductive Health Voucher	2006	Dennis et al. (2018)	2010–2013		X		X	X		No	DID	Medium
Kenya	Maternal Voucher Experiment	2013	Grépin, Habyarimana, and Jack (2019)	2013		X		X			Yes	SD	Low
Pakistan	Jhang Maternal Health Voucher	2010	Agha (2011)	2010–2011				X	X		No	DID	High
Pakistan	Marie Stopes Chakwal Voucher	2012	Ali et al. (2019)	2015	X						Yes	DID	Medium
Pakistan	Suraj	2008	Azmat et al. (2016)	2013	X						No	DID	High
Tanzania	Helping Poor Pregnant Women Access Better Health Care	2010	Kuwawenaruwa et al. (2019)	2013–2014		X		X	X		No	DID	Medium

(Continued)

171

Table 6A.1 continued

Country	Intervention name	Start year	Reference	Years post-treatment data collected	Indicators with impact estimates						Randomized	Statistical model	Risk of bias
					Modern family planning	4+ ANC checks	Maternal tetanus vaccination	Facility delivery	1+ PNC checks	Full child vaccination			
Uganda	HealthyBaby	2008	Obare et al. (2016)	2010–2011		X		X	X	X	No	DID	High
Conditional Cash Transfers													
Afghanistan	Ministry of Public Health Scheme	2016	Edmond et al. (2019)	2016–2017				X			No	DID	High
Bangladesh	Demand-Side Financing Program	2004	Keya et al. (2018)	2011–2012				X			No	DID	High
		2008	Nguyen et al. (2012)	2008–2009				X			No	DID	High
China	CHIMACA	2007	Hemminki et al. (2013)	2007–2009					X		Yes	SD	High
Honduras	Bono 10,000	2010	Benedetti, Ibarrarán, and McEwan (2016)	2012–2013			X		X	X	Yes	SD	Low
Honduras	Programa de Asignación Familiar (PRAF II)	2000	Morris et al. (2004)	2001–2002			X		X		Yes	DID	Low
India	Indira Gandhi Motherhood Support Scheme	2011	von Haaren and Klonner (2020)	2012–2016					X	X	No	DID	High
India	Janani Suraksha Yojana	2005	Debnath (2013)	2005–2008				X			No	DID	Medium
India		2005	Powell-Jackson, Mazumdar, and Mills (2015)	2005–2008				X			No	DID	High

(Continued)

Table 6A.1 *continued*

Country	Intervention name	Start year	Reference	Years post-treatment data collected	Modern family planning	4+ ANC checks	Maternal tetanus vaccination	Facility delivery	1+ PNC checks	Full child vaccination	Randomized	Statistical model	Risk of bias
Indonesia	Program Keluarga Harapan	2007–2008	Alatas (2011)	2008–2009		X		X		X	No	IV	High
			Cahyadi et al. (2018)	2007–2013				X		X	No	IV	Medium/High
			Kusuma et al. (2016)	2008–2009		X		X			Yes	DID	Medium
			Kusuma et al. (2017)	2009						X	Yes	DID	Low
			Triyana (2013)	2008–2009			X	X			Yes	DID	Low
Kenya	M-SIMU RCT	2013	Gibson et al. (2017)	2014–2015						X	Yes	SD	High
Kenya	Maternal Conditional Cash Transfer Experiment I	2013	Grépin, Habyarimana, and Jack (2019)	2013		X		X			Yes	SD	Low
Kenya	Maternal Conditional Cash Transfer Experiment II	2013	Grépin, Habyarimana, and Jack (2019)	2013				X			Yes	SD	Low
Kenya	Maternal Conditional Cash Transfer and Voucher Experiment	2013	Grépin, Habyarimana, and Jack (2019)	2013				X			Yes	SD	Low
Mali	Cash for Nutritional Awareness	2014	Adubra et al. (2019)	2014–2016				X	X	X	Yes	DID	Medium
Mexico	Progresa	1997	Barber and Gertler (2010)	1998–2003			X				Yes	SD	Low

(Continued)

Table 6A.1 *continued*

Country	Intervention name	Start year	Reference	Years post-treatment data collected	Modern family planning	4+ ANC checks	Maternal tetanus vaccination	Facility delivery	1+ PNC checks	Full child vaccination	Randomized	Statistical model	Risk of bias
Nicaragua	Red de Protección Social	2001	Barham and Maluccio (2009)	2001						X	Yes	DID	Low
			Handa and Maluccio (2010)	2001						X	Yes	SD	Medium
Nigeria	Maternal Cash Transfer Experiment	2017	Okeke, Wagner, and Abubakar (2020)	2017–2018				X			Yes	SD	Medium
Peru	Juntos	2005	Díaz and Saldarriaga (2017)	2006–2014		X		X	X		No	DDD	Medium
			Díaz and Saldarriaga (2019)	2005–2011			X				No	DID	Medium
Philippines	Pantawid Pamilya	2008	Kandpal et al. (2016)	2008–2011		X		X	X		Yes	SD	Low
Turkey	Social Risk Mitigation Project	2004	Ahmed et al. (2006); Ahmed et al. (2022)	2005–2006						X	No	RD	High
Zimbabwe	Manicaland HIV/STD Project	2010	Robertson et al. (2013)	2011						X	Yes	SD	Medium

Source: World Bank.

Note: Statistical model: DDD = triple difference; DID = double difference; IV = instrumental variables; SD = single difference. ANC = antenatal care; PBF = performance-based financing; PNC = postnatal care.

Table 6A.2 PBF and DFF interventions, by country, in the five countries in the pooled analysis of PBF versus DFF (Cameroon, Nigeria, Rwanda, Zambia, and Zimbabwe): Comparison of alternative financing approaches

Country	Arm of intervention	Description	Contract	Business plan	Quality evaluation	Review/ verification of service amounts	Payment	Management autonomy	Report
Cameroon	T1: PBF	Complete PBF with performance bonuses for medical personnel	Yes, classic PBF contract	PBF payments can be used based on priorities identified in their business plans, including to offer health worker performance or retention bonuses or to purchase inputs	Quality evaluation and feedback, accounting for quality in bonus payment	Review and verification of service quantities	Payments tied to performance	Management autonomy with control over all revenues	Monthly activity report submitted to district
	C1: Direct financing	PBF with subsidies that are not linked to performance	Yes, contract stipulating the conditions of PBF for verification and supervision	Facilities develop business plans	Quality evaluation with feedback as in T1, but no effect on payment	Review and verification of service quantities	Payments not tied to performance	Management autonomy with control over all revenues	Monthly activity report submitted to district
	C2: Enhanced supervision and monitoring	Only supervision, without bonuses or autonomy	Yes, contract stipulating technical support in the form of supervision	Simple business plan focused on intensified supervision	Quality evaluation with feedback as in T1	Review and verification of service quantities	No payment	No management autonomy, continuation of the status quo system	Monthly activity report submitted to district
	C3: Control group	Status quo	No contract	No business plan	Quality evaluation with written feedback twice a year	Single quarterly statement without verification of the quantity of services produced	No payment	No management autonomy, continuation of the status quo system	Monthly activity report submitted to district

(Continued)

Table 6A.2 *continued*

Country	Arm of intervention	Description	Contract	Business plan	Quality evaluation	Review/ verification of service amounts	Payment	Management autonomy	Report
Nigeria	PBF	PBF as part of the Nigeria State Health Investment Project	Yes, classic PBF contract	Yes, facilities could use these funds for: (1) health facility operational costs (about 50%), including maintenance and repair, drugs and consumables, outreach, and other quality enhancement measures; and (2) performance bonuses for health workers (up to 50%)	A quantitative supervisory checklist (QSC) that assessed structural and process quality of care was used by local government area supervisors and formed the basis of a quality bonus. The QSC was also verified by the external verification agency. An additional bonus was tied to the remoteness of the facility.	Health services indicators were reported monthly by the health facilities and verified quarterly by an external verification agency. A quarterly audit assessed structural and process quality at each facility using a comprehensive checklist. Bonuses were tied to quality indicators as measured through a comprehensive quality checklist, with further bonuses for facility remoteness.	Yes, quarterly payment contingent upon the delivery of a predefined set of health services under PBF	Money would be transferred electronically to the facility's bank account. The amount earned by the facility was transferred electronically to the facility's bank account for which the signatories were the officer in charge and the chair of the Ward Development Committee.	Monthly and verified quarterly

(Continued)

Table 6A.2 *continued*

Country	Arm of intervention	Description	Contract	Business plan	Quality evaluation	Review/ verification of service amounts	Payment	Management autonomy	Report
	DFF	DFF as part of the Nigeria State Health Investment Project	Yes, facilities were paid after the conditions, such as management arrangements, previous period fund utilization, and transparent use of funds had been met	Yes, the funds could be used to finance operational costs but not performance bonuses for staff	DFF facilities were not subject to third-party verification of quanity or quality.	DFF facilities were not subject to third-party verification of quanity or quality	Yes, quarterly DFF payments were calculated to be equal to the average funds earned by the PBF facilities net of the performance bonuses (50% of the average PBF payment). DFF facilities received half the amount the PBF facilities earned since DFF facilities were not allowed to pay performance bonuses to their staff.	The payments were provided directly to the facilities. DFF facilities had the same level of autonomy in using their funds as PBF facilities, they were supervised in a similar way, and they received funds into their bank accounts through electronic transfer.	As is the case for PBF facilities, DFF facilities send monthly reports of a comprehensive quality score checklist, but these reports were not verified on a quarterly basis.

(Continued)

Country	Arm of intervention	Description	Contract	Business plan	Quality evaluation	Review/ verification of service amounts	Payment	Management autonomy	Report
Rwanda	PBF	Performance pay: provides financial incentives for providers to increase the use and quality of care of maternal and child services	No contract. The government of Rwanda implemented a national performance pay scheme to supplement primary health care centers' input-based budgets with bonus payments based on the quantity and quality of key services.	No business plan	Every quarter, supervisors from the district hospital assess quality indicators through direct observation and review of patient records. At the end of the visit, they discuss their findings with the facility's personnel and provide recommendations to improve quality of services. The facility's overall quality is measured as an index of both structural and process measures of quality of care for various types of services. The quality indicators are assessed through the regular monitoring system, in which district hospitals monitor and supervise the quality of health centers in their districts.	Third-party auditors review the utilization registry and facility records each quarter. A comparison of facility records with face-to-face interviews of a random sample of patients reported very little false reporting.	Payment tied to performance	Performance payments go directly to facilities and are used at each facility's discretion	Facilities report their monthly indicators to the district PBF steering committee responsible for authorizing payment. For the referral indicators, the facility must also submit verification from the hospital that the referral was appropriate and the referred patient was treated.
	Control	C2 ("pure control" arm) group received nothing.	No contract	None	None	None	Business-as-usual in Rwanda includes enhanced facility financing	None	None

(Continued)

Table 6A.2 *continued*

Country	Arm of intervention	Description	Contract	Business plan	Quality evaluation	Review/ verification of service amounts	Payment	Management autonomy	Report
Zambia	PBF	PBF facilities received emergency obstetric and neonatal care equipment and PBF performance-based grants	Yes, "contracting-in" public health system using the existing government systems and structures in Zambia	Health facilities in the PBF districts were allowed to use a maximum of 60% of their PBF funds for staff incentives, and a minimum of 40% for investments and other recurrent/ operational costs at the health facilities and communities. The percentages allocated varied by health facility, both across districts and over time.	Monthly visits from district health teams to health facilities for quantity audit. Hospital quarterly visits to health facilities for quality audit. The evaluation was unannounced to the health facility teams and could take place anytime during a particular quarterly period. Hospital submits quality report to district medical offices.	For internal and external verification processes, reported data were extensively audited. District Results-Based Financing (RBF) Steering Committees were the internal verifiers, Provincial RBF Steering Committees were the purchasers, and the Ministry of Health headquarters was both the fund holder and regulator.	Payments were tied to performance. Ministry of Health facilitates payment after verifying data.	To promote fiscal decentralization and support autonomy of resources, PBF health facilities received performance-based payments directly into their bank accounts after the delivery of the pre-agreed indicators on quantity and quality.	District medical offices compile quality and quantity reports and submit provisional invoices to the district steering committee (DSC). District medical offices compile quality and quantity reports and submit provisional invoices to DSC. DSC verifies provisional invoices and submits validated invoices to Provincial RBF Steering Committee for approval.

(Continued)

Table 6A.2 *continued*

Country	Arm of intervention	Description	Contract	Business plan	Quality evaluation	Review/ verification of service amounts	Payment	Management autonomy	Report
	DFF	C1 group ("enhanced financing" arm) received emergency obstetric and neonatal care equipment exactly as in the PBF and the equivalent in money of the average PBF performance-related grants as input financing	Yes, "contracting-in" public health system using the existing government systems and structures in Zambia	The PBF matching grants that were disbursed to C1 districts had some restrictions on their spending, namely: (1) resources could only be used for meal allowances or per diems according to the number of days worked, and (2) activities had to be related to the delivery of maternal and child health interventions at the health facility level. The manner in which health facilities in C1 districts used the PBF matching grant was also dependent on how much was disbursed to the health facility by the district medical office.	None		Payments not tied to performance	Money disbursed to the health facilities in C1 districts was required to be spent down before replenishment. This was contrary to health facilities in the PBF arm where PBF payments were disbursed directly into the health center bank accounts and spending down previous funds was not required.	None
	Control	C2 ("pure control" arm) group received nothing	No contract	None	None	None	No payment	None	None

(Continued)

Country	Arm of intervention	Description	Contract	Business plan	Quality evaluation	Review/ verification of service amounts	Payment	Management autonomy	Report
Zimbabwe	PBF	PBF in Zimbabwe consists of three components: payment for quantity of services, payment for quality of services, and, if applicable, a remoteness bonus. For rural health centers, the quantity component consists of payment on a unit price basis for provision of selected indicators identified by the Ministry of Health and Child Care as mother and child health priorities. A facility's enrollment in the PBF intervention component was conditional on removing or waiving user fees for the partial package of services that are incentivized. Waiving of user fees was verified by an independent firm in implementing facilities.	Yes, contracting "pay for service conditional on quality" is done not only with the health facilities, but also other stakeholders such as the district and provincial health executives	A financial plan has been prepared, including adequate community arrangements, user charges for different services, transfer of funds to districts, allocation of premiums, and application of funds	The quality of services was measured using a balanced scorecard covering numerous aspects of structural and process quality, as well as organizational and management systems	Balanced scorecard filled out during verification visits by the District Health Executive for rural health centers, or the Province Health Executive for district hospitals every quarter	Payments for service conditional on quality	No autonomy over hiring and firing staff, but decentralized planning and decision making for investments at the facility level. The PBF facilities had the autonomy to utilize the PBF earnings in consultation with the Health Center Committees.	Reporting to supervision and verification by the health managers. Reporting to and verification by the beneficiary of the community.

(Continued)

Table 6A.2 *continued*

Country	Arm of intervention	Description	Contract	Business plan	Quality evaluation	Review/ verification of service amounts	Payment	Management autonomy	Report
	DFF	Control: for the last 18 months of the 24-month study period, facilities in control districts received equivalent fixed funding each quarter through the UNICEF-administered Health Transitions Fund, which was not tied to performance. User fees were also waived under the Health Transitions Fund.	No contract	None	None	None	Equivalent fixed payment not tied to performance	None	None

Sources: Cameroon: de Walque et al. 2021; Nigeria: Kandpal et al. 2019; Rwanda: Gertler et al. 2010; Zambia: Friedman et al. 2016; Zimbabwe: World Bank 2016c.

Note: C1 = direct financing; C2 = enhanced supervision and monitoring; C3 = control group; DFF = direct facility financing; DSC = district steering committee; PBF = performance-based financing; QSC = quantitative supervisory checklist; RBF = results-based financing; T1 = PBF arm of the intervention; UNICEF = United Nations Children's Fund.

Notes

1. Across intervention types, most programs were in various stages of piloting during evaluation, with only two PBF programs (Burundi's PBF and Rwanda's pay-for-performance scheme) and four CCT programs (India's Janani Suraksha Yojana (JSY), Mexico's Progresa, Peru's Juntos, and Turkey's Social Risk Mitigation programs) having nationwide or near nationwide scope. There is only a small number of programs (India's JSY, Kenya's Mobile Solutions for Immunization CCT pilot, and the Suraj and Chakwal vouchers in Pakistan) that incentivize only a single health service, as the other programs typically target a broad range of family planning and MCH indicators. Information on the magnitudes of incentives relative to baseline facility, health worker, and household incomes is often lacking or difficult to compare across programs, but where they are available, they indicate substantial variation. In the Tajik PBF pilot, for instance, incentive payments amount to 70 percent of base health worker salaries—more than twice the rate in the Afghanistan PBF pilot.

2. Moreover, relatively narrow service coverage variable definitions were used to identify the effect sizes eligible for this review, to minimize the risk of outcome variable heterogeneity as a confounding factor. Nevertheless, a degree of variation in—and uncertainty about—coverage variable definitions remains (see Neelsen et al. 2021, table 3). For instance, reports estimating impacts on modern family planning sometimes do not list the specific contraceptive types they include, and among studies with explicit reporting of contraceptive types, some differences (for example, whether condoms are included) can exist. However, examining the robustness of overall and subgroup-specific mean effect sizes to the omission of effect sizes with diverging indicator definitions does not lead to meaningful changes on effect size magnitudes or significance.

3. The Nigerian pilot leveraged the local Ward Development Committee for community oversight. This committee is a "pre-existing community group that addresses development challenges for a population of 10,000–20,000 people" (Khanna et al. 2021, 4).

References

Adubra, L., A. Le Port, Y. Kameli, S. Fortin, T. Mahamadou, M. T. Ruel, Y. Martin-Prevel, and M. Savy. 2019. "Conditional Cash Transfer and/or Lipid-Based Nutrient Supplement Targeting the First 1000 D of Life Increased Attendance at Preventive Care Services but Did Not Improve Linear Growth in Young Children in Rural Mali: Results of a Cluster-Randomized Controlled Trial." *American Journal of Clinical Nutrition* 110 (6): 1476–90.

Agha, S. 2011. "Changes in the Proportion of Facility-Based Deliveries and Related Maternal Health Services among the Poor in Rural Jhang, Pakistan: Results from a Demand-Side Financing Intervention." *International Journal for Equity in Health* 10 (1): 57.

Ahmed, A., D. Gilligan, A. Kudat, R. Colasan, H. Tatlidil, and B. Ozbilgin. 2006. "Interim Impact Evaluation of the Conditional Cash Transfer Program in Turkey: A Quantitative Assessment." International Food Policy Research Institute, Washington, DC.

Ahmed, T., A. Arur, D. de Walque, and G. Shapira. 2022. "Incentivizing Quantity and Quality of Care: Evidence from an Impact Evaluation of Performance-Based Financing in the Health Sector in Tajikistan." *Economic Development and Cultural Change*. https://doi.org/10.1086/713941.

Alatas, V. 2011. "Program Keluarga Harapan: Impact Evaluation of Indonesia's Pilot Household Conditional Cash Transfer Program." World Bank Office, Jakarta, Indonesia.

Ali, M., S. K. Azmat, H. B. Hamza, M. M. Rahman, and W. Hameed. 2019. "Are Family Planning Vouchers Effective in Increasing Use, Improving Equity and Reaching the Underserved? An Evaluation of a Voucher Program in Pakistan." *BMC Health Services Research* 19: Article 200.

Azmat, S. K., W. Hameed, H. B. Hamza, G. Mustafa, M. Ishaque, G. Abbas, O. F. Khan, et al. 2016. "Engaging with Community-Based Public and Private Mid-Level Providers for Promoting the Use of Modern Contraceptive Methods in Rural Pakistan: Results from Two Innovative Birth Spacing Interventions." *Reproductive Health* 13: Article 25.

Baird, S., C. McIntosh, and B. Özler. 2011. "Cash or Condition? Evidence from a Cash Transfer Experiment." *Quarterly Journal of Economics* 126 (4): 1709–53.

Bajracharya, A., L. Veasnakiry, T. Rathavy, and B. Bellows. 2016. Increasing Uptake of Long-Acting Reversible Contraceptives in Cambodia Through a Voucher Program: Evidence From a Difference-in-Differences Analysis. *Global Health: Science and Practice*; 4 Suppl 2: S109-21.

Barber, S. L., and P. J. Gertler. 2010. "Empowering Women: How Mexico's Conditional Cash Transfer Programme Raised Prenatal Care Quality and Birth Weight." *Journal of Development Effectiveness* 2 (1): 51–73.

Barham, T., and J. A. Maluccio. 2009. "Eradicating Diseases: The Effect of Conditional Cash Transfers on Vaccination Coverage in Rural Nicaragua." *Journal of Health Economics* 28 (3): 611–21.

Basinga, P., P. J. Gertler, A. Binagwaho, A. L. Soucat, J. Sturdy, and C. M. Vermeersch. 2011. "Effect on Maternal and Child Health Services in Rwanda of Payment to Primary Health-Care Providers for Performance: An Impact Evaluation." *The Lancet* 377 (9775): 1421–28.

Bassani, D. G., P. Arora, K. Wazny, M. F. Gaffey, L. Lenters, and Z. A. Bhutta. 2013. "Financial Incentives and Coverage of Child Health Interventions: A Systematic Review and Meta-Analysis." *BMC Public Health* 13 (3): 1–13.

Bauhoff, S., and E. Kandpal. 2021. "Information, Loss Framing, and Spillovers in Pay-for-Performance Contracts." Policy Research Working Paper 9687, World Bank, Washington, DC.

Belaid, L., A. Dumont, N. Chaillet, A. Zertal, and V. De Brouwere. 2016. "Effectiveness of Demand Generation Interventions on Use of Modern Contraceptives in Low- and Middle-Income Countries." *Tropical Medicine & International Health* 21 (10): 1240–54.

Bellows, B., C. Bulaya, S. Inambwae, C. L. Lissner, M. Ali, and A. Bajracharya. 2016. "Family Planning Vouchers in Low and Middle Income Countries: A Systematic Review." *Studies in Family Planning* 47 (4): 357–70.

Benedetti, F., P. Ibarrarán, and P. J. McEwan. 2016. "Do Education and Health Conditions Matter in a Large Cash Transfer? Evidence from a Honduran Experiment." *Economic Development and Cultural Change* 64 (4): 759–93.

Benhassine, N., F. Devoto, E. Duflo, P. Dupas, and V. Poulique. 2015. "Turning a Shove into a Nudge? A 'Labeled Cash Transfer' for Education." *American Economic Journal: Economic Policy* 7 (3): 86–125.

Binyaruka, P., E. Patouillard, T. Powell-Jackson, G. Greco, O. Maestad, and J. Borghi. 2015. "Effect of Paying for Performance on Utilisation, Quality, and User Costs of Health Services in Tanzania: A Controlled Before and After Study." *PLoS One* 10 (8): e0135013.

Björkman, M., and J. Svensson. 2009. "Power to the People: Evidence from a Randomized Field Experiment on Community-Based Monitoring in Uganda." *Quarterly Journal of Economics* 124 (2): 735–69.

Bonfrer, I., R. Soeters, E. Van de Poel, O. Basenya, G. Longin, F. van de Looij, and E. van Doorslaer. 2014. "Introduction of Performance-Based Financing in Burundi Was Associated with Improvements in Care and Quality." *Health Affairs* 33 (12): 2179–87.

Bonfrer, I., E. Van de Poel, and E. V. Doorslaer. 2014. "The Effects of Performance Incentives on the Utilization and Quality of Maternal and Child Care in Burundi." *Social Science & Medicine* 123: 96–104.

Borenstein, M., L. Hedges, and J. Higgins. 2009. *Introduction to Meta-Analysis.* Chichester, UK: John Wiley & Sons.

Bridges, K., and M. Woolcock. 2019. *"Implementing Adaptive Approaches in Real World Scenarios: A Nigeria Case Study, with Lessons for Theory and Practice."* Policy Research Working Paper 8904, World Bank, Washington, DC.

Cahyadi, N., R. Hanna, B. A. Olken, R. A. Prima, E. Satriawan, and E. Syamsulhakim. 2018. "Cumulative Impacts of Conditional Cash Transfer Programs: Experimental Evidence from Indonesia." NBER Working Paper 24670, National Bureau of Economic Research, Cambridge, MA.

Card, N. A. 2015. *Applied Meta-Analysis for Social Science Research.* New York: Guilford Press.

Chiba, Y., M. A. Oguttu, and T. Nakayama. 2012. "Quantitative and Qualitative Verification of Data Quality in the Childbirth Registers of Two Rural District Hospitals in Western Kenya." *Midwifery* 28 (3): 329–39.

Cullen, D., M. Sidebotham, J. Gamble, and J. Fenwick. 2016. "Young Student's Motivations to Choose an Undergraduate Midwifery Program." *Women and Birth* 29 (3): 234–39.

De Allegri, M., J. Lohmann, and M. Hillebrecht. 2018. "Results-Based Financing for Health Impact Evaluation in Burkina Faso: Results Report. Institute of Public Health, Heidelberg University, Germany.

de Souza Cruz, R. C., L. B. Azevedo de Moura, and J. J. Soares Neto. 2017. "Conditional Cash Transfers and the Creation of Equal Opportunities of Health for Children in Low and Middle-Income Countries: A Literature Review." *International Journal for Equity in Health* 16: Article 161.

de Walque, D., A. Chukwuma, N. Ayivi-Guedehoussou, and M. Koshkakaryan. 2022. "Invitations, Incentives, and Conditions. A Randomized Evaluation of Demand-Side Interventions for Health Screenings." *Social Science & Medicine* 296: 114763.

de Walque, D., J. Friedman, E. Kandpal, M. Saenz, and C. Vermeersch. 2022. "Performance-Based Financing versus Direct Facility Financing for Primary Health Service Delivery: Pooled Evidence from Five Sub-Saharan African Countries." World Bank, Washington, DC.

de Walque, D., P. J. Robyn, H. Saidou, G. Sorgho, and M. Steenland. 2021. "Looking into the Performance-Based Financing Black Box: Evidence from an Impact Evaluation in the Health Sector in Cameroon." *Health Policy and Planning* 36 (6): 835–47.

Debnath, S. 2013. "Improving Maternal Health with Incentives to Mothers vs. Health Workers: Evidence from India." University of Virginia, Charlottesville, VA.

Dennis, M. L., T. Abuya, O. M. R. Campbell, L. Benová, A. Baschieri, M. Quartagno, and B. Bellow. 2018. "Evaluating the Impact of a Maternal Health Voucher Programme on Service Use before and after the Introduction of Free Maternity Services in Kenya: A Quasi-Experimental Study." *BMJ Global Health* 3 (2).

Diaconu, K., J. Falconer, A. Verbel, A. Fretheim, and S. Witter. 2020. "Paying for Performance to Improve the Delivery of Health Interventions in Low- and Middle-Income Countries." *Cochrane Database of Systematic Reviews* 12: CD007899.

Díaz, J., and V. Saldarriaga. 2017. "Promoting Prenatal Health Care in Poor Rural Areas through Conditional Cash Transfers: Evidence from JUNTOS in Peru." Avances de Investigación 25. Lima, Peru: GRADE.

Díaz, J., and V. Saldarriaga. 2019. "Encouraging Use of Prenatal Care through Conditional Cash Transfers: Evidence from JUNTOS in Peru." *Health Economics* 28 (9): 1099–1113.

Doran, T., and M. Roland. 2011. "Lessons from Major Initiatives to Improve Primary Care in the United Kingdom." *Health Affairs* 29 (5): 1023–29.

Edmond, K. M., A. I. Foshanji, M. Naziri, A. Higgins-Steele, J. M. Burke, N. Strobel, and F. Farewar. 2019. "Conditional Cash Transfers to Improve Use of Health Facilities by Mothers and Newborns in Conflict Affected Countries, a Prospective Population Based Intervention Study from Afghanistan." *BMC Pregnancy and Childbirth* 19: Article 193.

Engineer, C. Y., E. Dale, A. Agarwal, A. Agarwal, O. Alonge, A. Edward, S. Gupta, et al. 2016. "Effectiveness of a Pay-for-Performance Intervention to Improve Maternal and Child Health Services in Afghanistan: A Cluster-Randomized Trial." *International Journal of Epidemiology* 45 (2): 451–59.

Falisse, J.-B., J. Ndayishimiye, V. Kamenyero, and M. Bossuyt. 2014. "Performance-Based Financing in the Context of Selective Free Health-Care: An Evaluation of Its Effects on the Use of Primary Health-Care Services in Burundi Using Routine Data." *Health Policy and Planning* 30: 1251–60.

Fehr, E., and L. Goette. 2007. "Do Workers Work More If Wages Are High? Evidence from a Randomized Field Experiment." *American Economic Review* 97 (1): 298–317.

Ferguson, L., R. Hasan, C. Boudreaux, H. Thomas, M. Jallow, and G. Fink. 2020. "Results-Based Financing to Increase Uptake of Skilled Delivery Services in The Gambia: Using the 'Three Delays' Model to Interpret Midline Evaluation Findings." *BMC Pregnancy and Childbirth* 20 (1): 712.

Filmer, D., and N. Schady. 2011. "Does More Cash in Conditional Cash Transfer Programs Always Lead to Larger Impacts on School Attendance?" *Journal of Development Economics* 96 (1): 150–57.

Friedman, J., A. Das, and R. Mutasa. 2017. "Rewarding Provider Performance to Improve Quality and Coverage of Maternal and Child Health Outcomes: Zimbabwe Results-Based Financing Pilot Program: Evidence to Inform Policy and Management Decisions." World Bank, Washington, DC.

Friedman, J., and E. Kandpal. 2021. "The Roles of Financial Incentives and Performance Monitoring in Improving the Quality of Health Care: Evidence from a National Pay-for-Performance Trial in the Kyrgyz Republic." World Bank, Washington, DC.

Friedman, J., J. Qamruddin, C. Chansa, and A. K. Das. 2016. "Impact Evaluation of Zambia's Health Results-Based Financing Pilot Project." World Bank, Washington, DC.

Friedman, J., and R. M. Scheffler. 2016. "Pay for Performance in Health Systems: Theory, Evidence and Case Studies." In *World Scientific Handbook of Global Health Economics and Public Policy: Volume 3: Health System Characteristics and Performance*, edited by R. M. Scheffler, 295–332. World Scientific.

Fritsche, G. B., R. Soeters, and B. Meessen. 2014. *Performance-Based Financing Toolkit*. Washington, DC: World Bank.

Gaarder, M. M., A. Glassman, and J. E. Todd. 2010. "Conditional Cash Transfers and Health: Unpacking the Causal Chain." *Journal of Development Effectiveness* 2 (1): 6–50.

Gage, A., and S. Bauhoff. 2021. "The Effects of Performance-Based Financing on Neonatal Health Outcomes in Burundi, Lesotho, Senegal, Zambia and Zimbabwe." *Health Policy and Planning* 36 (3): 332–40.

Gertler, P., P. Giovagnoli, and S. Martinez. 2014. "Rewarding Provider Performance to Enable a Healthy Start to Life: Evidence from Argentina's Plan Nacer." Policy Research Working Paper 6884, World Bank, Washington, DC.

Gertler, P. J., A. L. Soucat, C. M. Vermeersch, P. Basinga, A. Binagwaho, and J. R. Sturdy. 2010. "Paying Primary Health Care Centers for Performance in Rwanda." World Bank, Washington, DC.

Gertler, P., and C. Vermeersch. 2013. "Using Performance Incentives to Improve Medical Care Productivity and Health Outcomes." NBER Working Paper 19046, National Bureau of Economic Research, Cambridge, MA.

Gibson, D. G., B. Ochieng, E. W. Kagucia, J. Were, K. Hayford, L. H. Moulton, O. S. Levine, et al. 2017. "Mobile Phone-Delivered Reminders and Incentives to Improve Childhood Immunisation Coverage and Timeliness in Kenya (M-SIMU): A Cluster Randomised Controlled Trial." *Lancet Global Health* 5 (4): e428–e38.

Glassman, A., D. Duran, L. Fleisher, D. Singer, R. Sturke, G. Angeles, J. Charles, et al. 2013. "Impact of Conditional Cash Transfers on Maternal and Newborn Health." *Journal of Health, Population and Nutrition* 31 (4 Suppl 2): 48–66.

Goldberg, J. 2016. "Kwacha Gonna Do? Experimental Evidence about Labor Supply in Rural Malawi." *American Economic Journal: Applied Economics* 8 (1): 129–49.

Gopalan, S., R. Mutasa, J. Friedman, and A. Das. 2014. "Health Sector Demand-Side Financial Incentives in Low- and Middle-Income Countries: A Systematic

Review on Demand- and Supply-Side Effects." *Social Science & Medicine* 100: 72–83.

Grépin, K. A., J. Habyarimana, and W. Jack. 2019. "Cash on Delivery: Results of a Randomized Experiment to Promote Maternal Health Care in Kenya." *Journal of Health Economics* 65: 15–30.

Grover, D., S. Bauhoff, and J. Friedman. 2019. "Using Supervised Learning to Select Audit Targets in Performance-Based Financing in Health: An Example from Zambia." *PloS One* 14 (1): e0211262.

Hahn, D., P. Wanjala, and M. Marx. 2013. "Where Is Information Quality Lost at Clinical Level? A Mixed-Method Study on Information Systems and Data Quality in Three Urban Kenyan ANC Clinics." *Global Health Action* 6 (1): 21424.

Handa, S., and J. A. Maluccio. 2010. "Matching the Gold Standard: Comparing Experimental and Nonexperimental Evaluation Techniques for a Geographically Targeted Program." *Economic Development and Cultural Change* 58 (3): 415–47.

Hemminki, E., Q. Long, W.-H. Zhang, Z. Wu, J. Raven, F. Tao, H. Yan, et al. 2013. "Impact of Financial and Educational Interventions on Maternity Care: Results of Cluster Randomized Trials in Rural China, CHIMACA." *Maternal and Child Health Journal* 17 (2): 208–21.

Higgins, J., and S. Green, eds. 2011. *Cochrane Handbook for Systematic Reviews of Interventions Version 5.1.0.* Updated March 2011. London: The Cochrane Collaboration.

Huillery, E., and J. Seban. Forthcoming. "Performance-Based Financing, Motivation and Final Output in the Health Sector: Experimental Evidence from the Democratic Republic of Congo." *Economic Development and Cultural Change.*

Hunter, B., S. Harrison, A. Portela, and D. Bick. 2017. "The Effects of Cash Transfers and Vouchers on the Use and Quality of Maternity Care Services: A Systematic Review." *PLoS One* 12 (3): e0173068.

Ireland, M., E. Paul, and B. Dujardin. 2011. "Can Performance-Based Financing Be Used to Reform Health Systems in Developing Countries?" *Bulletin of the World Health Organization* 89: 695–98.

Kandpal, E., H. Alderman, J. Friedman, D. Filmer, J. Onishi, and J. Avalos. 2016. "A Conditional Cash Transfer Program in the Philippines Reduces Severe Stunting." *Journal of Nutrition* 149 (9): 1793–1800.

Kandpal, E., B. P. Loevinsohn, C. M. Vermeersch, E. Pradhan, M. Khanna, M. K. Conlon, and W. Zeng. 2019. "Impact Evaluation of Nigeria State Health Investment Project." No. 135384, World Bank, Washington, DC.

Keya, K. T., B. Bellows, U. Rob, and C. Warren. 2018. "Improving Access to Delivery Care and Reducing the Equity Gap through Voucher Program in Bangladesh: Evidence from Difference-in-Differences Analysis." *International Quarterly of Community Health Education* 38 (2): 137–45.

Khanna, M., B. Loevinsohn, E. Pradhan, O. Fadeyibi, K. McGee, O. Odutolu, G. B. Fristche, et al. 2021. "Improving Maternal and Neonatal Health in Nigeria: Performance-Based Financing versus Decentralized Facility Financing." *BMC Medicine* 19: Article 224.

Kusuma, D., J. Cohen, M. McConnell, and P. Berman. 2016. "Can Cash Transfers Improve Determinants of Maternal Mortality? Evidence from the

Household and Community Programs in Indonesia." *Social Science & Medicine* 163: 10–20.

Kusuma, D., H. Thabrany, B. Hidayat, M. McConnell, P. Berman, and J. Cohen. 2017. "New Evidence on the Impact of Large-Scale Conditional Cash Transfers on Child Vaccination Rates: The Case of a Clustered-Randomized Trial in Indonesia." *World Development* 98: 497–505.

Kuwawenaruwa, A., K. Ramsey, P. Binyaruka, J. Baraka, F. Manzi, and J. Borghi. 2019. "Implementation and Effectiveness of Free Health Insurance for the Poor Pregnant Women in Tanzania: A Mixed Methods Evaluation." *Social Science & Medicine* 225: 17–25.

Lannes, L., B. Meessen, A. Soucat, and P. Basinga. 2016. "Can Performance-Based Financing Help Reaching the Poor with Maternal and Child Health Services? The Experience of Rural Rwanda." *International Journal of Health Planning and Management* 31 (3): 309–48.

Leonard, K. L., and M. C. Masatu. 2010. "Professionalism and the Know-Do Gap: Exploring Intrinsic Motivation among Health Workers in Tanzania." *Health Economics* 19 (12): 1461–77.

Ma-Nitu, S. M., L. Tembey, E. Bigirimana, C. Y. Dossouvi, O. Basenya, E. Mago, P. M. Salongo, et al. 2018. "Towards Constructive Rethinking of PBF: Perspectives of Implementers in Sub-Saharan Africa." *BMJ Global Health* 3 (5): e001036.

Meessen, B., A. Soucat, and C. Sekabaraga. 2011. "Performance-Based Financing: Just a Donor Fad or a Catalyst towards Comprehensive Health-Care Reform?" *Bulletin of the World Health Organization* 89: 153–56. PMID:21346927. https://doi.org/10.2471/BLT.10.077339.

Morris, S. S., R. Flores, P. Olinto, and J. M. Medina. 2004. "Monetary Incentives in Primary Health Care and Effects on Use and Coverage of Preventive Health Care Interventions in Rural Honduras: Cluster Randomised Trial." *The Lancet* 364 (9450): 2030–37.

Mullen, K. J., R. G. Frank, and M. B. Rosenthal. 2010. "Can You Get What You Pay For? Pay-for-Performance and the Quality of Healthcare Providers." *Rand Journal of Economics* 41 (1): 64–91.

Neelsen, S., D. de Walque, J. Friedman, and A. Wagstaff. 2021. *"Financial Incentives to Increase Utilization of Reproductive, Maternal, and Child Health Services in Low- and Middle-Income Countries: A Systematic Review and Meta-Analysis."* Policy Research Working Paper 9793, World Bank, Washington, DC.

Nguyen, H. T. H., L. Hatt, M. Islam, N. L. Sloan, J. Chowdury, J.-O. Schmidt, A. Hossain, and H. Wang. 2012. "Encouraging Maternal Health Service Utilization: An Evaluation of the Bangladesh Voucher Program." *Social Science & Medicine* 74 (7): 989–96.

Obare, F., P. Okwero, L. Villegas, S. Mills, and B. Bellows. 2016. "Increased Coverage of Maternal Health Services among the Poor in Western Uganda in an Output-Based Aid Voucher Scheme." Policy Research Working Paper 7709, World Bank, Washington, DC.

Oettinger, G. S. 1999. "An Empirical Analysis of the Daily Labor Supply of Stadium Vendors." *Journal of Political Economy* 107 (2): 360–92.

Okeke, E. N., and A. V. Chari. 2015. "Can Institutional Deliveries Reduce Newborn Mortality? Evidence from Rwanda." RAND Corporation, Santa Monica, CA.

Okeke, E. N., Z. Wagner, and I. S. Abubakar. 2020. "Maternal Cash Transfers Led to Increases in Facility Deliveries and Improved Quality of Delivery Care in Nigeria." *Health Affairs* 39 (6): 1051–59.

Oyo-Ita, A., C. S. Wiysonge, C. Oringanje, C. E. Nwachukwu, O. Oduwole, and M. M. Meremikwu. 2016. "Interventions for Improving Coverage of Childhood Immunisation in Low- and Middle-Income Countries." *Cochrane Database of Systematic Reviews* 7 (7): CD008145.

Paul, E., L. Albert, B. N'Sambuka Bisala, O. Bodson, E. Bonnet, P. Bossyns, S. Colombo, et al. 2018. "Performance-Based Financing in Low-Income and Middle-Income Countries: Isn't It Time for a Rethink?" *BMJ Global Health* 3 (1): e00064.

Petersen, L. A., L. D. Woodard, T. Urech, C. Daw, and S. Sookanan. 2006. "Does Pay-for-Performance Improve the Quality of Health Care?" *Annals of Internal Medicine* 145 (4): 265–72.

Powell-Jackson, T., S. Mazumdar, and A. Mills. 2015. "Financial Incentives in Health: New Evidence from India's Janani Suraksha Yojana." *Journal of Health Economics* 43: 154–69.

Priedeman Skiles, M., S. L. Curtis, P. Basinga, and G. Angeles. 2013. "An Equity Analysis of Performance-Based Financing in Rwanda: Are Services Reaching the Poorest Women?" *Health Policy and Planning* 28 (8): 825–37.

Ridde, V., L. Gautier, A.-M. Turcotte-Tremblay, I. Sieleunou, and E. Paul. 2018. "Performance-Based Financing in Africa: Time to Test Measures for Equity." *International Journal of Health Services* 48 (3): 549–61.

Robertson, L., P. Mushati, J. W. Eaton, L. Dumba, G. Mavise, J. Makoni, C. Schumacher, et al. 2013. "Effects of Unconditional and Conditional Cash Transfers on Child Health and Development in Zimbabwe: A Cluster-Randomised Trial." *The Lancet* 381 (9874): 1283–92.

Rudasingwa, M., R. Soeters, and O. Basenya. 2017. "The Effect of Performance-Based Financing on Maternal Healthcare Use in Burundi: A Two-Wave Pooled Cross-Sectional Analysis." *Global Health Action* 10 (1): 1327241.

Ryan, R., and Cochrane Consumers and Communication Review Group. 2016. "Cochrane Consumers and Communication Group: Meta-Analysis." Cochrane Consumers and Communication Group, London.

Shapira, G., I. Kalisa, J. Condo, J. Humuza, C. Mugeni, D. Nkunda, and J. Walldorf. 2018. "Going beyond Incentivizing Formal Health Providers: Evidence from the Rwanda Community Performance-Based Financing Program." *Health Economics* 27 (12): 2087–2106.

Sharma, A., S. K. Rana, S. Prinja, and R. Kumar. 2016. "Quality of Health Management Information System for Maternal & Child Health Care in Haryana State, India." *PLoS One* 11 (2): e0148449.

Sherry, T. B., S. Bauhoff, and M. Mohanan. 2017. "Multitasking and Heterogeneous Treatment Effects in Pay-for-Performance in Health Care: Evidence from Rwanda." *American Journal of Health Economics* 3 (2).

Taaffe, J., A. Longosz, and D. Wilson. 2017. "The Impact of Cash Transfers on Livelihoods, Education, Health and HIV—What's the Evidence?" *Development Policy Review* 35: 601–19.

Triyana, M. 2013. *The Effects of Household and Community-Based Interventions: Evidence from Indonesia.* Chicago, IL: University of Chicago.

Valentine, J. C., T. D. Pigott, and H. R. Rothstein. 2010. "How Many Studies Do You Need? A Primer on Statistical Power for Meta-Analysis." *Journal of Educational and Behavioral Statistics* 35 (2): 215–47.

Van de Poel, E., G. Flores, P. Ir, and O. O'Donnell. 2016. "Impact of Performance-Based Financing in a Low-Resource Setting: A Decade of Experience in Cambodia." *Health Economics* 25 (6): 688–705.

Van de Poel, E., G. Flores, P. Ir, O. O'Donnell, and E. Van Doorslaer. 2014. "Can Vouchers Deliver? An Evaluation of Subsidies for Maternal Health Care in Cambodia." *Bulletin of the World Health Organization* 92 (5): 331–39.

von Haaren, P., and S. Klonner. 2020. "Maternal Cash for Better Child Health? The Impacts of India's IGMSY/PMMVY Maternity Benefit Scheme." Department of Economics, University of Heidelberg, Germany.

Waddington, H., H. White, B. Snilstveit, J. Garcia Hombrados, M. Vojtkova, P. Davies, A. Bhavsar, et al. 2012. "How to Do a Good Systematic Review of Effects in International Development: A Tool Kit." *Journal of Development Effectiveness* 4 (3): 359–87. https://doi.org/10.1080/19439342.2012.711765.

Wagstaff, A., and M. Claeson. 2004. *Rising to the Challenges: The Millennium Development Goals for Health.* Washington, DC: World Bank.

WHO (World Health Organization). 2020. "Noncommunicable diseases." WHO, Geneva (accessed May 28, 2020), https://www.who.int/news-room/fact-sheets/detail/noncommunicable-diseases.

World Bank. 2016a. "Impact Evaluation of Zambia's Health Results Based Financing Pilot Project." World Bank, Washington, DC.

World Bank. 2016b. *Rewarding Provider Performance to Improve Quality and Coverage of Maternal and Child Health Outcomes.* Washington, DC: World Bank.

World Bank. 2016c. "Rewarding Provider Performance to Improve Quality and Coverage of Maternal and Child Health Outcomes: Zimbabwe Results-Based Financing Pilot Programme Evidence to Inform Policy and Management Decisions." World Bank, Washington, DC.

Zeng, W., E. Pradhan, M. Khanna, O. Fadeyibi, G. Fritsche, and O. Odutolu. 2021. "Cost-Effectiveness Analysis of the Decentralized Facility Financing and Performance-Based Financing Program in Nigeria." *Journal of Hospital Management and Health Policy.* https://doi.org/10.21037/jhmhp-20-82.

Zeng, W., D. S. Shepard, J. de Dieu Rusatira, A. P. Blaakman, and B. M. Nsitou. 2018. "Evaluation of Results-Based Financing in the Republic of the Congo: A Comparison Group Pre-Post Study." *Health Policy and Planning* 33 (3): 392–400.

Zeng, W., D. S. Shepard, H. Nguyen, C. Chansa, A. K. Das, J. Qamruddin, and J. Friedman. 2018. "Cost-Effectiveness of Results-Based Financing, Zambia: A Cluster Randomized Trial." *Bulletin of the World Health Organization* 96 (11): 760–71.

CHAPTER 7

Performance-Based Financing as a Health System Reform and Cautionary Evidence on Performance Pay and Irrelevant Care

Introduction

Performance-based financing (PBF) is often just one component of a broader health system reform. As health systems develop, not just the quantity, but also the quality of care dispensed and the cost of delivering such care play a central role in improving health outcomes and ensuring that public health care provision remains sustainable. This chapter points to emerging issues and open questions that it foresees arising as this health system transformation occurs.

First, the chapter draws attention to a topic on which there is comparatively little research: the problem of provision of irrelevant or nonindicated care in low- and middle-income countries (LMICs). In the early stages of health system development, when capacities and coverage are low, many quality improvement measures rightly focus on increasing insufficient levels of care. As a result, in typical pay-for-performance schemes in LMICs, there can be few safeguards against overprovision. However, the provision of unnecessary care and misallocated resources are widespread even in health care systems in low-income countries. Moreover, as health budgets become less constrained and demand-side interventions decrease the cost of care to patients, the misuse of prescription medications, expensive diagnostics, and overall cost inflation are likely to become more prevalent and in the long run affect sustainability: the pressing problem of steeply rising health care costs is well known from high-income countries. When PBF programs are being scaled up, they should therefore be designed to counter *both* the underuse of needed care and the provision of nonindicated care, with adjustments over time toward a greater focus on the latter to ensure the continued sustainability and cost efficiency of delivering effective coverage for all.

In this context, the chapter briefly discusses to what extent the quality measurement methods introduced in chapter 3 may be used in designing effective performance incentives for providers. Such incentives should counteract both the underprovision of needed care and the overprovision of nonindicated care. The chapter argues that measuring effective coverage and quality of care should become an integral part of both health policy research and any health system reform, and quality measurement should be built into health data collection systems, with an eye to supporting health financing initiatives as well as continued policy research to expand the evidence base.

Second, the chapter discusses the timing and design of evaluations that aim to inform policy makers on the health system impacts of PBF programs at scale. As PBF reaches scale, it is important to move beyond proof-of-concept studies based on time-limited pilots, toward understanding PBF's full impact on the health system. For example, even in national-level pilots, there might sometimes be insufficient capacity building on the ground due to a project-based approach that is not always conducive to decentralized implementation and management. Given that PBF approaches influence the entire health system, a criticism of impact evaluations of PBF pilots is that they fail to assess the entirety of the impacts generated. The chapter therefore also discusses the timing and design of evaluations that aim to inform policy makers on the health system impacts of PBF programs at scale.

Provision of nonindicated treatment in the context of financial incentives

Many times, low quality of care leads not only to the undersupply of needed treatment, but also to the provision of nonindicated or "mismatched" treatment; that is, the patient receives treatment other than what is needed, or in excess of what is needed. The unnecessary prescription and supply of medications and diagnostics are increasingly recognized as affecting not only high-income countries, but also LMICs (Brownlee et al. 2017; Busfield 2015; Holloway et al. 2013; WHO 2009).

While the main priority of any quality of care initiative in LMICs is typically to reduce undertreatment and expand coverage, there are several reasons why policy makers and researchers should not lose sight of overprovision in these settings. For one, the evidence summarized below shows that nonindicated care often occurs alongside insufficient care. Thus, when budgets are tight and human capital and materials are in short supply, there is a real concern that providing unnecessary care in one part of the health care system diverts resources away from patients elsewhere who urgently need them. Preventing unnecessary treatment may therefore directly contribute to reducing underuse. In addition to wasting resources, nonindicated care may also cause medical harm: to the patients themselves, by causing side effects, drug interactions, or trauma from invasive procedures, and to the public at large, by furthering resistant pathogens. Indeed, the World Health Organization (WHO) has declared antimicrobial resistance "one of the top 10 global public health threats facing humanity" (WHO 2020). Last, the chapter argues that preexisting incentives to supply nonindicated care may increase as countries become wealthier and their health systems less budget constrained, and these drivers may be reinforced by pay-for-performance schemes that reward the quantity of care without verifying whether such care is needed.

The problem of nonindicated or overly expensive treatment may be more familiar, and perhaps considered more pressing, in high-income countries, but it is pervasive across health care systems and a widespread problem for many conditions and medications. As early as 2009, the WHO compiled a database of 679 studies published from 1990 to 2006 reporting on common medicine use indicators in 97 countries. The findings were summarized in a Fact Book (WHO 2009) that was later updated to include studies until 2009 (Holloway et al. 2013). Most of the cited studies focus on public sector care,[2] where it might be expected that the minimum standards for the availability of diagnostic tools, provider training, and medicine use would be poor. For example, over 40 percent of pneumonia cases were not treated with an antibiotic (as they should be in almost all cases), while nearly 50 percent of upper respiratory tract infections received one (constituting nonindicated care). Analogously, irrelevant care was provided for malaria and diarrhea, most often simultaneously with substantial undertreatment. Overall, 40 percent or fewer cases were treated according to the standard guidelines (Holloway et al. 2013).

This chapter begins by summarizing the evidence on nonindicated treatment in LMICs, especially in curative care, drawing frequently on data collected for a study of malaria treatment at community health clinics in Bamako, Mali in 2016, which is described in box 3.1, in chapter 3 (Lopez, Sautmann, and Schaner 2022a, 2022b). It then turns to a discussion of how performance pay interacts with the provision of nonindicated care. Finally, the data on antenatal care (ANC) from chapter 4 are used to show that PBF may worsen the provision of preventive measures such as vaccines, including in ways that could harm the patient.

Incorrect diagnosis and nonindicated treatment in LMICs

Nonindicated care is an important manifestation of low health care quality. Many arms in the "effective coverage tree" lead to the patient receiving irrelevant care, instead of or in addition to relevant care for their condition, as illustrated in figure 7.1. Relative to preventive care, where the needs

Figure 7.1 Nonindicated care for a specific condition in the effective coverage tree

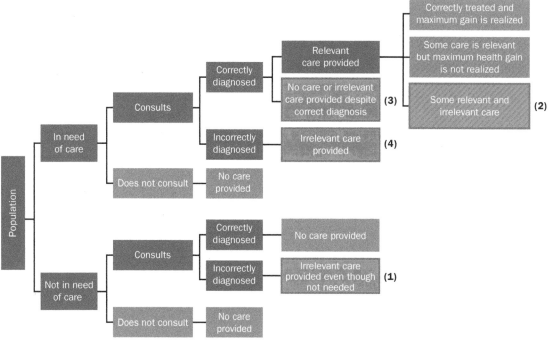

Source: World Bank.

Note: At the end of each branch of the tree, the green color denotes a desirable outcome, and orange denotes an undesirable outcome. Purple border around box indicates irrelevant care that uses scarce resources without health benefits or even causing harm.

assessment is often comparatively straightforward (for example, all children under five should be vaccinated), curative care is particularly at risk of misdiagnosis and consequently nonindicated care. Thus, an important task of the health care system is to provide an accurate diagnosis ensuring that each condition receives the appropriate treatment. Nonindicated care occurs (often alongside undertreatment) when the patient is misdiagnosed and treated for the wrong condition, when the provider treats several conditions at once to "cover their bases," or when the provider reaches for a more powerful, more invasive, or more expensive treatment than is needed, such as giving an injection instead of an oral tablet.

Consider the example of treatment for *P. falciparum* malaria. The treatment for uncomplicated or *simple malaria* is artemisinin-based combination therapy (ACT), usually given in tablet form. In *severe malaria* cases, the patient will initially receive parenteral (intravenous or intramuscular) antimalarials and should be admitted to intensive care (Pasvol 2005; Trampuz et al. 2003). Nonindicated treatment for malaria can occur in multiple ways. A patient may be mistakenly diagnosed with malaria, for example, if the provider conducts a microscopy test and misinterprets the result (branch 1 in figure 7.1).[1] Even if the patient has malaria and is correctly diagnosed, the doctor may provide nonindicated care, such as treatment for severe malaria in the case of an uncomplicated malaria infection (branch 2). The provider might even knowingly substitute irrelevant for relevant care, for example, by giving an antibiotic instead of an antimalarial because the clinic is stocked out of ACTs (branch 3). Last, the provider might mistake the diffuse symptoms of uncomplicated malaria for a different illness, such as a bacterial infection, and wrongly prescribe an antibiotic (branch 4).

Identifying misuse of care requires a third-party diagnosis for verification, which is not always possible. An exception is presented by malaria rapid detection tests (RDTs), which can be easily and quickly administered with minimal training and detect parasite antigens even after treatment has started. This approach makes it possible to measure treatment received conditional on true malaria status. Researchers took advantage of this in the studies that form the basis of the case study in box 3.1, in chapter 3 (Lopez, Sautmann, and Schaner 2022a, 2022b).

The malaria data from Mali are used as a case study and referred to throughout the chapter. Patient intake and exit interviews were conducted at 60 community health clinics in the capital of Mali, Bamako. Table 7.1 summarizes the characteristics of the clinics. Although some of the clinics

Table 7.1 Overview of clinics in the malaria case study in Mali

Variable	Mean	SD
Self-reported patient load per day	29.7	22.1
Clinic has a laboratory for malaria microscopy	83%	38%
Clinic has a pharmacy/dispensary	100%	n.a.
Average number of staff who can prescribe antimalarials	11.1	4.4
Days with stockouts of any malaria test materials	31%	46%
Days with stockouts of all malaria test materials	0.8%	9.1%
Days with stockouts of any malaria drugs	69%	47%
Days with stockouts of all malaria drugs	1.7%	13%

Sources: World Bank, using data from Lopez, Sautmann, and Schaner 2022a, 2022b.

Note: The study included 60 public clinics (Centres de Santé Communautaire) in Bamako, Mali. Data were collected in a baseline survey and on six observation days per clinic. Baseline information is missing for one study clinic. n.a. = not applicable; SD = standard deviation.

are large, during a given shift there are typically one to three physicians on staff, along with nurses, midwives, a pharmacist, a lab technician, and some nonmedical staff. In a novel approach to measuring the misallocation of treatment, the patients with acute symptoms were "re-diagnosed" by conducting a malaria test in a follow-up visit at the patient's home one day after their clinic visit. The RDT used in these visits, CareStart HRP2(Pf), performed well in quality checks, with less than 1 percent false positives and 91 and 100 percent correct detection rates for low and high parasite loads, respectively (WHO 2015).

Figure 7.2 shows the results for the correct allocation of treatment. The quality of malaria care that patients receive is worryingly low. On the one hand, there is a large amount of nonindicated care, corresponding to branches 1 and 2 in figure 7.1. Although purchase rates are lower than prescription rates, 40 percent of patients with a negative malaria test at home took a malaria treatment, and nearly 50 percent of them received an intravenous line or injection, which, according to official treatment guidelines, is only indicated for severe malaria cases (Ministère de la Santé 2013). Among those with a positive test, over 65 percent (correctly) received treatment, but a large majority of these patients received more expensive severe malaria care. This is despite few reports of severe symptoms in the intake interviews and an estimated rate of severe malaria in this population of 10 percent of malaria cases (PMI 2015). Remarkably, although these are patients who decided to visit a clinic and seek care, there is parallel substantial undertreatment: more than 20 percent of the patients with a positive

Figure 7.2 Malaria treatment prescriptions and purchases, conditional on a positive (left) or negative malaria RDT taken at home

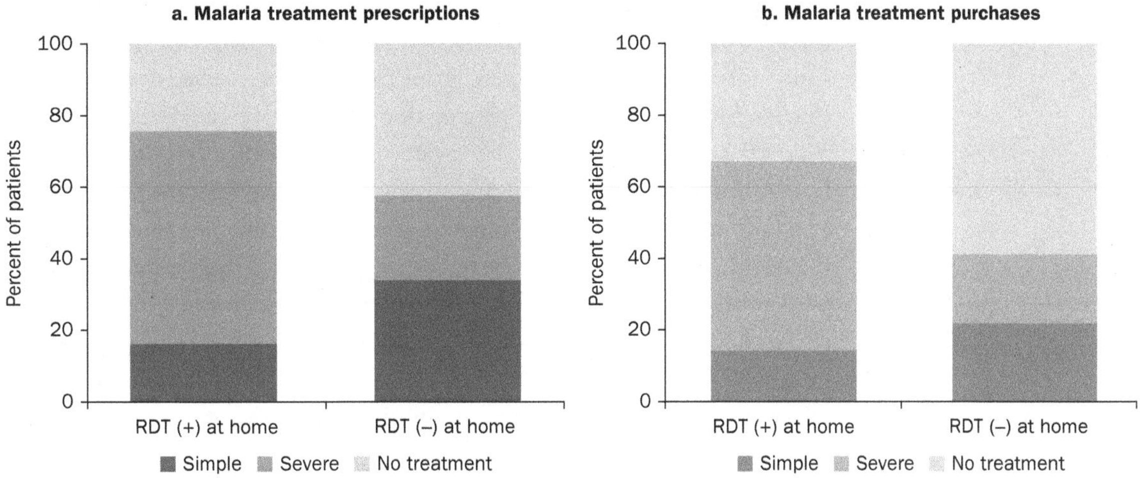

a. Malaria treatment prescriptions

b. Malaria treatment purchases

Source: World Bank, using data from Lopez, Sautmann, and Schaner 2022a, 2022b.

Note: "Simple treatment" refers to the recommended treatment course of artemisinin combination therapy, given orally. "Severe treatment" refers to any treatment involving antimalarial injections, usually reserved for severe malaria, which occurs in approximately 10 percent of cases. RDT = rapid detection test.

malaria test at home did not receive an antimalarial prescription, and an even greater share did not purchase malaria treatment (branch 3 or 4). These numbers suggest a sizable gap between malaria care coverage and effective coverage.

The mismatch of need for care and care received can have grave consequences for individual and societal welfare. For example, treatment, especially for severe malaria, can have dangerous side effects, and the overuse of antimalarial medication furthers microbial resistance.[3] Exact numbers on the share of doctor-patient interactions where this type of medical harm occurs are often not available. However, in a standardized patient study on respiratory illness in 227 health facilities in Tanzania in 2018, King et al. (2021) estimate that the care received was clinically harmful to the patient in 6 percent of the cases and harmful to public health in 67 percent of the cases because the patient received nonindicated antibacterial or antimalarial drugs.[4] An audit study on diarrhea treatment in Bihar (India) showed that 72 percent of health care providers prescribed potentially harmful treatments (Mohanan et al. 2015). Research summarized in Hussam et al. (2020) using standardized patients from China, India, and Kenya shows that between 48 and 89 percent of cases receive entirely incorrect treatment

(Daniels et al. 2017; Das, Chowdhury, et al. 2016; Das et al. 2015; Das, Holla, et al. 2016; Kwan et al. 2018; Sylvia et al. 2017).

Even if there are no negative health consequences for the patient or the public, nonindicated treatment uses up valuable resources. In the Tanzania study, for example, fully 81 percent of the patients received such wasteful care, and in the standardized patient studies in Hussam et al. (2020), more than 70 percent of health care expenses were medically not indicated. In LMICs, where basic health care coverage continues to be low, unnecessary care for one person may imply that another person does not receive the care they need. The regular stockouts in Bamako's public clinics demonstrate that even in urban areas, medication and materials are often scarce (table 7.1).

To capture the opportunity costs of nonindicated care, this chapter proposes a back-of-the-envelope calculation of the "efficiency" of providing effective coverage, as illustrated in figure 7.3. This measure expresses what

Figure 7.3   Efficiency of effective coverage provision

(i) Individuals who consult and receive appropriate care (%)

(iii) Per person cost of appropriate care

(ii) Actual per person cost of care

Source: World Bank.

Note: The efficiency of effective coverage provision is calculated based on (i) the share of patients who consult and do (versus do not) receive the correct care, (ii) the actual cost of health care per person, and (iii) the cost of providing the optimal level of care per person. The product of (i) and (iii) divided by (ii) gives the share of total expenditure going toward appropriate care.

proportion of health care expenditure goes toward care that fills a correctly identified health care need. As touched on in chapter 3, it is generally very difficult to calculate this share without data specifically gathered for this purpose. However, table 7.2 illustrates the idea using the malaria case study, with approximations from the data. Table 7.2 shows the share of patients who tested positive for malaria and received malaria treatment as well as the share of patients who tested negative and did not receive malaria treatment. These are the patients who (in approximation) received appropriate care. The table shows that these are only 51 percent of all patients. In addition, exit interview data on payments were used to obtain the per-person price of care for these two groups. The lower per-person price of care of patients who (correctly) did not receive an antimalarial reflects that malaria care is relatively expensive. In these data, the average per-person price for all patients was CFA 5,396, or approximately US$8.99 at 2016 exchange rates (CFA 600 per US dollar). Using this number in the denominator, the share of expenses going toward treatment that correctly matches malaria status is approximately 45 percent, implying that 55 percent of health care spending by patients is at least partially wasteful.

The calculation uses patient prices rather than true cost, and the observed price of care when malaria treatment choices match malaria status rather than the true price of appropriate care. Several caveats are therefore in order. First, public health care in Mali is at least partly subsidized.

Table 7.2 Approximating the efficiency of health care provision using data from 60 community health centers in Bamako, Mali

Description	Indicator
Appropriate treatment	
Positive match: malaria test was positive and the patient received malaria treatment as part of the prescription.	19% of patients, at visit cost of CFA 5,507 each
Negative match: malaria test was negative and the patient did not receive malaria treatment.	32% of patients, at visit cost of CFA 4,312 each
All treatment	
Per person average visit cost	CFA 5,396
Share of patient expenditure going to appropriate care	
Calculation: (19% x 5,507 + 32% x 4,312) / 5,396	Efficiency: 45%

Source: World Bank, using data from Lopez, Sautmann, and Schaner 2022a, 2022b.

Note: This table uses data from clinic exit interviews on prescriptions received and the price paid for treatment, combined with information from a malaria test conducted in a follow-up visit at home. The average exchange rate was approximately CFA 600 per US$.

Unless the prices that patients pay are proportional to the true cost of services, the 45 percent expenditure share may not represent the share of the total social cost that goes toward providing appropriate care. Second, health care providers would likely have to spend more diagnostic effort per patient to improve the allocation of care for all patients. As a result, the labor cost of providing appropriate care is higher than the current labor cost per visit.

Last, the study assumed that the cost of care for appropriate malaria treatment is CFA 5,507, or equivalently what malaria-positive patients who receive an antimalarial spend. However, an unusually high share of these patients received treatment that indicates severe malaria (and this treatment tends to be more expensive than a simple ACT). Similarly, the study assumes that the cost of care for appropriate treatment for conditions other than malaria is given by the observed price of visits that did not include malaria. However, 63 percent of the patients in the study received an antibiotic, often prescribed for respiratory issues or diarrhea, and it is likely that some of these drug prescriptions were not indicated. Both factors imply that the cost of providing appropriate medications may be lower than the observed medication costs. Chapter 3 briefly discusses how the efficiency of care might be measured in a more complete manner.

Although these numbers are therefore not precise, a key takeaway from the efficiency-of-care indicator is that even in basic primary care in low-income countries, resources go to waste because patients are treated for illnesses they do not have. The problem of nonindicated care is even more serious in high-income countries, partly driven by differences in medicine use patterns due to epidemiology and age profiles. Overuse is particularly severe for high-cost diagnostic testing, such as colonoscopy (Kruse et al. 2015) and medical imaging (FDA 2010), and for surgical procedures (Chan et al. 2011), and there is systemic growth in the nonindicated use of medications for psychological and degenerative conditions. Busfield (2015) highlights that many drugs prescribed to large percentages of the population and heavily promoted by pharmaceutical companies may have few proven benefits, such as antihypertensives (Diao et al. 2012), antidepressants (Ioannidis 2008), and antipsychotics for dementia (Banerjee 2009). The evidence overwhelmingly shows that poor quality of care in the form of overprescription and overdiagnosis is a pressing problem in mature health systems. Correspondingly, it is likely that growing issues with nonindicated care will be seen in LMICs as their health systems begin to transform. The following subsections discuss the reasons in more detail.

Multiple factors contribute to the provision of unnecessary or inappropriate care. Building on the effective coverage framework, the patient may be incorrectly diagnosed (branch 1) and as a result receive a treatment that is not needed. Alternatively, the doctor's diagnosis may be accurate—or at least, the doctor may be capable of accurately diagnosing—but he or she is choosing to provide inappropriate care (branches 2 and 3). Correspondingly, along the lines of chapter 3, the causes of nonindicated care are classified into knowledge and capacity gaps versus provider effort.

Knowledge and capacity gaps versus provider choice

Errors in diagnosis—or in prescription choice after diagnosis—may be the result of knowledge or capacity gaps. For example, the provider may not know the diagnostic protocols or may follow the protocols but draw faulty conclusions. Providers who are uncertain about the correct treatment often perceive the risks of overtreating to be lower than the risk of undertreating (see, for example, Krockow et al. 2019) and therefore tend to overprescribe. In the malaria case study, for example, there are many signs that diagnostics are poor and physicians overtreat as a result. Figure 7.4 splits treatment outcomes by the type of malaria test that was administered at the clinic: no test, RDT only, or microscopy test. In general, microscopy tests carried out by an experienced technician are considered the "gold standard" of malaria testing. However, in field conditions, microscopy can perform poorly, for example because dust particles may be mistaken for malaria parasites. Panel a in figure 7.4 shows the malaria rates for the home RDT test and the share of patients who bought an antimalarial. Panel b shows the match between malaria treatment received and malaria status. Patients who received a microscopy test at the clinic (alone or in combination with an RDT) had relatively low rates of malaria in the home test and yet in nearly 80 percent of the cases received an antimalarial. As a result, compared with patients who did not receive a test at all, patients who were tested with microscopy had very low match rates between malaria status and malaria treatment. This is largely due to very high rates of overtreatment and low shares of patients with a "negative match" (that is, patients who did not have malaria and correctly did not receive an antimalarial).

Interestingly, both positive and negative match rates are higher when only an RDT is used than when microscopy is conducted. Moreover, the study found that providing training to clinic staff on the accuracy of RDTs

Figure 7.4 Malaria incidence and treatment outcomes by type of test conducted at the clinic

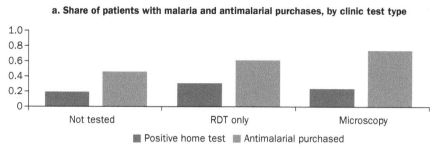

a. Share of patients with malaria and antimalarial purchases, by clinic test type

■ Positive home test ■ Antimalarial purchased

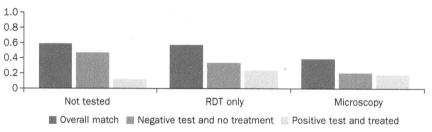

b. Match between malaria test result and treatment, by clinic test type

■ Overall match ■ Negative test and no treatment ■ Positive test and treated

Source: World Bank, using data from Lopez, Sautmann, and Schaner 2022a, 2022b.

Note: Panel a shows the share of patients who tested positive for malaria at home and the share who received an antimalarial. Panel b shows the match between treatment for malaria and malaria home test result. From left to right, antimalarial purchases increase from under 50 percent to over 70 percent, but the share of patients who were correctly treated worsens from 60 to 40 percent, largely due to overtreatment. RDT = rapid detection test.

reduces "duplicate testing" with both RDT and microscopy and significantly improves both positive and negative match rates (Lopez, Sautmann, and Schaner 2022a; see also figure 3.1, in chapter 3). This evidence, along with the high mismatch rates under microscopy testing, suggests that doctors may be treating based on incorrectly interpreted blood smears.

Of course, another explanation for nonindicated care may be that the facility simply does not have the required diagnostic tools and materials available. Table 7.1 shows that the clinics in the sample of the malaria case study were stocked out of some malaria test materials 31 percent of the time. Figure 7.4 shows that nearly 50 percent of patients without a malaria test nonetheless received an antimalarial, perhaps due to providers writing prescriptions when a test was unavailable. Knowledge gaps and capacity gaps may respond to PBF in the long run if facility directors respond to these incentives by training or hiring their staff more thoroughly and managing their supply chain better. These changes are likely to take time.

However, the treatment rates for untested patients in figure 7.4 could also indicate that at least some doctors choose not to carry out a test, even if the materials are available, and prescribe based on clinical diagnosis alone. Some doctors may also order lab or RDT tests but then ignore the results. This is the *effort* or *provider choice* component of quality of care. The providers in the case study clinics may not test or may override a test result that does not conform to their assessment and prescribe an antimalarial anyway, despite clear health policies requiring a positive malaria test for an antimalarial prescription (Ministère de la Santé 2013).[5]

Further evidence that doctors choose not to follow diagnostic protocol and provide care that is not needed, despite having the knowledge and resources to do so, comes from the audit and standardized patient studies. These studies compare the actual diagnostic steps taken in daily clinical practice with behavior in a hypothetical vignette. They show that doctors only complete a fraction of the essential case-specific checks and prescribe treatment for conditions the patient does not have, against their better knowledge (see, for example, Das and Hammer (2007) for an early such study). Strikingly, doctors in India who practice both in public facilities and their own private practices deliver very different quality of care in the two settings and are 15 percent more likely to diagnose the patient correctly and 37 percent more likely to offer the correct treatment in their private office (Das, Holla, et al. 2016). The authors argue that the fee-for-service provision of health care in the private sector holds doctors more accountable and incentivizes them to provide higher quality care. Lack of provider effort and misaligned incentives are clearly important contributors to low quality health care and specifically the provision of nonindicated care.

Financial and nonmonetary incentives to prescribe and the role of PBF

The role of provider incentives in connection with the overprovision of care is twofold. First, providers often lack incentives for diagnostic accuracy or low expenditure and therefore do not explicitly work to avoid overuse. Second, there is a range of external incentives that tend to encourage providers to sell medications or services that are not needed. In this context, PBF has the potential to improve incentives for accurate diagnosis and treatment allocation, but in practice the nature of the incentives offered often reinforces existing incentives to oversell. This problem relates to the challenges of evaluating the quality of health care allocation and accurately rewarding desired behavior. As health systems develop, outside incentives for overprovision may become even stronger and reinforce performance pay incentives further. This subsection discusses the evidence for incentives to provide nonindicated care in LMIC health systems and in economies in transition, using the examples of China and India. It also briefly points to the potential touchpoints with PBF. The next subsection returns to the example of ANC from chapter 4 and shows evidence of nonindicated care in response to PBF.

Financial incentives are most often cited as the main driver of what is termed "physician-induced demand." Induced demand occurs when the provider "influences a patient's demand for care against the physician's interpretation of the best interests of the patient" (McGuire 2000, 504). The provider can influence what the patient wants because health care is, in many aspects, a credence good, meaning that the patient does not observe the benefits and harms of the treatment directly and must rely on the judgment of the "expert," here the health care provider. Even professional and altruistic providers may act against what they deem is in the patient's best interests if other interests strongly compel them. There is ample evidence that providers respond to direct or indirect financial incentives, for example, by increasing prescription rates to boost sales profits. In a standardized patient study in China, prescription rates were 55 percent when the provider's clinic benefited from the sale, compared with 10 percent when the patient indicated they would purchase a prescribed antibiotic at a nonaffiliated pharmacy (Currie, Lin, and Meng 2014).

But even if the volume of sales is not financially incentivized, as in most public health facilities and for salaried physicians,[6] providers may be tempted to furnish nonindicated care. Concern about their reputation may motivate them to offer treatment rather than asking the patient to "wait and see" (Das, Hammer, and Leonard 2008). This is related to an often reported, but less often rigorously studied, cause for overprescription, namely, patients' demand for powerful treatment. The theory of "induced demand" assumes that doctors work to persuade reluctant patients to buy more than they need, yet providers often report that patients arrive at the consultations with expectations about receiving specific treatments (Kotwani, Chaudhury, and Holloway 2012; Linder et al. 2014; van Staa and Hardon 1996). In the malaria case study, 57 percent of the health workers reported pressure from patients to prescribe unnecessary medications, and many named antibiotics and antimalarials specifically. Meanwhile, 55 percent of the patients said they believed they had malaria even before consulting with a physician.

A main motivation of the research that forms the basis of the malaria case study was to test the effects of patient demand on provider prescription practices. The authors conducted an experiment where they gave out vouchers that reduced the price of a simple ACT for malaria but varied on randomly selected days whether patients were informed about this discount or whether doctors could mention it at their discretion (Lopez, Sautmann, and Schaner 2022b). In the treatment arm where patients knew about the discount, antimalarial prescription rates were significantly higher and the match between treatment and illness was worse. Moreover, among the randomly selected clinics where providers received training and the allocation of malaria treatment improved, patient satisfaction declined. This suggests that, at least in this context, some nonindicated care is the result of "induced demand": a nonnegligible share of patients demand malaria care despite not having malaria, and it is *doctors* who reluctantly bend to patient preferences.

Performance-based incentives can reinforce financial or other external incentives and increase the problem of overprovision when they reward the volume of care provided, which is often the case (Miller and Babiarz 2014). An incentive based on carrying out a procedure without verifying its appropriateness acts as piece-rate pay and encourages quantity over quality. This is more of an issue in curative care, where an important aspect of quality of care is to allocate treatment to the right recipients rather than give it to as many recipients as possible; however, as the next subsection shows, it also occurs in preventive care (here using the example of ANC).

The experience of high-income countries provides a preview of the problems to come in the overprovision of care when health systems become less resource constrained. The incentives to provide nonindicated care are further reinforced when patients have high incomes and therefore a high willingness to pay. Moreover, health policies that increase access and protect patients from unexpected shocks, such as health insurance coverage and subsidized public health care, also create a wedge between the costs patients face and the value they receive. In this situation, patients are willing to accept expensive treatments or diagnostics even if they provide only moderate benefits.

To give an example, the high rates of medication use in China are often attributed to the pharmaceutical policy that was historically aimed at promoting local drug companies, leading to uneven price regulation and high markups (Sun et al. 2008). As a result, drug sale revenues at provider-owned pharmacies effectively cross-subsidized other health services (see also

Currie, Lin, and Meng 2014), and physicians were heavily incentivized to increase drug sales (Dupas and Miguel 2017). The abuse of antibiotics and corticosteroids was particularly severe, with between 55 and 85 percent of drug prescriptions containing an antibiotic (Currie, Lin, and Meng 2014; Currie, Lin, and Zhang 2011; Li et al. 2012; Sun et al. 2008). In a recent paper, Fang et al. (2021) describe the effects of the "zero markup policy" that was implemented in public hospitals to curb the problem. The policy was introduced in a staggered rollout across China starting in 2009, and in response, physicians shifted their treatment regimen so that patients' drug expenses were substituted by nondrug expenses, keeping hospital revenues the same.

Another example is the ongoing shift in India to paying for health care with public health insurance but procuring it through private hospitals. Evidence from Rajasthan shows that changes in the fixed reimbursement rates for different types of services led to significant shifts in the supply of those services as well as to changes in (prohibited) charges to patients and rates of false claims (Jain 2021). These findings echo longstanding evidence, for example, from physician response to reimbursement policies in the US Medicare system (Cabral, Geruso, and Mahoney 2018; Rice 1983).

It is imperative to anticipate the rising costs of health care and the increased provision of nonindicated diagnostics and care in LMICs as their health systems transform and to design policies that can address both the underprovision and overprovision of health care. Pay-for-performance schemes can support these efforts if they can disincentivize nonindicated care while promoting needed care. An example of an intervention that had moderate success in reducing the use of antibiotics in rural China was a joint capitation and performance pay scheme piloted in Ningxia province (Yip et al. 2014).

Inappropriate or irrelevant care in ANC visits and the effects of PBF

An inherent danger of PBF is that paying for certain actions can cause health workers to do them even if they are not strictly necessary or even harmful (Cors et al. 2011; Lyu et al. 2017; Morgan et al. 2019). This subsection explores overuse in the context of ANC using the three-gap framework and data presented in chapter 4. As touched on in chapter 4, although the available ANC data were not geared toward picking up overuse, there are indications of unnecessary treatment even at baseline, before the introduction of any PBF interventions.

The subsection revisits the same indicators of overuse discussed in chapter 4—too early initiation of preventive malaria treatment and too early provision of the tetanus vaccine. These measures are defined as (1) initiating preventive malaria treatment and (2) providing the tetanus vaccine in the first trimester, while the WHO guidelines state that it should only be provided in the second trimester or later. Further, the too-early provision of preventive malaria treatment is not only an instance of unnecessary care that is an inefficient use of resources, but also harmful to the growing fetus (Peters et al. 2007; Hernandes-Diaz et al. 2000).

As discussed in detail in chapters 5 and 6, the Nigerian and Cameroonian PBF pilots included business-as-usual as well as a direct facility financing (DFF) arm for comparison. In the latter, facilities were provided enhanced financing and autonomy over the expenditure of the additional budget but were not allowed to use it for staff remuneration. Figure 7.5 presents the evidence from Cameroon and Nigeria on the impacts of PBF on overuse compared with the business-as-usual and DFF arms. Relative to business-as-usual, in Nigeria, the suggestions that the PBF intervention may have led to increases in the overuse of malaria treatment and tetanus shot provision were imprecisely estimated. Tetanus shots were explicitly incentivized

Figure 7.5 Assessing the impact of PBF on indicators of overuse in antenatal care

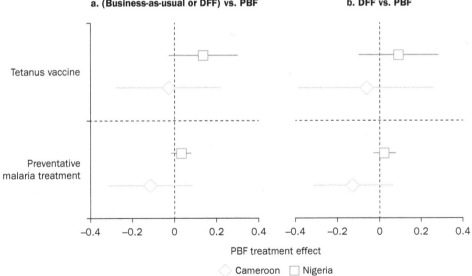

Sources: World Bank, based on Khanna et al. 2021 and de Walque et al. 2021.

Note: "Whiskers" represent 95% confidence intervals. SE clustered at the treatment level. DFF = direct facility financing; PBF = performance-based financing; SE = standard errors.

under the payment scheme (Khanna et al. 2021). In Cameroon, the intervention also purchased the provision of tetanus vaccines in pregnancy. Relative to both business-as-usual and DFF, PBF does not appear to increase the overuse of tetanus shots, although again neither effect is precisely estimated. Relative to DFF in Nigeria, PBF led to smaller and again insignificant impacts on malaria treatment as well as tetanus vaccination.

Quality measurement to inform incentives at scale

The chapter has argued that financial incentives that reward quantity indiscriminately can actually *lower* the quality of care. This implies that well-designed incentive schemes must appropriately measure and reward quality rather than quantity. Chapter 3 provides an overview of the various ways of measuring quality of care used in research; when adapting such measures to implement performance-based incentives, policy makers must carefully consider two things: first, what aspect of quality and effort to reward and how; and second, what the potential advantages and drawbacks of the various measurement methods are in the context of implementing incentives. The optimal at-scale design of performance-based incentives in health care remains an important question for future research, but some lessons can be drawn from existing studies.

A series of seminal contributions in economics considers the problem of incentivizing performance by an "agent"—here, the health worker—in environments where effort is hard to assess and the agent performs multiple complex tasks (Baker, Gibbons, and Murphy 1994; Holmström 1979; Holmström and Milgrom 1991, 1994). Some of the lessons are useful for thinking about incentives in health care. The first insight is that it is usually best to reward the ultimate outcome of interest, such as the population's overall health and happiness, especially when it is difficult to observe and evaluate the "inputs" into this output—such as the quality of the individual provider-patient interaction. However, when the output is only very indirectly related to the agent's actions, an outcome-based incentive effectively holds the agent responsible for bad outcomes that they have no power to prevent (say, the outbreak of a viral disease), and this risk puts limits on making pay dependent on outcomes. In this setting, it is best to use *all* the information that contributes to a more complete picture of the agent's actions, including directly observing them (for example, via standardized patient visits). Subjective assessments, such as patient satisfaction surveys or supervisor evaluations, may be preferred to objective, quantitative metrics when some aspects of performance are much harder to measure than others, such as pain levels or care for chronic illness.

Finally, when important aspects of care cannot be measured, financial incentives can be counterproductive because they divert the health worker's attention away from the unmeasured quality aspects to the measured ones. A well-calibrated system of financial incentives therefore likely combines a variety of subjective as well as objective quality measures, such as patient interviews, population surveys, and standardized patient visits, and may provide a variety of incentive structures for different types or specialties of providers, depending on the tasks these groups are expected to perform. In addition, performance metrics should be adjustable over time and account for overuse as an aspect of quality. Each specific implementation should be accompanied by research that assesses long-run health outcomes and may trigger a readjustment.

An important consideration for the practical implementation will also be whether a specific measurement approach can assess quality of care in a reliable and unbiased manner. As an example, when using direct clinical observation for research purposes, researchers find that physicians seem to return quickly to their usual conduct and practice (Leonard and Masatu 2010). However, this is likely not true in situations where the physician knows that she or he is being evaluated with the purpose of determining performance-based pay. Thus, basing the incentive on clinical observation will reward the provider's knowledge and skill but not their day-to-day effort.

Another example is the use of patient satisfaction surveys to evaluate providers in the context of overuse. In many contexts, patient surveys can be very informative, for instance, about aspects of quality such as the provider's general conduct and approachability or the time spent with the patient as well as the price of care. However, in the malaria case study, patient satisfaction was overall *lower* when patients received unnecessary malaria treatment less often (Lopez, Sautmann, and Schaner 2022a). More generally, patients may demand overtreatment and therefore paradoxically *low* quality of care. It is necessary to validate carefully whether a given indicator truly rewards the desired behavior by the physician. An important aspect of any performance-based incentive scheme should thus be the cost of providing a given level of care or the efficiency of care. Performance-linked payments may otherwise lead to misaligned incentives that generate rapid cost increases.

PBF as a health system reform

Chapters 5 and 6 in this report discuss how PBF pilot interventions affected the coverage and quality of care patients received. However, these studies may not capture the full effects of carrying out such pilots on the health system as a whole. Even temporary PBF interventions can have a considerable impact on the development of health systems. They provide examples of what can work, how, and why. Input-based financing of health systems has historically performed poorly (Leslie et al. 2018; Kutzin 2012), and it has not been designed to incentivize efficiency, access, or quality of service provision. In this historical context, introducing PBF, even if through a vertical financing modality—where a central purchaser channels payment through the public financial management system all the way down to individual facilities and workers—can offer policy makers a glimpse as to what can be achieved through system building.

For example, PBF reforms in many countries have shown that in most contexts, it is possible to provide access to financial services and build capacity for facility managers to use these resources prudently. Good accounting and reporting, although not health outputs per se, are important steps on the road toward a health system that delivers quality services efficiently. The PBF experience may also provide evidence that the increased fiduciary risk of delegating responsibility to facility managers may pay off as they can respond to changing needs. In addition, PBF can show that flexibility of resource use does not necessarily expose the public financial management system to greater fiduciary risk and at the same time allows for efficiency gains because spending is not locked into input-based categories. All these lessons can be integrated into the design of health systems. This does not mean that there needs to be a radical shift toward full fee for service, but the experience can inform what a transition away from a purely input-based system to a mixed payment system could look like.

Another benefit of PBF pilots is the introduction of data collection and data-sharing systems. Knowing what services were delivered where and to which patient is unequivocally an essential building block of health systems and thus should be tracked systematically, for instance, through a unified health management information system. Often, PBF systems provide such tracking data through dashboards or portals that facilities use to report performance. Of course, such portals can be adopted without the strategic purchasing component and simply be linked to the health management information system instead. Budget provisions to facilities should at least in part reflect that such spending can be reoriented for greater efficiency, equity, and quality of services. Building such capacity takes time, but it can be part of the PBF verification process, through which a facility's performance reports are audited or verified by a third party (neither the government purchasing agency nor the facility itself).

To reiterate, the PBF initiatives reviewed elsewhere in this report have meticulously documented their performance. Thanks to rigorous impact evaluations, it is clear where and to what degree the approach has worked. However, most of the impact evaluations of the PBF schemes reviewed in this report evaluate a handful of indicators of success—all measured at the health facility, worker, or population catchment level—whereas PBF is promoted as a health system intervention (Shroff et al. 2017). Indeed, the potentially transformative sectorwide impacts are often discussed as both a benefit (Meessen, Soucat, and Sekabaraga 2011) and a criticism (Paul et al. 2018) of PBF schemes. Among the reasons PBF is hypothesized to be a systemwide intervention are the autonomy, accountability, and transparency aspects, which may indeed accrue at a higher level than the health facility. There may be important effects on the Public Expenditure Tracking System, which are not captured by impact evaluations. Finally, there may also be important political economy considerations as governments must be willing to invest scarce resources in the health sector. Tying payments to results can make PBF politically feasible and a conduit for health sector investments—the so-called flypaper effect (Devarajan and Swaroop 1998).

A related question is whether it is possible to measure the effects of different components of PBF separately. What is known from the studies discussed earlier is the effect of the set of interventions implemented as part of the PBF package, vis-à-vis the status quo or other packages, like decentralized financing or supportive supervision and autonomy. What a health system practitioner might be most interested in, however, is the marginal effect of any one of the above-mentioned changes since they might be interested in pursuing individual measures separately. For example, what is the effect of allowing greater facility autonomy, and what might it take to get there? Can facilities be introduced one by one into the government chart of accounts? Sending funds to providers might require training them in accounting and reporting. Is this realistic, and what would be the effect on accountability and service delivery? It may be most useful for practitioners to understand these individual effects, rather than the effect of the PBF package as a whole, to pursue meaningful reforms in the public financial management space. These may mimic specific PBF processes and would affect health system reform and how the health budget is managed. At the same time, most LMIC health systems may face constraints at several points in the underlying production function for effective coverage. For instance, there may be inadequate training of health workers, insufficient capacity, or demand-side barriers. A PBF program intervenes at one point or constraint—the health facility. It may be the case, however, that alleviating some of these other constraints may also lead to improved effectiveness of the PBF intervention. Thus, understanding the time horizon and observational unit capturing all—or even most—of the PBF impacts and the complementarity with other approaches is key to documenting any system-level impacts of PBF interventions.

Another important question is what to measure as an end outcome. Improvements in health systems are believed to contribute to effective coverage at a lower cost down the line (Vaz et al. 2020). If this is the case, then seeing gains in intermediate steps to effective coverage could be indicative that down the line, enough system-level gains would accrue that would lead to improvements in effective coverage and health outcomes. Thus, changes in health systems—timeliness of payments, accountability, and transparency—may be worth tracking even without concomitant improvements in effective coverage or health outcomes. This challenge is essentially that of an incomplete time cycle in using impact evaluations to study an intervention that is trying to change a system—such changes take time to implement, but it is typically infeasible, possibly even unethical, to maintain a counterfactual for an extended period. Thus, if it is believed that PBF interventions have system-level impacts and that such impacts can improve effective coverage, then it is important to track health system development as an end goal in and of itself as part of evaluative research.

One way to understand a PBF pilot's broader impact is to study what the government chooses to invest its resources in after a donor-funded PBF pilot has reached completion. Such an approach would assess concerns around the fungibility of donor aid and government resources. The concern with the fungibility of aid is identifying what the government would have spent resources on in the absence of donor aid. If donor aid is simply displacing government funding, then outcomes might have been identical even without the intervention (Devarajan and Swaroop 1998; van de Walle and Mu 2007). This of course presents a challenge for the sort of evaluative research discussed here. One way to assess the impact of a PBF pilot in the face of such fungibility concerns might be to examine what aspects of the pilot are scaled up. Sometimes, even when the PBF intervention is not scaled up, individual elements may be. Policy makers must then decide whether the PBF pilot can be deemed to have been a success. This was the case, for example, in Tanzania, where the accountability mechanism was adopted at scale even as the strategic purchasing of services was not (Binyaruka, Lohmann, and De Allegri 2020; Binyaruka 2020). However, as Wagstaff (2011) shows, given diminishing returns to spending and that not all areas—or sectors—are equally funded, it is possible even for fully fungible aid to increase total benefits relative to when aid is completely nonfungible.

In summary, individual impact evaluations may encounter difficulties in capturing issues surrounding the fungibility of aid, the flypaper effect, and incomplete time cycles. Evaluative research could fruitfully broaden its scope for a better understanding of whether health financing reforms such as PBF and DFF indeed have any system-level effects.

Conclusion

It is important to understand the optimal design of financial incentives in health care and the best way to measure quality of care at scale to support such incentive schemes. Aligning performance incentives in a manner so that it is in the provider's best financial interest to arrive at the correct diagnosis and administer the appropriate level of care, with neither undersupplying nor oversupplying, is a difficult policy problem in which many open questions remain. However, in the long run, performance-based incentives can only be successful if they can solve this problem. An important area of research in this context is the question of how to prevent the provision of nonindicated care more effectively. The reason that nonindicated care is damaging, especially in LMIC contexts, is partly that overprovision and underuse are directly connected. Mechanically, when resources are scare, nonindicated care for one patient means a lack of indicated care for another. But patients also may lose trust in the health care system when they feel that the quality of care is low and they are being frequently overcharged, and then they may opt not to seek care (Hussam et al. 2020). They may also simply not be able to afford care if the average doctor visit is prohibitively expensive. Another gap in the literature relates to the potential effects of PBF reforms that go beyond immediate improvements in quality of care and effective coverage due to the provider response to incentives As this chapter laid out, the health system changes initiated by PBF interventions may have additional impacts that only manifest indirectly or more slowly than typical impact evaluations last.

Even with many questions still unanswered, a key contribution of this report is to highlight research findings on the limits to the impacts of PBF interventions, particularly in isolation and when compared with policy options that include DFF and cash transfers to bolster demand. The final chapter of the report provides some concluding thoughts on how to translate these research findings into operational implications for the design of health system financing interventions.

Notes

1. Even though microscopy is often treated as the gold standard, overdiagnosis is common in blood smear testing in clinical practice, especially with inexperienced technicians. For example, evidence from Uganda shows very high false positive rates both in private and public facilities (Mutabazi et al. 2021; Nankabirwa et al. 2009).
2. Only about 15 percent of the studies in the Fact Book look at medicine use in pharmacy shops or non-licensed shops.
3. Resistant parasites have already rendered past generations of malaria drugs ineffective (Arrow, Panosian, and Gelband 2004).
4. The study used standardized patients who completed 909 visits and presented cases of asthma, nonmalarial fever, tuberculosis, and upper respiratory tract infection.
5. Providers are likely to choose if and how to test for malaria partly based on their a priori assessment of how likely the patient is to have malaria. In the malaria case study, survey evidence indicates that doctors believe that RDTs only reliably detect high parasite loads and therefore use them more often on "obvious" malaria cases. This is consistent with the differences in malaria prevalence across tests, and it implies once more that providers may often not follow up a negative test result.
6. An example is the doctors and nurses in the malaria case study. In Mali, most providers receive a salary, although the clinic director's remuneration may depend on the performance of the clinic overall. Salaried employees may also feel responsible for the clinic's financial health.

References

Arrow, K., C. Panosian, and H. Gelband, eds. 2004. *Saving Lives, Buying Time: Economics of Malaria Drugs in an Age of Resistance.* Washington, DC: Institute of Medicine, National Academies Press.

Baker, G., R. Gibbons, and K. J. Murphy. 1994. "Subjective Performance Measures in Optimal Incentive Contracts." *Quarterly Journal of Economics* 109 (4): 1125–56. https://doi.org/10.2307/2118358.

Banerjee, S. 2009. *The Use of Antipsychotic Medication for People with Dementia.* London: Department of Health.

Binyaruka, P., Lohmann, J., and De Allegri, M. 2020. "Performance-Based Financing in Low-Income and Middle-Income Countries: The Need to Look beyond Average Effect." *BMJ Global Health* 5 (8): e003136. https://doi.org/10.1136/bmjgh-2020-003136.

Binyaruka, P., J. Lohmann, and M. De Allegri. 2020. "Evaluating Performance-Based Financing in Low-Income and Middle-Income Countries: The Need to Look beyond Average Effect." *BMJ Global Health* 5 (8): e003136.

Brownlee, S., K. Chalkidou, J. Doust, A. G. Elshaug, P. Glasziou, I. Heath, S. Nagpal, et al. 2017. "Evidence for Overuse of Medical Services around the World." *The Lancet* 390 (10090): 156–68. https://doi.org/10.1016/S0140-6736(16)32585-5.

Busfield, J. 2015. "Assessing the Overuse of Medicines." *Social Science & Medicine* 131: 199–206. https://doi.org/10.1016/j.socscimed.2014.10.061.

Cabral, M., M. Geruso, and N. Mahoney. 2018. "Do Larger Health Insurance Subsidies Benefit Patients or Producers? Evidence from Medicare Advantage." *American Economic Review* 108 (8): 2048–87. https://doi.org/10.1257/aer.20151362.

Chan, P. S., M. R. Patel, L. W. Klein, R. J. Krone, G. J. Dehmer, K. Kennedy, B. K. Nallamothu, et al. 2011. "Appropriateness of Percutaneous Coronary Intervention." *JAMA* 306 (1): 53–61. https://doi.org/10.1001/jama.2011.916.

Cors, W. K., and Sagin, T. 2011. "Overtreatment in Health Care: How Much Is Too Much?" *Physician Executive* 37 (5): 10.

Currie, J., W. Lin, and J. Meng. 2014. "Addressing Antibiotic Abuse in China: An Experimental Audit Study." *Journal of Development Economics* 110: 39–51. https://doi.org/10.1016/j.jdeveco.2014.05.006.

Currie, J., W. Lin, and W. Zhang. 2011. "Patient Knowledge and Antibiotic Abuse: Evidence from an Audit Study in China." *Journal of Health Economics* 30 (5): 933–49. https://doi.org/10.1016/j.jhealeco.2011.05.009.

Daniels, B., A. Dolinger, G. Bedoya, K. Rogo, A. Goicoechea, J. Coarasa, F. Wafula, et al. 2017. "Use of Standardised Patients to Assess Quality of Healthcare in Nairobi, Kenya: A Pilot, Cross-Sectional Study with International Comparisons." *BMJ Global Health* 2 (2): e000333. https://doi.org/10.1136/bmjgh-2017-000333.

Das, J., A. Chowdhury, R. Hussam, and A. V. Banerjee. 2016. "The Impact of Training Informal Health Care Providers in India: A Randomized Controlled Trial." *Science* 354 (6308): aaf7384. https://doi.org/10.1126/science.aaf7384.

Das, J., and J. Hammer. 2007. "Money for Nothing: The Dire Straits of Medical Practice in Delhi, India." *Journal of Development Economics* 83 (1): 1–36. https://doi.org/10.1016/j.jdeveco.2006.05.004.

Das, J., J. Hammer, and K. Leonard. 2008. "The Quality of Medical Advice in Low-Income Countries." *Journal of Economic Perspectives* 22 (2): 93–114.

Das, J., A. Holla, A. Mohpal, and K. Muralidharan. 2016. "Quality and Accountability in Health Care Delivery: Audit-Study Evidence from Primary Care in India." *American Economic Review* 106 (12): 3765–99. https://doi.org/10.1257/aer.20151138.

Das, J., A. Kwan, B. Daniels, S. Satyanarayana, R. Subbaraman, S. Bergkvist, R. K. Das, et al. 2015. "Use of Standardised Patients to Assess Quality of Tuberculosis Care: A Pilot, Cross-Sectional Study." *The Lancet Infectious Diseases* 15 (11): 1305–13. https://doi.org/10.1016/S1473-3099(15)00077-8.

de Walque, D., P. J. Robyn, H. Saidou, G. Sorgho, and M. Steenland. 2021. "Looking into the Performance-Based Financing Black Box: Evidence from an Impact Evaluation in the Health Sector in Cameroon." *Health Policy and Planning* 36 (6): 835–47.

Devarajan, S., and V. Swaroop. 1998. *The Implications of Foreign Aid Fungibility for Development Assistance.* Washington, DC: World Bank.

Diao, D., J. M. Wright, D. K. Cundiff, and F. Gueyffier. 2012. "Pharmacotherapy for Mild Hypertension." *Cochrane Database of Systematic Reviews* (8): CD006742. https://doi.org/10.1002/14651858.CD006742.pub2.

Dupas, P., and E. Miguel. 2017. "Impacts and Determinants of Health Levels in Low-Income Countries." In *Handbook of Economic Field Experiments, Vol. 2,* edited by E. Duflo and A. Banerjee, 3–93. Amsterdam, Netherlands: Elsevier.

Fang, H., X. Lei, J. Shi, and X. Yi. 2021. "Physician-Induced Demand: Evidence from China's Drug Price Zero-Markup Policy." NBER Working Paper 28998, National Bureau of Economic Research, Cambridge, MA.

FDA (US Food and Drug Administration). 2010. "Initiative to Reduce Unnecessary Radiation Exposure from Medical Imaging." White Paper, FDA, Silver Spring, MD.

Holloway, K. A., V. Ivanovska, A. K. Wagner, C. Vialle-Valentin, and D. Ross-Degnan. 2013. "Have We Improved Use of Medicines in Developing and Transitional Countries and Do We Know How To? Two Decades of Evidence." *Tropical Medicine & International Health* 18 (6): 656–64. https://doi.org/10.1111/tmi.12123.

Holmström, B. 1979. "Moral Hazard and Observability." *Bell Journal of Economics* 10 (1): 74–91. https://doi.org/10.2307/3003320.

Holmström, B., and P. Milgrom. 1991. "Multitask Principal-Agent Analyses: Incentive Contracts, Asset Ownership, and Job Design." *Journal of Law, Economics, & Organization* 7: 24–52.

Holmström, B., and P. Milgrom. 1994. "The Firm as an Incentive System." *American Economic Review* 84 (4): 972–91.

Hussam, R., A. Banerjee, J. Das, J. Hammer, and A. Mohpal. 2020. "The Market for Healthcare in Low-Income Countries." Working Paper, Harvard Business School, Boston, MA.

Ioannidis, J. P. A. 2008. "Effectiveness of Antidepressants: An Evidence Myth Constructed from a Thousand Randomized Trials?" *Philosophy, Ethics, and Humanities in Medicine* 3: Article 14. https://doi.org/10.1186/1747-5341-3-14.

Jain, R. 2021. "Private Hospital Behavior under Government Health Insurance in India." Working Paper, Freeman Spogli Institute for International Studies, Stanford, CA.

Khanna, M., B. Loevinsohn, E. Pradhan, O. Fadeyibi, K. McGee, O. Odutolu, G. B. Fritsche, et al. 2021. "Decentralized Facility Financing versus Performance-Based Payments in Primary Health Care: A Large-Scale Randomized Controlled Trial in Nigeria." *BMC Medicine* 19 (1): 1–12.

King, J. J. C., T. Powell-Jackson, C. Makungu, J. Hargreaves, and C. Goodman. 2021. "How Much Healthcare Is Wasted? A Cross-Sectional Study of Outpatient Overprovision in Private-for-Profit and Faith-Based Health Facilities in Tanzania." *Health Policy and Planning* 36 (5): 695–706. https://doi.org/10.1093/heapol/czab039.

Kotwani, A., R. R. Chaudhury, and K. Holloway. 2012. "Antibiotic-Prescribing Practices of Primary Care Prescribers for Acute Diarrhea in New Delhi, India." *Value in Health* 15 (1): S116–S119. https://doi.org/10.1016/j.jval.2011.11.008.

Krockow, E. M., A. M. Colman, E. Chattoe-Brown, D. R. Jenkins, N. Perera, S. Mehtar, and C. Tarrant. 2019. "Balancing the Risks to Individual and Society: A Systematic Review and Synthesis of Qualitative Research on Antibiotic Prescribing Behaviour in Hospitals." *Journal of Hospital Infection* 101 (4): 428–39. https://doi.org/10.1016/j.jhin.2018.08.007.

Kruse, G. R., S. M. Khan, A. M. Zaslavsky, J. Z. Ayanian, and T. D. Sequist. 2015. "Overuse of Colonoscopy for Colorectal Cancer Screening and Surveillance." *Journal of General Internal Medicine* 30 (3): 277–83. https://doi.org/10.1007/s11606-014-3015-6.

Kutzin, J. 2012. "Anything Goes on the Path to Universal Health Coverage? No." *Bulletin of the World Health Organization* 90: 867–68.

Kwan, A., B. Daniels, V. Saria, S. Satyanarayana, R. Subbaraman, A. McDowell, S. Bergkvist, et al. 2018. "Variations in the Quality of Tuberculosis Care in Urban India: A Cross-Sectional, Standardized Patient Study in Two Cities." *PLoS Medicine* 15 (9): e1002653. https://doi.org/10.1371/journal.pmed.1002653.

Leonard, K. L., and M. C. Masatu. 2010. "Using the Hawthorne Effect to Examine the Gap between a Doctor's Best Possible Practice and Actual Performance." *Journal of Development Economics* 93: 226–34.

Leslie, H. H., L. R. Hirschhorn, T. Marchant, S. V. Doubova, O. Gureje, M. E. Kruk. 2018. "Health Systems Thinking: A New Generation of Research to Improve Healthcare Quality." *PLoS Medicine* 10 15(10): e1002682.

Li, Y., J. Xu, F. Wang, B. Wang, L. Liu, W. Hou, H. Fan, et al. 2012. "Overprescribing in China, Driven by Financial Incentives, Results in Very High Use of Antibiotics, Injections, and Corticosteroids." *Health Affairs* 31 (5): 1075–82.

Linder, J. A., J. N. Doctor, M. W. Friedberg, H. R. Nieva, C. Birks, D. Meeker, and C. R. Fox. 2014. "Time of Day and the Decision to Prescribe Antibiotics." *JAMA Internal Medicine* 174 (12): 2029–31.

Lopez, C., A. Sautmann, and S. Schaner. 2022a. "Do Patients Value High-Quality Care? Patient Satisfaction and the Allocation of Malaria Treatment." University of Southern California, Los Angeles.

Lopez, C., A. Sautmann, and S. Schaner. 2022b. "Does Patient Demand Contribute to the Overuse of Prescription Drugs?" *American Economic Journal: Applied Economics* 14 (1): 225–60. https://doi.org/10.1257/app.20190722.

Lyu, H., T. Xu, D. Brotman, B. Mayer-Blackwell, M. Cooper, M. Daniel, E. C. Wick, et al. 2017. "Overtreatment in the United States." *PLoS ONE* 12 (9): e0181970. https://doi.org/10.1371/journal.pone.0181970.

McGuire, T. G. 2000. "Physician Agency." In *Handbook of Health Economics, Vol. 1, Part 1*, edited by A. J. Culyer and J. P. Newhouse, 461–536. Amsterdam, Netherlands: Elsevier.

Meessen, B., A. Soucat, and C. Sekabaraga. 2011. "Performance-Based Financing: Just a Donor Fad or a Catalyst towards Comprehensive Health-Care Reform?" *Bulletin of the World Health Organization* 89: 153–56.

Miller, G., and K. S. Babiarz. 2014. "Pay-for-Performance Incentives in Low- and Middle-Income Country Health Programs." In *Encyclopedia of Health Economics*, edited by A. J. Culyer, 457–66. San Diego, CA: Elsevier.

Ministère de la Santé. 2013. "Politique nationale de lutte contre le paludisme." Ministry of Health, Conakry, Guinea.

Mohanan, M., M. Vera-Hernández, V. Das, S. Giardili, J. D. Goldhaber-Fiebert, T. L. Rabin, S. S. Raj, et al. 2015. "The Know-Do Gap in Quality of Health Care for Childhood Diarrhea and Pneumonia in Rural India." *JAMA Pediatrics* 169 (4): 349–57. https://doi.org/10.1001/jamapediatrics.2014.3445.

Morgan, D. J., S. S. Dhruva, E. R. Coon, S. M. Wright, and D. Korenstein. 2019. "2019 Update on Medical Overuse: A Review." *JAMA Internal Medicine* 179 (11): 1568–74.

Mutabazi, T., E. Arinaitwe, A. Ndyabakira, E. Sendaula, A. Kakeeto, P. Okimat, P. Orishaba, et al. 2021. "Assessment of the Accuracy of Malaria Microscopy in Private Health Facilities in Entebbe Municipality, Uganda: A Cross-Sectional Study." *Malaria Journal* 20 (1): 250. https://doi.org/10.1186/s12936-021-03787-y.

Nankabirwa, J., D. Zurovac, J. N. Njogu, J. B. Rwakimari, H. Counihan, R. W. Snow, and J. K. Tibenderana. 2009. "Malaria Misdiagnosis in Uganda—Implications for Policy Change." *Malaria Journal* 8 (1): 66. https://doi.org/10.1186/1475-2875-8-66.

Pasvol, G. 2005. "The Treatment of Complicated and Severe Malaria." *British Medical Bulletin* 75–76 (1): 29–47. https://doi.org/10.1093/bmb/ldh059.

Paul, E., L. Albert, B. N. S. Bisala, O. Bodson, E. Bonnet, P. Bossyns, S. Colombo, et al. 2018. "Performance-Based Financing in Low-Income and Middle-Income Countries: Isn't It Time for a Rethink?" *BMJ Global Health* 3 (1): p.e000664.

Peters P. J., M. C. Thigpen, M. E. Parise, and R. D. Newman. 2007. "Safety and Toxicity of Sulfadoxine/Pyrimethamine: Implications for Malaria Prevention in Pregnancy Using Intermittent Preventive Treatment." *Drug Safety* 30 (6): 481–501.

PMI (US President's Malaria Initiative). 2015. "President's Malaria Initiative Mali: Malaria Operational Plan FY 2016." US Agency for International Development, Washington, DC.

Rice, T. H. 1983. "The Impact of Changing Medicare Reimbursement Rates on Physician-Induced Demand." *Medical Care* 21 (8): 803–15.

Shroff, Z. C., M. Bigdeli, and B. Meessen. 2017. "From Scheme to System (Part 2): Findings from Ten Countries on the Policy Evolution of Results-Based Financing in Health Systems." *Health Systems & Reform* 3 (2): 137–47.

Sun, Q., M. A. Santoro, Q. Meng, C. Liu, and K. Eggleston. 2008. "Pharmaceutical Policy in China." *Health Affairs* 27 (4): 1042–50. https://doi.org/10.1377/hlthaff.27.4.1042.

Sylvia, S., H. Xue, C. Zhou, Y. Shi, H. Yi, H. Zhou, S. Rozelle, et al. 2017. "Tuberculosis Detection and the Challenges of Integrated Care in Rural China: A Cross-Sectional Standardized Patient Study." *PLoS Medicine* 14 (10): e1002405. https://doi.org/10.1371/journal.pmed.1002405.

Trampuz, A., M. Jereb, I. Muzlovic, and R. M. Prabhu. 2003. "Clinical Review: Severe Malaria." *Critical Care* 7 (4): 315–23. https://doi.org/10.1186/cc2183.

van de Walle, D., and R. Mu. 2007. "Fungibility and the Flypaper Effect of Project Aid: Micro-Evidence for Vietnam." *Journal of Development Economics* 84 (2): 667–85.

van Staa, A. L., and A. Hardon. 1996. "Injection Practices in the Developing World." World Health Organization, Geneva.

Vaz, L. M., L. Franco, T. Guenther, K. Simmons, S. Herrera, and S. N. Wall. 2020. "Operationalising Health Systems Thinking: A Pathway to High Effective Coverage." *Health Research Policy and Systems* 18 (1): 1–17.

Wagstaff, A. 2011. "Fungibility and the Impact of Development Assistance: Evidence from Vietnam's Health Sector." *Journal of Development Economics* 94 (1): 62–73.

World Health Organization. 2009. *Medicines Use in Primary Care in Developing and Transitional Countries: Fact Book Summarizing Results from Studies Reported between 1990 and 2006.* Geneva: WHO.

World Health Organization. 2015. *Malaria Rapid Diagnostic Test Performance: Results of WHO Product Testing of Malaria RDTs: Round 6 (2014–2015).* Geneva: WHO.

World Health Organization. 2020. "Antimicrobial Resistance." WHO, Geneva (accessed August 5, 2021), https://www.who.int/news-room/fact-sheets/detail/antimicrobial-resistance.

Yip, W., T. Powell-Jackson, W. Chen, M. Hu, E. Fe, M. Hu, W. Jian, et al. 2014. "Capitation Combined with Pay-for-Performance Improves Antibiotic Prescribing Practices in Rural China." *Health Affairs* 33 (3): 502–10. https://doi.org/10.1377/hlthaff.2013.0702.

CHAPTER 8

Conclusion and Operational Implications

This report has provided a frank overview of the evidence. Yet, it has not taken a firm position for or against the continuation of performance-based financing (PBF) operations. Instead, it recognized the importance of nuance, context, and the principles underlying health financing reform. The nature of health financing is complex, with multiple fund flows, actors, and institutional relationships. In many such settings, PBF has introduced and fostered principles around sending funds to the frontlines, provider autonomy, financial management capacity, accountability, and an output orientation of the payment system. These are all fundamental to the efficient functioning of a health system that provides quality health services.

The report presented several key findings on the topic of financing for effective coverage in primary health care in low- and middle-income country (LMIC) settings. It revealed that gaps in effective coverage are driven by low utilization and poor content of care. Focusing on the determinants of the content of care, it showed that poor clinical quality is driven by three factors: (1) structural constraints (inadequate infrastructure, drugs, supplies, and equipment), (2) poor health worker knowledge, and (3) low effort by health workers. It then proceeded to study interventions that financially incentivize improvements in effective coverage: focusing first on PBF of health facilities.

Taking a deep dive into the PBF schemes implemented by the World Bank in primary maternal and neonatal health care, the report found that PBF schemes remove structural capacity constraints across the board but have limited effects on content of care. A systematic review and meta-analysis of supply-side (PBF) and demand-side (conditional cash transfer) financial incentives show that incentives have significant but modest impacts on effective coverage. Supply-side incentives in the form of PBF may, if anything, lead to smaller impacts than vouchers and cash transfers would have. In addition, the comparison between PBF and direct facility financing (DFF) shows that budget equalization providing unconditional increases in facility financing as well as autonomy may lead to comparable impacts at lower cost than PBF. The findings thus highlight the complexities of a PBF intervention and suggest that thinking of DFF, PBF, and demand-side cash transfers as a menu of potentially reinforcing policy options, rather than substitutes for each other, may be a fruitful means for increasing effective coverage.

However, as discussed in chapters 6 and 7, a fundamental change brought about by PBF, relative to other methods of health system financing, is the autonomous role of the health facility. The central role of the facility as an autonomous unit, with a budget to control, is a marked difference in paradigm and has had significant impacts on health systems across many LMICs. Since PBF requires health facilities to be able to receive and use funds directly, the health facility as an entity has received renewed attention. This is an important departure for many countries where health facilities previously only received in-kind support from higher levels of the administration. Recognizing health facilities as stand-alone entities explicitly means that these facilities must have access to financial services and requires facility managers to account for and report on the use of funds. This requires some information and communications technology investments and capacity-building efforts. Therefore, many PBF designs accommodate greater flexibility of resource use than was commonplace in many countries in the prevailing public financial management (PFM) structures. For example, facility managers generally do not require an onerous approval process to reallocate PBF funds as long as these remain within given parameters. Another change is that facilities now receive budgetary allocations against performance measures instead of on an input basis. This has several important consequences. One is that the facility receives funds as reimbursement *after* the services are provided, and another is that the budgetary allocation is contingent on outputs or services delivered. Sending funds directly to facilities and including an output orientation has stimulated a purchasing reform dialogue in many countries that can incentivize efficiency and access to quality services. Finally, rigorous third-party verification of results is another introduction by PBF that is necessitated by its direct relationship to the subsequent budget and the risks of gaming associated with the use of self-reported administrative data for making payments. Linking payments to verified outputs can be costly, but it has been particularly popular among donors who appreciate the direct relationship between payment, results, and accountability. Because of the popularity of the PBF mechanisms among donors, the overall investment in health in LMICs is likely to have increased.

This chapter builds on past experience to provide a forward-looking perspective. The following four messages emerge: (1) sustainability of interventions, particularly those geared at revamping the financing of entire health systems, is critical and about more than just money; (2) the four facility tenets—provider autonomy, financial management capacity, unified payment systems, and output orientation—should be systematically supported to build health systems; (3) PBF incentives should be understood in the broader health financing context; and (4) the potential of technological advances to facilitate provider payment reform should be better examined and exploited. These key messages call for the development of a new research agenda that is more focused on the design and implementation of PBF reforms and their role in health systems strengthening.

Message 1: Recognize that sustainability is about more than just money

Fiscal space for health is always constrained, but this is particularly the case as countries are struggling with the economic consequences of COVID-19 and increased expenditure pressures across all sectors. Domestic contributions to PBF engagements may therefore become more difficult to mobilize, although they may provide essential contributions to basic primary care services, and many of these reforms are recognized as quintessential for health system reform by academics and practitioners alike (Barroy et al. 2019). As long as the PBF engagement is conducted in parallel to regular PFM processes, such financial contributions may be at risk. As governments can no longer afford to finance both the regular budget and off-budget schemes, the off-budget schemes are likely to be cut. If PBF reforms were financed through off-budget schemes, this risks the sustainability of the reforms. If all the aforementioned changes (provider autonomy, flexibility of fund use, output orientation of budget, and so forth) relate only to the PBF financing streams, all of this risks being undone and the health system might return to the legacy PFM processes.

Therefore, sustainability is not only about whether funds are directed to off-budget PBF schemes and whether such PBF schemes have been "institutionalized" in a systematic manner. Rather, the question should be whether PBF principles (or, more broadly, facility financing principles) are mainstreamed into general PFM practices. PFM reform is a longer term endeavor, and changes tend to occur incrementally (Diamond 2013). However, once changes are made, they become difficult to reverse; therefore, if PBF principles can be mainstreamed into PFM structures, these will likely be sustainable. For example, on the one hand, a facility may receive funds directly through an off-budget PBF scheme, which empowers the facility while this financing modality is in place, but it also disappoints when it is undone. On the other hand, if facilities are recognized explicitly in the budget, it becomes necessary to discuss facility budget allocations through the legislative process, and decisions must be made that carry the force of law. The budget is a legal instrument and should be implemented; if it is not, questions will be asked by the legislature. Once this process is set up, it will become difficult to reverse, especially once facility managers and communities realize the benefits.

It will be important to understand the current PFM environment and how facility financing principles can be aligned. A recent paper proposes a diagnostic framework on how to identify the current state of alignment to PFM systems and how to develop a reform roadmap (Piatti-Fünfkirchen, Hadley, and Mathivet 2021). Exploring where and how PBF differs from PFM systems and identifying what reforms could be pursued offer an opportunity for mainstreaming PBF principles and therefore strengthening sustainability. Some PFM reforms, such as the introduction of program budgeting, may lend themselves particularly well to mainstreaming PBF principles. Careful attention will be required for fully understanding how a program budgeting reform will be implemented and how it can reflect PBF principles. This will require active collaboration of PFM and health finance practitioners.

For countries with off-budget social health insurance (SHI) schemes, the PBF experience can be fully absorbed within the SHI. In this case, it may not be necessary to align PBF with the PFM system, but clear separation of functions is necessary to facilitate sustainability. It is then necessary to determine clearly what services can be financed through PFM structures and what can be financed through the SHI. However, if the SHI is not better at raising funds or pooling risks than is done by tax authorities or through the budget, it may not be advisable to support such a system (Yazbeck et al. 2020; Yazbeck 2021). The only advantage of the SHI remains that it gives authorities greater flexibility in terms of purchasing than a typical PFM system allows. Rather than retaining an entirely separate scheme, it may be more efficient to reform the PFM system to mimic purchasing functions.

Concerns about sustainability differ depending on countries' public health budgets and health systems. In countries such as Tanzania, for example, the PBF experience contributed to a process of rethinking facility financing through government channels. In other, more fragile and donor-dependent countries, such as the Central African Republic or Chad, for example, the sustainability agenda—at least in the short term—should revolve much more around reducing the government's transaction costs in dealing with external resources and reducing the risk of discontinuation of services due to donor-specific funding cycles or budget cuts through greater use of pooled financing mechanisms.

Message 2: Support the four facility financing tenets

How health facilities operate within a health system is a central aspect of health financing reform. Therefore, creating an enabling environment is key and can lead to important gains in efficiency and access to quality services. This can be done by supporting the facility financing tenets identified in a forthcoming WHO paper on direct facility financing (O'Dougherty et al. 2022).

Tenet A: Health facilities require budget autonomy and spending flexibility

Incentives can only be effective if facilities have the decision space to react to them. Whether facilities will promote utilization or efficiency will be a function of their ability to react to the incentives set by the purchasing mechanism. Therefore, provider autonomy is a fundamental facility financing tenet, including for PBF. This does not mean that facilities need to be private, as they can have autonomy within a public sector setting. Autonomy is also not binary. Issues that affect autonomy relate to a facility's legal status, its ability to receive and spend funds, and its ability to make decisions on human resource management, including hiring, firing, provision of incentive payments, and taking corrective action.

On the use of funds, there are significant variations and the level of autonomy may differ by expenditure type. For example, salaries may be paid centrally, drugs procured by a central medical store, and investment spending managed by the district administration. This would only leave autonomy over other nonwage recurrent spending. The degree to which facilities should have autonomy over various spending items will vary by country context, but it is an important factor to consider. Facilities should be limited in purchasing items that fall outside the remits of their level of care (for example, a primary care provider should not have the autonomy to procure a magnetic resonance imaging scanner).

Tenet B: Health facilities require adequate financial management capacity

It is important that facilities can manage funds prudently and carefully account for and report on the use of funds to ensure accountability and inform decision making. Although it is preferred that facilities are paid against outputs, this does not relieve them of the need to account for and report on spending against inputs. Ledgers on revenue and expenditures must be maintained carefully and audited periodically. Further, due process is required for the procurement of products and services to ensure value for money. These aspects are akin to basic business management. As financial management capacity at the facility level grows, ministries of finance are likely to be more willing to extend greater degrees of autonomy to facilities. As such, this is likely a sequential reform process over the medium term.

Emerging technologies can be explored to minimize capacity-building needs. For example, it may not be desirable to hire accountants at every facility. Instead, payments made through smartcards or mobile money that automatically captures spending categories would greatly reduce the financial management burden on facility managers who in turn can focus on patients instead.

Tenet C: A unified payment system supports facility management

Health facilities often draw on multiple sources for payment. These may include input-based budget provisions from the government budget, revenue from user fees, payment from insurance funds, and support from various development partners. These multiple sources fragment the payment environment and can lead to conflicting incentives and inefficiencies. They also place an undue burden of accounting and reporting requirements on health service providers and make strategic planning difficult (Piatti-Fünfkirchen, O'Dougherty, and Ally 2020). Unifying payment streams therefore becomes critical. If pooling resources at a higher level is not possible, it may be desirable to ensure that there is a common facility plan that includes anticipated revenue from all the financing sources and that budget execution protocols are harmonized such that there are no significant differences in how money can be used across financing sources. Furthermore, unifying the payment system is important to make the output orientation of the budget effective as the design of the payment system and underpinning incentive structures need to consider all financing sources.

Tenet D: Health facility payments should be output oriented

Input-based budget provisions alone cannot adequately serve health sector needs as they are designed to ensure financial accountability and budget control rather than incentivize the behavior of health providers. An output-oriented payment system, in contrast, reimburses facilities based on the number of people served and the types and volumes of services provided. This can help incentivize the efficiency of provider management and utilization of services. Relating payments to outputs also shifts the accountability relationship from accountability of financing inputs to accountability of the provision of services.

An output-oriented payment system introduces significant flexibility. First, the facility operating budget becomes a function of the workload rather than being predetermined at the beginning of the year. Second, there are inherently fewer input-based controls, and facilities can reorient spending according to need. Transitioning toward an output-based payment system is therefore desirable. In practice this may not be possible for all spending items. For example, the wage bill may still be paid on an input basis, and there are inherent economy of scale advantages in purchasing drugs in bulk. In addition, most payment systems are mixed payment systems. To make these effective, it is critical to make it a purposeful mixed payment system with incentive structures that are mutually supportive. The output orientation can inform the operational budget and be a combination of simple capitation supported by performance indicators.

Message 3: Understand PBF incentives in a broader health system context

Typically, financial incentives are most efficiently used at the margin to incentivize behavior changes that are not possible with other, simpler financing mechanisms. However, many low-income countries suffer from underfunded health systems: low salaries, low (or sometimes even inexistent) operational budgets, shortages of key inputs, and so forth. Flexible resources from PBF are often used to fill these gaps, and hence the question arises whether the results could be provided through less transaction-heavy mechanisms (see the PBF-DFF comparison in chapter 6). For a better understanding of the potential for direct financing approaches, it is important to consider the full scope of facility financing mechanisms before designing any incentive-based formulas on top of them. This will require a careful analysis of public expenditure data combined with survey data to map out the relative importance of different financing mechanisms and the cause behind low coverage of certain service interventions.

The broader health system context also includes the role of development partners. Especially in low- and lower-middle-income countries, they can contribute to a sizable amount of total health spending, often matching or exceeding government contributions. Therefore, understanding how various external financing flows are reaching facilities is important. To reduce transaction costs and foster efficiency, an effort should be made to utilize government systems to the extent possible. PBF is most effective at the margin. To understand where the margin lies and introduce a purposeful performance orientation to the payment system, it is critical to have a full overview of financing flows to facilities, domestic and external alike.

Message 4: Explore opportunities of maturing technologies

Many technologies have matured and become readily available at low cost (O'Dougherty et al. 2022). The choice of technology and their deployment can directly affect the design and implementation of PBF operations. Innovations in the fintech space could, for example, change how facilities receive funds and make accounting and reporting easier, thereby alleviating nursing staff from an undue financial management burden. Mobile money has penetrated many parts of Africa, which provides opportunities for extending financial services to remote and rural health facilities. Blockchain technology has become increasingly affordable and available to low-capacity environments and can create accountability and transparency in payment and supply chain management processes (Talary et al., forthcoming). Machine learning algorithms can be deployed to automate data analyses and facilitate risk-based verification for reduced costs. Smart contracts can be set up that automate contractual arrangements between parties that could, for example, trigger PBF payments upon fulfillment of certain terms. Last, rapid advances in identity management and the low-cost availability of fingerprint technology are significant since they can facilitate the foundation for patient history records.

To look for examples of how these technologies have been successfully deployed requires looking beyond the health sector. For example, there are few examples of governments using mobile money to extend financial access to remote health facilities. However, there are plenty of examples of governments sending cash transfers to the poor and vulnerable in remote locations through mobile money balances. Important lessons can be drawn from social protection programs on how that was made possible and what challenges had to be overcome. This is the approach the Zimbabwe health sector is taking in exploring opportunities in health finance by learning from the experience of a cash transfer program. Similarly, blockchain technology is being used increasingly in the agriculture sector. Last-mile verification of farm equipment is being done in a low-capacity environment in Pakistan (Hanna, Mullainathan, and Schwartzstein 2012), suggesting that a similar process could be done for last-mile verification of drugs or personal protective equipment in the health sector to prevent leakage. Insurance agencies in the United States are already exploring blockchain technology to support claims management.

Building on this experience, management in the Côte d'Ivoire health sector is looking to minimize the cost of verification of services and build a health management information system with data integrity. Finding solutions for a particular problem may require looking beyond the obvious health sector experience or hard evidence from clinical trials. It may require looking at how other sectors and countries deal with administrative processes, identifying opportunities, working with small-scale pilots to explore what a technological solution may look like, and determining how this would address the problem at hand. It may also require exploring a set of different tools. Box 8.1 explores an example drawing on a set of innovations in Côte d'Ivoire and Zimbabwe.

Box 8.1   In Focus: Combining technological innovations to facilitate strategic purchasing

Data are essential for strategic purchasing, especially data on the types and volumes of services provided. Evidence based on data should be an important factor for determining budget allocations to health providers. However, routine data collection in prevailing systems is not always guaranteed, and if the service providers benefit directly from the data they report, there is an incentive to manipulate the data or overestimate expenditures and not be transparent about the use of the budget allocations. To ensure integrity of data and reporting, third-party data verification is often required, which can be prohibitively expensive and adds to the complexity of data audit processes.

This problem with routine data collection is inherent to performance-based financing. The following approach is explored to address this problem, drawing on a set of innovations in Côte d'Ivoire and Zimbabwe:

- Every registered patient needs to be identified, registered, and recorded as they enter a health facility.
- Electronic identification of all actors in the work process (patients and providers) can be enabled through fingerprint sensors and camera imaging technologies at low cost with minimal hardware investments.
- A mobile phone number associated with the SIM card of the mobile phone used to collect and transmit the data is linked to the use case actor's account to enable communication and verification of transactions between the digital identities of the service providers and patients and to link this with the identity of the device that is collecting the data.
- Once a patient receives a service, the service provider enters information that describes the service provided digitally on a blockchain (for example, using a tablet connected to the web over the internet or

via text messaging an application interface to the blockchain).
- A message is automatically sent to the patient to inquire whether this service was indeed provided. The patient can respond "yes" or "no" using their mobile phone to confirm when, where, and what services have been provided.
- If the patient responds with "yes," the service provision is recorded as completed and verified on the blockchain.
- If the patient responds with "no," the lack of service provision is recorded, and an alert is triggered to the administrator to investigate and verify.
- The information on what services were provided in which health facilities is subsequently stored in the health management information system and given the verification process and decentralized ledger, there is confidence in the integrity of the data.
- Payment to the providers can be triggered through a smart contract.
- Payment to remote providers can be made through the use of mobile money.

Through such a process, a health management information system with integrity is created. This can then form the basis for facility budget allocations or facility payments against an output-informed formula. Data are stored on decentralized ledgers and are immutable, minimizing the risk of gaming. Verification may still be necessary but would be much less costly as the system can identify high-risk transactions. If desired, patient utilization data can be recorded in the process of verification, which strengthens the basis for future diagnoses and efficiency in the health sector. Access to the information can be controlled by the permissioning features of blockchain technology so that patient data protection issues can be maintained.

The example in box 8.1 shows how processes can be supported through various technological innovations that together facilitate a more efficient, transparent, and accountable way to engage through means that were previously unimaginable. An important first step in this process is a feasibility assessment that explores the cost and realism of such an approach and identifies any potential downside risks. This assessment must also consider the policy environment, local capacity, political economy, and how such an approach would build on existing infrastructure.

While technological advances are rapid and hold promise, these should be explored with caution. An enabling policy environment is necessary for making such investments effective, and this is not always a given. Political economy and change management considerations are necessary as such investments can be disruptive and challenge power relationships. Further, there are potential downside risks, such as the use of personal identity data for the wrong purposes, that need to be fully understood and mitigated.

Building a forward-looking research agenda

Many PBF initiatives have meticulously documented their performance, and thanks to rigorous impact evaluations, it can be seen where the approach has worked. However, the PBF initiatives studied in these impact evaluations are a set of interventions that include aspects like autonomy, community engagement, decentralization, and enhanced supervision—not just the purchasing mechanism. These studies have revealed the effects of the set of interventions vis-à-vis the status quo or against another counterfactual package of interventions, such as DFF. However, a health system or PFM practitioner might be most interested in the marginal effect of any one of the above-mentioned changes. For example, what is the effect of allowing greater facility autonomy, and what might it take to get there? Can facilities be introduced one by one into the government's chart of accounts? Sending funds to providers might require training them in accounting and reporting. Is this realistic, and how would it affect accountability and service delivery?

It may be most useful for practitioners to understand these individual effects and view PBF as a point on a continuum of DFF. When viewed as a continuum and broken down into its component parts, each aspect can be addressed and studied individually to pursue meaningful reforms in the PFM space. These may mimic specific PBF processes and would affect health system reform and the way the health budget is managed. One such study was conducted in Malawi that explores how well the PFM system supports a purchasing environment through the budget and provides recommendations for a stepwise reform process (Piatti-Fünfkirchen, Chansa, and Nkhoma 2021). While this study does not address PBF specifically, the approach and principles apply more broadly.

PBF schemes offer strong accountability toward external donors, and this has been an important reason for their popularity in recent years in low-income countries. If, for above-mentioned reasons of sustainability and efficiency, "lighter" payment mechanisms such as DFF appear more appropriate, it will be important to consider alternative measures of accountability that satisfy the reporting demands of donors. This is especially the case in heavily donor-dependent countries where it could be argued that—at least in the short term—PBF schemes should serve as a tool for improving donor alignment around a package of services, much more than a tool for changing the public provider payment function. Although PBF-type schemes offer the potential for increased pooling and alignment of external resources, this potential has not been fully realized in many countries. Further research into what are the bottlenecks to aligning around these schemes would be important. Especially in the current macro-fiscal context with limited potential for raising more domestic revenue, increasing the efficiency of external resources is critical.

References

Barroy, H., M. Piatti-Fünfkirchen, F. Sergent, E. Dale, S. O'Dougherty, G. Mtei, G. Kabaniha, and J. Lakin. 2019. *World Bank Blog: Let Managers Manage. A Health Service Provider's Perspective on Public Financial Management*, September 9, 2019. https://blogs.worldbank.org/health/let-managers -manage-health-service-providers-perspective-public-financial-management.

Diamond, J. 2013. "Good Practice Note on Sequencing PFM Reforms." PEFA Secretariat, World Bank, Washington, DC. https://www.pefa.org/sites/pefa /files/resources/downloads/v8-Good_Practice_Note_on_Sequencing_PFM _Reforms_%28Jack_Diamond__January_2013%29_1.pdf.

Hanna, R., S. Mullainathan, and J. Schwartzstein. 2012. "Learning through Noticing: Theory and Experimental Evidence in Farming." No. w18401, National Bureau of Economic Research, Cambridge, MA.

O'Dougherty, S., H. Barroy, M. Piatti-Fünfkirchen, J. Kutzin, and G. Mtei. 2022. "Policy Brief on Direct Facility Financing." World Health Organization, Geneva. https://www.who.int/publications/i/item/9789240043374.

Piatti-Fünfkirchen, M., C. Chansa, and D. Nkhoma. 2021. "Public Financial Management in the Health Sector: An Assessment at the Local Government Level in Malawi." World Bank, Washington, DC. https://openknowledge .worldbank.org/handle/10986/35925.

Piatti-Fünfkirchen, M., S. Hadley, and B. Mathivet. 2021. "Alignment of Performance-Based Financing in Health with the Government Budget: A Principle Based Approach." Health, Nutrition, and Population Discussion Paper, World Bank, Washington, DC.

Piatti-Fünfkirchen, M., S. O'Dougherty, and M. Ally. 2020. *World Bank Blog: Why Strategic Purchasing in Health and Public Financial Management Are Two Sides of the Same Coin*, August 12, 2020. https://blogs.worldbank.org/health/why-strat egic-purchasing-health-and-public-financial-management-are-two-sides -same-coin.

Talary, M., M. Piatti-Fünfkirchen, A. Liang, M. Chandrahas Karajgi, C. Lao Pena, and C. N. Sisimayi. Forthcoming. "Introducing Blockchain for Efficiency, Transparency and Accountability in Healthcare Provision." World Bank, Washington, DC.

Yazbeck, A. 2021. "Debunking the Idealized World of Market-Based Health Insurance." Health Finance and Governance Project, US Agency for International Development, Washington, DC. https://medium.com/health -finance-and-governance/debunking-the-idealized-world-of -market-based-health-insurance-98f0cbb9c72b.

Yazbeck, A. S., W. D. Savedoff, W. C. Hsiao, J. Kutzin, A. Soucat, A. Tandon, A. Wagstaff, and W. Chi-Man Yip. 2020. "The Case Against Labor-Tax-Financed Social Health Insurance for Low- and Low-Middle-Income Countries." *Health Affairs* 39 (5): 892–97.